Aquarium

The Career and Defection of a
Soviet Military Spy

VIKTOR SUVOROV

Translated from the Russian by
DAVID FLOYD

HAMISH HAMILTON
London

First published in Great Britain 1985
by Hamish Hamilton Ltd
Garden House 57–59 Long Acre London WC2E 9JZ

British Library Cataloguing in Publication Data

Suvorov, Viktor
  The aquarium.
  1. Suvorov, Viktor   2. Intelligence officers
  —Soviet Unon—Biography
  I. Title
  355.3′432′0924   UB271.R9ZS/
  ISBN 0-241-11545-0

Typeset by Computape (Pickering) Ltd
Printed and bound in Great Britain by
Richard Clay (The Chaucer Press) Ltd, Bungay, Suffolk

Aquarium

By the same Author

The Liberators
Inside the Soviet Army
Soviet Military Intelligence

For Tanya

Prologue

'We have a very simple rule: it's a rouble to get in, but two to get out. That means that it's difficult to join the organisation, but a lot more difficult to get out of it. Theoretically there's only one way out for any member of the organisation – through the chimney of the crematorium. For some it is an honourable exit, but for others it is a shameful and terrible way to go, but there's only the one chimney for all of us. That's the only way we can leave this organisation. That's the chimney over there . . . ' the man with grey hair points towards a huge picture window taking up the whole wall. 'Have a good look at it.'

At the level of the ninth floor I have a panoramic view of the vast, unbounded and deserted airfield stretching to the horizon. And if I look straight down I can see below me a labyrinth of sand-covered pathways running between thick rows of shrubs. The green of the plants in the garden and the burnt-up grass of the airfield are separated by an indestructible concrete wall protected by a thick network of barbed wire.

'That's it over there . . . . ' Grey-hair points to a fat square chimney, no more than ten metres high, built on top of a flat asphalt roof. The black roof floats among the greenery of the lilac bushes like a raft in the ocean or an old-fashioned battleship, sitting low in the water with its funnel quite out of proportion. A thin transparent smoke is rising from the chimney.

'Is that someone leaving the organisation?'

'No.' Grey-hair laughs. 'The chimney is not only our way out; it is also a source of energy for us and the guardian of our secrets. At the moment they are simply burning secret papers. It's better, you know, to burn them than to keep them. When somebody leaves the organisation the smoke is not like that; it is dense and oily. If you join the organisation you too will one day rise into the sky through that chimney. But that's not what we're here for now. The organisation is giving you a last chance to change your mind, a final opportunity to consider your choice. And to give you something to think about, I'll show you a film. Sit down.'

He presses a knob on the control panel and sits down in an armchair alongside me. With a faint scraping noise, heavy brown shutters cover the huge windows and immediately a picture appears on the screen without any title or other explanation. It is a black and white film, obviously old and rather scratched. It has no sound track, and the regular clicking noise of the projector can be clearly heard.

1

On the screen there appears a high, gloomy room without windows, something between a factory workshop and a boiler house. In the foreground there is a furnace with fire-doors looking like the gates of a small castle, with grooves running into the furnace like rails into a tunnel. People in grey protective gowns are standing near the furnace. Boilermen. Then they showed a coffin. So this is a crematorium too. Probably the same one I have just been looking at out of the window. The men in gowns lift the coffin and place it on the guide rails. The fire doors open smoothly to each side, the coffin is given a gentle push and it bears its unknown occupant into the roaring flames. Then the camera gives a close-up of a living person. A face swimming in perspiration. It is probably very hot near the furnace. The face is displayed from all sides of what seems an eternity. At last the camera pulls back to show the person full length. He is not in a gown. He is dressed in an expensive black suit, terribly crumpled. His tie is tightly screwed round his neck. The man himself is bound fast with steel wire to a stretcher, and the stretcher has been propped up against the wall so that the man can see the furnace.

Next all the attendants suddenly turn their attention to the bound man. Their attention obviously gives him no pleasure. He lets out a scream. A terrible scream. There is no sound, but I can tell it is a scream that would make the windows rattle. Four of the attendants carefully lower the stretcher to the floor and then raise it again. The bound man makes an incredible effort to prevent this. The titanic strain is apparent in the expression on his face. A vein on his forehead stands out as though it is about to burst. But his effort to bite the hand of an attendant is in vain. His teeth only bite into his own lip, and a black trickle of blood begins to run down his chin. He certainly has sharp teeth. His body is firmly tied down, but it is wriggling about like that of a captured lizard. Submitting to an animal instinct, he begins to beat his head against the wooden handle of the stretcher and so assist his body. He is not fighting for his life, but for an easy death. His calculation is clear: to rock the stretcher over so as to fall with it off the guide rails and onto the concrete floor. This will mean either an easy death or loss of consciousness. You don't fear even the flames if you are unconscious. But the attendants know their job. The simply hold on to the handles of the stretcher to stop it rocking. And the prisoner cannot get at their hands with his teeth even if he breaks his neck.

They say that at the last moment of his life a man can perform miracles. Prompted by the instinct of self-preservation, all his muscles, all his mental and psychological resources, all his determination to live are suddenly concentrated into one supreme physical effort to survive. The man is making that last effort. He strains his whole body to try to get free. He sits like a fox which, caught in a trap, bites and tears off its own bloody paw. Even the metal guide rails begin to shake. He strains to the point of breaking his own bones, and tearing his own tendons and muscles. It is a superhuman effort. But the wire does not give. And the stretcher slides smoothly along the rails. The furnace doors move aside again and the fire casts a white light on the soles of the man's dirty patent leather shoes. He tries to bend his knees in an effort to increase the

2

distance between his feet and the roaring fire. But he can't. The cameraman then shows the man's fingers in close-up. The wire has bitten deeply into them. But the tips of his fingers are free, and with them too he is trying to slow down the movement towards the fire. His fingertips are spread out and tensed. If they could only come up against something the man would certainly hold on.

Then suddenly the stretcher comes to a halt at the furnace itself. A new figure appears on the screen dressed in a gown like the other attendants and gives them a signal with his hand. The attendants obediently remove the stretcher from the guide rails and stand it again on its handles against the wall. What is wrong? Why the hold-up? It soon becomes clear. Another coffin is wheeled into the crematorium on a low trolley. It is already nailed down and very elegant, with a decorative fringe. It is the coffin of some highly esteemed person. Make way for it! The attendants lift it on to the guide rails and send it off on its last journey. Then there is an unbelievably long wait while it is consumed by the flames. At last it is the turn of the man bound to the stretcher, which is again placed on the rails. And once again I hear that silent scream which is probably enough to lift the furnace doors off their hinges. I study the man's face in the hope of finding there signs of madness. It's easier for madmen in this world. But there are no such signs on that handsome manly face. It is not distorted by the imprint of madness. It is simply that he doesn't want to go into the furnace and is trying somehow to make that clear. But what can he do except scream? So he screams. Fortunately that scream is not recorded for posterity. Then his patent-leather shoes go into the fire, and that is that. The fire flares up. Oxygen being pumped in, no doubt. The two attendants at the front jump away to the side, while the two at the end give the stretcher a good push into the depths of the furnace. The furnace doors close and the sound of the projector dies out.

'Who was he?' I don't really know why I ask such a question.

'He was a colonel, a former colonel. He worked in our organisation in important posts. But he deceived us. So he was turned out of the organisation. And he left. That's the law here. We don't force anybody to come into the organisation. If you don't want to join you can simply refuse. But once you've joined you belong to the organisation lock, stock and barrel. Along with your shoes and your tie. So there you are . . . . I am giving you a last opportunity to change your mind. A minute to reflect.'

'But I don't need a minute for reflection.'

'That's the rule. Even if you don't need that minute the organisation is obliged to let you have it. So sit down and keep quiet.' Grey-hair presses a switch and a long thin hand begins to move round the bright face of the clock. Once again I can see before me the colonel's face at the very last moment when his feet are already in the fire, but his head is still living, blood is still circulating and his eyes still reflect the powerful intellect, the fear of death, the cruel torture and an unconquerable desire to live. If they are going to admit me into that organisation I am ready to serve it loyally. It is a serious and powerful organisation, and I like their ways. But I know damned well in advance that, if

3

I am to depart through the short square chimney, it will never be in a coffin with fancy frills. That is not in my character. I am not the sort to get fancy treatment . . . . Not me.

'Time's up. Do you want more time to think?'

'No.'

'Another minute?'

'No.'

'All right, then, captain, I have the honour to be the first to congratulate you on joining our secret brotherhood, known as the Chief Directorate of Intelligence of the General Staff, or the GRU for short. The next move is for you to meet Colonel-General Meshcheryakov, the deputy head of the GRU and to call on Colonel-General Lemzenko at the Central Committee of the Party. I think they will take to you. Don't try to be too clever, although it's better on these occasions to ask a question than to remain silent. In the course of the examinations and psychological tests that we set you questions sometimes seem to force themselves upon you. Don't let it worry you. Ask the question. Behave as you behaved here today and then everything will be all right. I wish you well, captain.'

Chapter One

If you should ever think of making your career in the KGB, simply make your way to any provincial centre. There you will be sure to find a statue of Lenin on the main square. Behind it there will be, just as surely, a huge building with a colonnaded façade. That will be the headquarters of the regional committee of the Communist Party. And somewhere close by you will find the regional headquarters of the KGB. Just ask anybody on the square: anyone will show you. Yes, that grey, gloomy building over there, the one that Lenin is pointing at with his reinforced concrete hand.

But you don't necessarily have to apply to the regional headquarters. You can enquire in the 'special department' at your place of work. There too everybody will help you: straight along the corridor and then to the right, the door covered in black leather.

There are even easier ways of becoming an employee of the KGB. Just apply to the man in charge of the special department. There's one to be found in every god-forsaken railway station and in every factory, sometimes in every workshop. There's one in every regiment, in every college, in every prison, in every Party committee, in every design bureau, and masses of them in the Communist youth movement, the trade unions, and the social organisations. Just go up to them and say: I want to join the KGB! It's another question whether they'll take you in or not (of course they will!). But the path to the KGB is open for everybody and there's no need at all to go looking for it.

It's by no means so easy to get into the GRU. Who do you apply to? Who do you ask for advice? Which door do you knock at? At the police station, maybe? But the police would only shrug their shoulders: never heard of it. In Georgia the police even issue car number plates with the letters 'GRU', never suspecting that they could have some other, less obvious significance. A car with a 'GRU' plate could travel all over the country without causing any surprise and without anyone paying it special attention. For the honest citizen, as for the whole of the Soviet police force, those letters mean nothing and have no special associations.

The KGB can count its voluntary workers in millions. The GRU has none. That is the main difference. The GRU is entirely secret. Since nobody knows about it, nobody can enter it on his own initiative. Even supposing that some volunteer were to come along, how would he set about finding the right door to knock at, to request admission? Would he be accepted? Not likely. Volunteers are not needed. In fact, a volunteer would be arrested at once and subjected to a long and very painful interrogation. He would have a lot of questions to answer. Where have you heard those three letters mentioned? How have you managed to find us? But most important: who helped you? Who? Who? Answer, you bastard! The GRU knows how to get the right answers out of people. They'll get an answer out of anybody. I can guarantee that. They would inevitably discover who helped the volunteer. Then the interrogation would begin over again. Who talked to *you*, you skunk, about the GRU? Where did you hear about it? Sooner or later they would get back to the original source. It might turn out to be someone entrusted with the secret whose tongue had overstepped the mark. Oh, the GRU knows how to rip such tongues out! It tears them off along with the heads. This is something that everyone who has got into the GRU knows very well. Anxious to save their own necks, the first thing they ensure is that they guard their tongues. You can talk about the GRU only inside the GRU. And you can talk only so long as your voice is not heard on the other side of the transparent walls of the building on the Khodinka. Everyone who gets into the GRU observes the law of the Aquarium, the name by which the headquarters is known to initiates. Everything we talk about inside stays inside. Not a single word must go beyond the transparent walls. And since such rules exist, there are very few people outside the transparent walls who know what goes on inside them. And since anyone who does know keeps his mouth shut, I personally had never heard anything about the GRU.

I was a company commander. Following our liberating campaign in Czechoslovakia a wave of new appointments swept me up and dropped me into the 318th motorised infantry division of the 13th Army of the Carpathian military district. I was put in command of the 2nd tank company in a tank battalion of the 910th motorised infantry regiment.

My company did not shine in performance, but it was also not reckoned among the laggards. My life seemed to be cut out for me for many years ahead. After commanding the company I would be chief of staff of a battalion. After that I should have to get myself accepted into the Malinovsky tank academy, and from there I might rise to command a battalion, then a regiment, and then maybe even higher. Deviations from this course might affect the speed at which I advanced, but not the direction. I had chosen that direction for myself, and I had no intention of changing it. But fate decided otherwise.

On 13 April 1969, at ten minutes past four in the morning, my orderly shook me gently by the shoulder and said: 'Get up, lieutenant, great deeds await you.' Then he quickly remembered that I didn't take easily to jokes on being awakened, and in a very different tone said curtly: 'Action stations!'

It took me three and a half minutes to get myself ready: off with my blanket and on with my trousers, socks and boots. I slipped into my tunic without buttoning it up – I could do that on the move. I strapped my shoulder-belt on as tight as I could, and put my officer's document case over my shoulder and my cap on my head. I ran my hand along the peak of my cap to make sure that the hat badge was in line with my nose. Then off at the run. My pistol was in the regimental duty officer's room, and I grabbed it out of the huge safe near the entrance to the regimental barracks. My rucksack, greatcoat, overalls and padded helmet were always kept in the tank. So down the stairs two at a time. It would have been good to get under a shower at that point, and to have run a razor over my cheeks. But there was no time. Actions stations! The snub-nosed truck was already practically full of young officers and their even younger orderlies. In the sky above the stars were beginning to fade. They were sneaking away quietly without saying goodbye, as people go out of our lives whose memory disturbs us.

The tank park reverberated with the deafening roar of hundreds of engines. A grey mist and the bitter smell of the exhausts hung over everything. Then the growl of the tanks as they moved from their places. The grey-green monsters trundled along the dirty concrete roadway and formed into an endless line. At the front the wide-bodied tanks of the reconnaissance company moved smoothly along, followed by the armoured personnel carriers of the staff and the signals company, then an armoured battalion, and beyond them round the corner three motorised infantry battalions formed into columns, and after them came the regimental artillery, the anti-aircraft and anti-tank batteries, the sappers, the chemical warfare troops and the repair units. There was no room for the support units in the huge park. They would start to form their columns only after the leading units had moved far ahead.

I ran past the columns of tanks towards my own company. The regimental chief of staff was having words with the company commanders, shouting above the noise of the engines. I kept running, as did the other officers. Quick was the word. There was my company. Three tanks in the first platoon, three in the second and another three in the third. And my tank, the command tank, was out in front. All ten were in place and I could hear the roar of my ten engines. I could distinguish them from among the general roar. Each engine has its own ways, its own character, its own voice. Not one of them was out of tune.

Not bad for a start. When I came up to my own tank I quickened my steps, jumped smartly on to the sloping front armour plate and ran up to the turret. The hatch was open and the radio operator handed me my helmet, already connected to the communication network. The helmet transported me out of the world of engine roar and the growl of tanks to one of peace and quiet. But the headphones almost immediately came to life, destroying the fragile illusion of tranquillity. The radio operator sitting beside me informed me of the latest instructions (otherwise he would have had to shout into my ear). Nothing of any importance. I cut him off with the most important question. Is it war or training? Goodness knows, he replied with a shrug of the shoulders.

Whatever the situation, my company was ready for battle and had to be moved immediately out of the tank park. That was the rule. The concentration of hundreds of tanks and vehicles in an enclosed park was the sort of target our enemies dreamed of. I looked out in front, could hardly make anything out.

The first tank company was standing in front of me. The commander had probably not yet arrived. All the others ahead of me were also waiting. I jumped up onto the top of the turret to get a better view. It looked as though one of the tanks in the reconnaissance company had stalled and was blocking the way for the whole regiment. I looked at my watch. Our regimental commander – our lord and master – still had eight minutes left. If in eight minutes' time the regiment's columns were not on the move, the commander would be cashiered and kicked out of the Army without a pension, like an old dog. But there were no signs of any tractor coming through from the repair company. The whole of the central road running between the dull grey garages was jammed full of tanks from end to end. There was a road off to the right with some emergency gates at the end. But the road was broken by a deep trench: they had started to lay some kind of cable or pipeline and there was no way through.

I jumped down into the turret and at the top of my voice ordered the driver: 'Left wheel and ahead!' And at the same time to the whole company: 'Do as I do!' There was no gateway to the left. There was only a brick wall running between the long blocks of repair shops. But in the command tank I had the best driver in the company. That had long been the rule throughout the Army. I shouted at him over the intercom: 'You're the best in the company! I chose you, you scoundrel. I conferred on you, you rascal, the highest honour – to care for and cherish the command tank. Don't disgrace your commander's choice! Or I'll flatten you and let you rot!'

My driver didn't have a chance to reply. Over a very short stretch of ground he whipped our armoured dinosaur up to a breakneck pace, changing gear at lightning speed. The body shook, the engine screamed. There was a terrifying shock as the tank hit the brick wall. Everything we had in the tank shuddered and began to rattle and squeak. The bricks descended in an avalanche on to the armour plate, wrecking the headlights, and aerials, ripping off boxes of spare instruments and denting the external spare fuel tanks. But my tank let out a roar and, wrapped in a web of barbed wire, burst its way out of a cloud of brick dust into the sleepy side street of a peaceful Ukrainian town. I looked out through the rear porthole and saw my tanks cheerfully passing through the gap behind me. The tank park's duty officer was running towards the gap in the wall, waving his hands and shouting something. It was like a silent film: you could only guess by his gestures what he was saying. His mouth was wide open, but you couldn't possibly hear what he was shouting. I guessed he was cursing. They were exceedingly vulgar gestures. No mistake about it.

When the tenth tank of my company had passed through the gap, the traffic control appeared: black uniforms with white belts and helmets. They would bring order into the situation. They knew who to let through first. Reconnaissance units first. Every regiment has its special reconnaissance company with special equipment and special troops and officers. But apart from that every motorised infantry and tank battalion in a regiment has another specially trained company which does not have special equipment or special troops but

8

which can also be used for carrying out reconnaissance. These companies have to be allowed to go ahead. Come on, you white-helmeted boys, let us get on the move! We've got to be out there in front.

To an outsider all the companies in a division or a regiment look exactly the same. But they're not. The first company in every battalion really is the first. However many poor quality soldiers there are in a battalion, the commander makes sure that everything and everybody of the best goes into the first company. And if there's a shortage of officers the fresh intake has to be given to the first company. Because the first company always forms the main axis of the battalion. It is the first to clash with the enemy head-on. And a great deal depends on how the first move in a battle is engaged and on its outcome.

The second company in any battalion is usually mediocre. The officers in second companies are without any special distinction, like me, and so are the troops. But every second company has additional reconnaissance training. It has a sort of second profession. It is primarily a fighting unit, but in case of need it can carry out reconnaissance on behalf of its battalion, and can even serve the regiment by replacing or supplementing the special reconnaissance company.

There are in the Soviet Army 2,400 motorised infantry and tank battalions, and each of them has a third company which is third not only in order. The people who serve in third companies are usually those who did not get into either the first or the second companies: very young and inexperienced officers or those who have been passed over and have little future. There is always a shortage of soldiers in the third companies. In fact, the overwhelming majority of third companies don't have any soldiers at all. Their battle equipment is kept permanently in mothballs. If war breaks out thousands of such companies will immediately be reinforced by the call-up of reservists and will quickly reach the level of normal fighting units. There is profound good sense in this system: to add reservists to an existing division is a thousand times better than forming new divisions wholly from reservists.

My second tank company continued to advance at top speed. As we were making the turn I looked back and counted the tanks. So far they were all keeping up with us. Close on the tail of the last tank of my company, making the sparks fly off the concrete, was a tracked personnel carrier with a little white flag. That was a great relief for me. The little white flag meant that there were umpires present. And that in turn meant that we were on manoeuvres and were not going to war. So we could live another day.

A military helicopter – a 'dragonfly' – appeared right above my head, lost height and swung round into the wind to hold its position. It hovered to the right of me. I stood on the turret cover with my right hand above my head. The pilot was a real redhead, with a face like a magpie's egg, covered with freckles. His white teeth gleamed as he smiled down at me. He knew, that man in the chopper, that the commanders to whom he was transmitting orders were not going to have the best of days. The helicopter suddenly shot upwards and away, the red-headed pilot still grinning, his teeth still reflecting the light of the rising sun.

My broad-fronted tank was cutting a path through everything that came in its way. Branches and undergrowth flew in all directions. The row inside the tank was hellish. The whole machine roared like a raging ocean, prancing about like a fury. I had my map on my knees, and the situation was fairly clear to me. A whole division had been thrown into the breach and was advancing at breakneck speed westwards. But it was not clear where the enemy was. The map was no use there. For that reason twenty companies were rushing ahead of the division, mine among them. These companies were like the fingers of a hand spread out, and their task was to detect the most vulnerable place in the enemy's defences, into which the divisional commander would thrust his thousand-ton fist. The enemy's weak spot had to be sought for over vast areas, and consequently each of the companies sent ahead operated entirely on its own. I knew that other companies like mine were also racing forward alongside me but avoiding centres of resistance in villages and towns. My company also took care to avoid getting involved in exhausting clashes. If it came upon the enemy it simply informed the staff, dodged round him as fast as possible and moved on ahead. Meanwhile, somewhere behind our main force was moving like a roaring river bursting through a dam. Forward, my boys, forward. Westwards!

The personnel carrier with the white flag was not dropping behind. The damned thing had only half the weight of a tank but practically the same enormous horse-power. Twice I tried to break away from it, on the grounds that high speed is a guarantee of victory. But it didn't come off. When I was in command of a platoon such tricks were perfectly possible, but not with a company. It would only break up the column and get the tanks stranded in the marshes, which would not get you any sympathy. It would certainly get you relieved of your company, however. To hell with the umpires, I thought, let them observe us to their heart's content; I'm not going to let the company get spread out.

'There's a crane ahead . . .' came a call from the commander of the sixth tank, sent ahead.

A crane? A lifting crane? Yes! A crane! A beautiful green crane, all camouflaged with tree branches. When do you ever come across a crane on a battlefield? Of course! With a missile battery! You don't get a bit of luck like that every day!

'Company,' I shouted. 'A missile battery . . . . Into action . . . . Advance!'

My lads already know exactly how to deal with missile batteries. The first platoon overtook me and spread out in battle formation. The second platoon

10

accelerated violently and took off to the right, its tracks spraying mud in all directions. The third platoon turned off to the left and in a wide sweep attacked the battery from the flank.

'Full speed ahead,' I shouted. But the drivers knew what was needed without my telling them. Every driver now had his foot hard down on the armour-plated floor, pressing the pedal to its limit, making the engines scream as if they were out of control. Hence the noise and the clouds of smoke: the fuel didn't have time to burn up completely in the motors, so it came belching thick and oily, out of the exhausts.

'Reconnaissance . . . completed . . . square 13–41 . . . initial position . . . am going into action . . . . ' That was my radio-operator-gun-loader sending what might well be our last message over the air. Missile units and enemy staffs had to be attacked as soon as they were met, without any commands being issued, whatever the chances of success and whatever the cost.

The gun-loader switched off the intercom and thrust the first shell into the carriage. It slid smoothly into the breech and a powerful breech block closed the barrel with a heart-rending shock, like the blade of a guillotine. The turret swung round to one side, and beneath my feet I caught a glimpse of the driver-mechanic and the stock of shells. With a shudder the breech of the gun swung upwards. The gun-layer gripped the firing console with both hands, and the powerful stabilisers, obeying his horny hands, controlled the gun and the turret in short sharp movements, preventing them from repeating the wild dance of the tank which seemed to have gone mad as it flew over tree-trunks and branches. With the thumb of his right hand the gun-layer pressed firmly on the trigger. So that the noise should not be transmitted to our ears without warning, there was a sharp click in the headphones, making our eardrums contract ahead of the great shock as the mighty gun fired. The click in our helmets came only hundredths of a second before the shot, so that we did not hear the shot itself.

The forty-ton hulk of our tank shuddered as it raced ahead. The gun-barrel sprang back and threw out the ringing, smoking shell-case. And immediately, following the example of the commander's gun, all the others started to bark in rapid succession. Meanwhile my gun-layer had already put a second shell in the carriage.

'Full speed ahead,' I shouted again.

The tank-tracks were throwing up fountains of mud, and the crunch of the tracks was louder even than the gunfire. Then a click in the helmet headphones told us that the gun-layer was about to press the trigger again. Once again we did not hear the sound of our own shot. We only saw the barrel spring back and heard the shell case make its frightening clang as it hit the baffle plate. We could hear the firing only of the guns of the tanks nearby. And they could hear ours. This shellfire whipped my valiant Asians into a fury. They became like wild beasts. I knew every single one of them. In the fifth tank, in between shots, the gun-layer was gnawing at the rubber strap on the sight out of sheer delight. Everybody knew this, not only in the company but in the battalion too. It was bad, that: it diverted attention from observing the situation. He had almost been transferred to the gun-loaders for that. But he was a very good shot, the scoundrel. In the eighth tank the commander always took an axe with him so that whenever his gun got choked through rapid firing he could bring the axe-head down on the armour plating. On our last sortie, the commander of the third tank had switched on his radio transmitter and forgotten to switch it off, ruining communications throughout the company. The whole company could hear him grinding his teeth and howling like a wolf.

'Hit 'em for six!' I said quietly. But my whisper was carried thirty kilometres by radio, as though I was whispering the words into the ear of every one of my dear ferocious Asians. And they understood. Their Russian was terrible, but they understood 'Hit 'em.'

Another click in our ears and another shell case clattered out. The smell of the expended shells made your head spin. The poisonous smell had a powerful, brutalising effect. My soldiers were intoxicated by the deafening noise, the power of their motors and the rattle of the machine-gun fire. No force in the world could hold them back now. All the drivers were behaving as though they had just been slipped off a leash. They yanked the driving levers with their great coarse hands, manhandled their machines and drove them straight into the heat of battle. Meanwhile I looked back, to make sure we were not being overtaken. Far away in the rear was the transporter with the white flag. It had dropped back, fallen by the wayside. I was sorry for the people in it: they had no powerful gun, no deafening noise, no intoxicating smells. They got no pleasure from life, didn't know what it was. That was why their driver was so cowardly, carefully dodging stones and tree trunks. But there was no need to be afraid. You had to grab the machine with both hands, take it and throw it about. An armour-plated tank is a gentle thing. But if it feels that it is being ridden by a really strong man it will go wild too. It will take you at the gallop over granite boulders, trunks of ancient oaks, through craters and ditches. Don't worry about ripping off the tracks or breaking a shaft. Just give it all you've got and it will sweep you along like a bird. A tank simply revels in battle: that is what it's made for. Onwards!

'*Take your company out of the battle line . . .*'

Sparks flew from under the tank tracks. The company rushed down on the defences of the missile battery. There was a crunching noise in my ears: either the tracks going across a steel plate or the gun-layer's teeth grinding in my headphones.

'*. . . take your company out of the battle line . . .*'

So as not to find themselves firing at each other, without further orders the tanks ceased fire and just went on growling like wolves tearing a deer to pieces. They were going head-on with their armoured breastplates into the fragile missile transporters and the cranes on the launch pads and were pushing the pride and glory of the missile artillery into the sticky black earth. Full speed ahead!

'*. . . take your company out of the battle line . . .*'

Once again I could hear somebody's distant squeaky voice and suddenly I realised that it was addressed to me. Damn! Who on earth, at such a moment of supreme, and almost sexual bliss, would want to drag people away from their favourite occupation? That blasted observer would make my stallions impotent! Who gave him the right to ruin a first-class tank company? An enemy of the people or a bourgeois saboteur? To hell with him!

'Company – full speed ahead!'

Then, banging my fist on the armour-plate and hurling into the air curses on the whole gang of staff officers who had never in their offices had the smell of powder in their nostrils, I gave the order:

'Company – break away! Left wheel into the meadow in platoons!'

My driver angrily pulled the left lever right over, nearly turning the heavy tank over on its right side and destroying a beautiful silver birch. Then he skilfully changed gears, put the tank quickly into top gear and sent it rushing through the bushes and over deep holes towards the meadow. Having swung the tank right round, he dropped the engine speed to a minimum so that it stood quietly in place, far ahead of the others, like an aircraft which has braked suddenly at the end of a runway. With a roar of disappointment the rest of the tanks thrust their way one after the other out of the forest and, breaking convulsively, formed up in a straight line.

'Disarm! Guns open for inspection!' I gave the order and then ripped the plug of the headphones out of its socket. The gun-layer cut off the intercom.

The APC with the group of observers had fallen a long way behind. While it was trying to catch up with us I had time to check the equipment, to receive a report on the state of the tanks and the quantity of fuel and ammunition that had been used, and to draw up the company and hold it in the middle of the meadow ready to make my report. As we stood there I worked out in my mind the pluses and minuses, what I might be praised for and what punished. The company had started to leave the tank park eight minutes before its set time, and that was praiseworthy, something for which a company commander might sometimes be slipped a gold watch. At the beginning of a war they reckon in seconds. All tanks, all aircraft and all staff headquarters have to get out of danger at top speed, so that the enemy's first terrible blow is delivered on deserted military camps. Eight minutes! Definitely a plus for me. All my tanks were in good shape and had remained so throughout the morning. That was a plus for my technical deputy. It was a pity that, due to the shortage of officers, I had no technical deputy: I had to do his work. We had avoided the strongholds in swift manoeuvres and had reported on them in good time and precisely. That was a plus for the commander of the first platoon. It was a pity that we didn't have one: again the shortage. We had not missed the missile battery, we had sniffed it out and flattened it into the ground. And a missile battery, even the most broken-down one, could produce a couple of Hiroshimas. But, by

13

stopping reconnaissance and throwing my boxes of metal against the missiles, I had averted those Hiroshimas. For such action in a war they pin a very big medal on your chest and refer to it approvingly at lectures for a long time afterwards.

At last the observer, a colonel, appeared. Hands white and spotlessly clean, boots glistening in the sun. With a look of distaste on his face he picked his way carefully, like a cat, round the puddles. The regimental commander, our chief, was also a colonel, only his huge hands were callused and obviously accustomed to hard work. His face was burnt brown with exposure to the frost, the sun and the winds of all the training grounds and ranges that I knew, unlike the pale features of the observing officer.

'Straighten up! Easy! Dressing by the right!'

But the colonel paid no heed to my report, cutting me off in the middle of a word: 'You have fun, don't you, lieutenant, in action! Like a little boy!'

I remained silent, smiling at him. He didn't seem to be finding fault with me; more like giving me a medal. But my smile seemed to make him even fiercer. The officers accompanying him remained grimly silent. They knew that Clause 97 of the Disciplinary Code did not permit him to criticise me in the presence of my subordinates. The majors and lieutenant-colonels knew that, by criticising me in the presence of my subordinates, the colonel was undermining not only my authority as a commander but the authority of the whole officer contingent of the glorious Soviet Army, including his own authority as a colonel. I seemed to be in the clear. So I went on smiling.

'It is quite disgraceful, senior lieutenant, not to hear orders and not to carry them out.'

My dear idiot colonel, I thought to myself, I would hang people who do not enjoy themselves in action and who are not intoxicated by the smell of blood – hang them on the gun barrels. This was just training, but if in a real battle the tracks of our tanks were spattered with real blood and not make-believe my Asians would have become even more excited. That was not a sign of weakness. That was their strength. Nobody in the world would be able to stop them.

'And then there's the wall! You knocked down the wall of the park! That's a serious offence!'

I had forgotten altogether about the wall. Big deal. It had probably already been rebuilt. Wouldn't take long. They only had to get ten prisoners from the glasshouse and they'd put a new wall up in a couple of hours. And how, my dear colonel, was I to know whether it was just an exercise or the real thing? And if it was war and the wall had remained standing, and 2000 men and hundreds of first-class fighting vehicles had been destroyed in one group? Eh, colonel? You have a big title, you are known as the Chief of Intelligence of the 13th Army, so just enquire how many targets my Uzbeks discovered in one day. They don't even speak Russian properly, but they know perfectly how to seek out targets. Praise them, colonel! Never mind about me, but give them a smile. And I kept smiling at him. I was standing with my back to the company and I could not possibly turn to look at them. But I knew very well that my whole company was smiling. Simply smiling, without any special reason. That's what they were like, ready to display their teeth in any circumstances.

The colonel was not pleased. He probably thought we were laughing at him. It made him furious. He ground his teeth, like the gun-layer in action. He was not capable of understanding or assessing our smiles. So he bawled straight at me:

'Young man, you are not fit to command a company. I am removing you. Hand your company over to your deputy and have him take the company back to barracks!'

'I don't have a deputy at the moment,' I told him, smiling.

'Then hand over to the commander of the first platoon!'

'There isn't one.' And, to save the colonel going through all the lower rank commanders, I explained: 'I am the only officer in the company.'

The colonel calmed down. All the fire went out of him, as though it had never been. The situation in which there is only one officer in a company is, in our Army, especially within the territory of the Soviet Union, practically universal. There are plenty of people who want to be officers, but they all want to be colonels. Very few are attracted by the idea of going in as a lieutenant. That's why there is a shortage at the lower end. There is a cruel shortage of officers. But people seem to forget about this at the top, in the headquarters staffs. That's why it didn't occur to the colonel that I could be the only officer in the whole company. He had removed me from my command, as he had a right to do. But the company had to be returned to barracks. And it was impossible to send a company, especially a tank company, dozens of kilometres without any officers. That was an offence. It would probably be regarded as an attempt at a *coup d'état*. So it was up to the colonel to take the fatal decision. Having removed a commander in circumstances where he had no deputy, he had taken personal responsibility for the company, and did not have the right to entrust the company to anyone else. If such a right were granted then every divisional commander could lead his troops out into the field, remove the commanders and replace them by others to suit his taste. Thus a *coup* could be carried out. But we don't have *coups*, because by no means everyone is permitted to handle the delicate question of selecting and appointing key people. He had the right to dismiss people. To dismiss is easy. Everyone had the right to dismiss people. It was easy as killing a man. But to restore commanders to their posts is as difficult as returning a dead man to life. Well, colonel, I said to myself, do you think you can put me in charge of the company again? It won't work. I am not worthy. Everybody heard you say that. You don't have the right to put an unworthy man in charge of a company. And what if your superiors get to know that, close to the state frontier, you were removing properly appointed commanders from tank companies and putting unworthy officers in their place? What would happen to you?

At this point it would have suited the colonel to get in touch with the commander of my battalion or regiment and ask him to take over his delinquent company. But the exercises were over. They had ended as suddenly as they had begun. Who would allow wartime communications to be used after the exercises were over? Officers who took such liberties in 1937 were shot. After that, no one was likely to get up to such tricks. So what about it colonel? Go on, take command of the company. But perhaps you've already forgotten how to lead a company? Maybe you've never led one? A whole career in staff jobs. There are plenty of such colonels. Every other job appears quite trifling. There doesn't seem to be anything very complicated about leading a tank company. But the commands have to be given as laid down in the new regulations. The men in the company are not Russians, they won't understand otherwise. Even worse if they misunderstand a command. Then your search troops will never find them, even with a helicopter over the forests and marshes. A tank is a heavy thing: it can run over a man, run off a bridge or sink in a bog. And the commander's come-uppance is always the same.

I was no longer smiling. The situation was serious and there was nothing to laugh about. I would have liked at that moment to have saluted smartly and said: 'May I be dismissed, comrade colonel?' After all, I had no status; I was neither a commander nor a subordinate. He had got himself into a mess and it was up to him to get himself out. He had wanted to take command, so let him command. But the pleasure of seeing him in a tough spot soon faded in me. It was my very own company, my men and my machines. I was no longer responsible for the company, but I wasn't going to drop it just like that.

'Permit me, comrade colonel,' I said, saluting smartly. 'Allow me to lead the company for the last time. A sort of farewell to it.'

'Yes,' he said, curtly. For a moment it seemed to me as though out of habit he was going to give me the usual advice – don't go too fast, don't play about, don't let the column get spread out. But he didn't.

'Yes, yes, you lead the company. Consider my order not having come into force. Take the company to barracks and hand it over there.'

'Very good!' I turned about sharply, but not without noticing the smiles on the faces of the colonel's suite. What on earth was that: taking command for the time being? His officers knew very well that there was no such order as 'command for the time being'. An officer was either worthy of commanding his unit and was entirely responsible for it, or he was not worthy and was removed immediately. To command for the time being – that was not a solution. His handling of the situation might cost the colonel dear. That was clear to me, and to his officers. But I hadn't time to bother with it for the moment. I had a serious matter on hand. I was commanding the company. And I couldn't care less who thought what, who did what or who was going to be punished for it.

Before he gives the first command a commander has to assert his authority over his unit. He has to cast his eye over his troops in such a way that a slight movement runs through the ranks which freezes into silence, when everyone is aware that the commander's orders are about to follow. But in tank troops commands are given in silence. There were two flags in my hands. I gave my orders with them.

I held up the white flag. That was my first command. With that short sharp gesture I was in fact conveying a quite long message to my company: 'I am now in command of the company! I forbid all transmissions by radio until we meet the enemy. Attention.' There are preliminary commands and executive commands. With a preliminary command an officer is, so to speak, taking hold of his subordinates with the reins of his own will. Then, having tightened the reins, the commander has to wait five seconds before giving the main command. His formation has to freeze in expectation, each man straining at the metal bit, quivering slightly, muscles flinching as if before a sharp blow, everyone awaiting the executive command as a good horse expects the whip.

I raised the red flag and then dropped both of them to my sides together. The company burst into life, broke formation and began to clatter with the sound of heavy boots on the armour-plate.

Maybe it was because the company was taking leave of me, or because they wanted to demonstrate their skills to the observers, or because they were just feeling angry and had no other way of expressing their anger. If only I had switched on a stop-watch! But even without it I knew immediately that my company was breaking the record for the division and perhaps doing even better than that. I knew that there were many genuine tank officers accompanying the colonel and that every one of them was admiring my Asians. I had seen a lot of records broken by tank units and I knew what they were worth. I had also seen hands broken and teeth knocked out. But all was going well for my lads at that moment. And I seemed to know in advance that not one of them would stumble or slip as he leapt into the hatch. I knew that nobody was going to get his fingers crushed by the lid. Not on this occasion.

Ten engines started to whine in harmony. I climbed into the command hatch. Now the white flag held high in my hand meant: 'I am ready!' Nine flags went up in reply: 'Ready! Ready! Ready!' I swept the flag in a circle above my head and then pointed clearly to the east: 'Follow me!' And that was all. Elementary. Primitive? Yes. But there is no form of radio reconnaissance that can detect even four tank armies moving off at the same time. And against other forms of detection there are equally primitive but effective devices. That is why we always turn up unexpectedly. We may make the right or the wrong move, but it's always unexpected. Even in Czechoslovakia, even with seven armies at once.

The colonel-observer scrambled up onto his personnel carrier, his officers after him. The machine roared into life, made a sharp turn and set off for the camp by another route.

The colonel's suite of officers obviously loathed him. Otherwise they would have suggested that he ought to follow immediately behind my tank. After all, I was now a nobody, an impostor. To entrust the company to me was like a police chief entrusting a policeman he had dismissed with the arrest of a major criminal. Having had such an idea, he should at least have remained alongside, ready to intervene. Having handed the company over to someone else because you can't lead it yourself, you should at least stay near to step on the brakes if

17

need be. But no one had pointed out to the colonel that he had put his life into the hands of a young senior lieutenant. And a senior lieutenant who had been relieved of his command could play all sorts of dirty tricks, since he no longer belonged to the company. The colonel would have to carry the can. Perhaps his officers were confident that the senior lieutenant would bring the company back without any accidents, that he would not ruin the colonel's future. But he could have done.

It often happens that a divison is whipped into action with an emergency alarm, rushes out into the fields and is then returned home. It makes very good sense. It becomes a habit. It means that when the division sets out on the real thing it acts as if it were going on maneouvres, without over-excitement. At the same time the enemy becomes less vigilant. Soviet divisions frequently burst out of their camps unexpectedly. So the enemy ceases to react.

The roads were jammed with tank columns. The order to withdraw had obviously been given to the whole division simultaneously. Who could tell how many divisions had been called into action by the alarm and how many were now making their way back to camp! Maybe just one division, maybe three, maybe five. For all we knew as many as a hundred divisions could have been activated at the same time.

A band was blaring forth at the entrance to the camp.

The officer commanding our regiment was standing on a tank, welcoming his columns back. He had an experienced eye, quick to detect faults. A single glance was sufficient for him to form an opinion of a company, a battery, a battalion, all their commanders. The officers shrank under their master's leaden gaze. He was a big fine-looking man, his shoulder belt done up on the last holes, barely coming together. The upper part of his enormous boots were slit open a little to enable him to pull them over his mighty calves. He had a fist as big as a kettle, and he was waving to someone with it. Probably at the commander of the third motorised infantry battalion whose armoured personnel carriers were just making their way through the gates. Next came the mortar battery from that battalion and then it was my turn. And although I knew that all my tanks were following behind me, and although it was now all the same to me whether they were coming or not, since I was no longer in command, I still looked round at the very last moment. Yes, they were all there. Not one had dropped back. So I quickly faced forward again and brought my right hand quickly up to my helmet; the commanders of the other nine tanks repeated the greeting.

The regimental commander was still shouting something offensive and threatening at the column of the third battalion. At last he directed a ferocious look at my company. Who could withstand such a look, the look of a gorilla in the jungle or a Cossack bandit in the steppes? As my eyes caught his I suddenly and to my own surprise decided to look at him straight. And he opened his

18

hand and brought the wide spade-like palm up to his cap-peak. I had not expected that. I looked blank for a moment, then blinked my eyes. My tank had already gone past him, but I swung my head round and looked at the commander. Suddenly he smiled at me. His face was so swarthy that his white-toothed smile was visible to my whole company and probably also to the howitzer battery which was behind me and which he was about to greet.

You do not realise, commander, I said to myself, that I'm no longer in charge of the company. I have been dismissed. Dismissed in disgrace. A sort of public reproach. That, commander, is nothing. Do you think I'm going to cry? Never in my life. I shall be smiling. Always. To spite everybody. I shall smile happily and proudly, just as I am smiling at you now, commander. I shall soon get a new company. There's a shortage of officers, as you well know. Only it's a pity to have to part from my Asians. We managed to get together a very friendly bunch of lads. But we shall survive. As far as I am concerned it is enough that the regiment was on the move in good time and that you, my commander, have not been dismissed from the regiment. Stand there and take the salute with your great fist. That's your job. We don't need any other commander in this regiment. We can forgive you your tough ways. And if need be we will follow you wherever you lead us. I too will follow you in command, if not of a company, then of a platoon. Or even as a simple gun-layer.

When a combat vehicle returns to its park, what is the first thing that has to be done? Of course. It has to be refuelled. Whether it is in good order or bad, it must be full of fuel. Who can tell when the next alarm will hit us? Every combat vehicle must be ready to repeat the exercise from the beginning at a moment's notice. For that reason the tank park was again full of noise. Hundreds of vehicles were being refuelled. Every tank needed a minimum of a ton of fuel. The APCs are also very thirsty and so are the artillery tractors. All the transport vehicles had to be filled up. At the same time the fighting vehicles had to have their ammunition replenished. Each tank shell weighs 30 kilograms. Hundreds of them were brought up, two shells to a box. Each box had to be taken off its transport, the shells taken out and the packing removed from each one. Then each one had to be cleaned, the factory's protective grease removed, and the shell placed in the tank. Cartridges also came in boxes, 880 to a box, and they had to be loaded into belts. In each machine-gun belt there were 250 rounds. The belts had to be loaded into their magazines, and there were thirteen of them in every tank. Then all the empty shell cases had to be picked up, and put in boxes and handed in to the stores. Gun barrels would be cleaned later. Each tank's gun barrel in turn was polished for several hours a day and for several days in a row. But for the moment the barrels had only to be oiled. Then the tanks had to be washed down: a rough clean-up now and a thorough wash and clean later. Next the troops had to be fed. They had had no mid-day meal, so that they would have lunch and supper together. After supper

19

everybody would be put on to servicing the vehicles. Everything had to be checked by the morning: motors, transmissions, suspensions and tracks. Where necessary the tracks would be replaced. In the fourth tank the torsion bar was broken on the left side. On the eighth the reduction gear was out of order. In the first tank company two motors had to be changed at once. Early the next morning the business of cleaning the barrels would begin. Everything must be in good order! Full speed! But then suddenly I had an empty feeling in my heart. I remembered that it would not be my job next morning to check on the servicing in my company. Tomorrow they might not even let me into the tank park. I knew that all the documents on my case had already been prepared and that I would be dismissed officially that same evening, not the next morning. I also knew that it was laid down that an officer should appear for his dismissal as smartly turned-out as he would to receive a decoration. My company knew that too. For that reason, while I was having words with the men filling the tanks, while I was checking the reports on ammunition used, and while I was crawling under tank number three, someone else was already putting a mirror polish on my boots, pressing my trousers and sewing a clean collar into my tunic. I got out of my dirty overalls and stepped quickly under a shower. Then I shaved carefully and slowly. At that moment an orderly arrived from regimental headquarters.

The park still resounded with noise. A tractor was hauling a damaged transporter through the gates. There was the clang of empty shell cases. The huge 'Ural' lorries rumbled along loaded to the top with empty shell boxes. An electric welder was throwing up a firework display of sparks. By morning everything would be dazzlingly bright. For the moment there was nothing but mud, mud all around, noise and din, as on a big construction site. There was nothing to distinguish officers from soldiers. They were all in overalls, all filthy and all cursing. Through all this chaos came Senior Lieutenant Suvorov, the officer thinking about his career, his uniform pressed to perfection, with every button gleaming. The grease-stained tankmen stared after me. Everybody could see that the senior lieutenant was on his way to be dismissed. Nobody knew why he had been removed. On another occasion the senior lieutenant would not have been noticed by the other companies or, if they had noticed, they would have pretended not to. They would have fiddled about in their engines, sticking out their greasy backsides. But this man was on his way to be dismissed. So tankmen from other companies, unknown to me, raised their dirty hands to their grimy caps to greet me. And I returned their greeting and smiled at them. They smiled back as if to say: it could be worse, don't give in.

Outside the walls of the tank park was a whole military camp, surrounded by three rows of chestnut trees. Some new recruits were singing very loudly but not very harmoniously. They were doing their best but were still not in tune. A very keen corporal was shouting at them. Then the recruits saluted me. They were still very raw and understood nothing. For them a senior lieutenant was a very important figure, even higher than their corporal. With boots that seemed to have a very special shine on them: probably on his way to some celebration.

20

I reached the headquarters building, where all was clean and quiet. The stairs were of marble, built by the Rumanians before the war. All the corridors were carpeted. I came to a semi-oval room brightly lit. In a transparent bullet-proof cone sealed with a crest was the regimental standard. Beneath the standard a soldier stood on guard. His short flat bayonet split up the last rays of the sun and scattered them in flashes of light on the marble. I saluted the regimental standard and an orderly saluted me. But the man on guard did not stir. Because he was holding a sub-machine gun, and a man bearing arms does not have to use any other form of greeting. His weapon is his greeting to everybody.

The orderly led me down the corridor straight to the office of the regimental commander. Strange. Why not to the chief of staff? The orderly knocked on the commanding officer's door, entered and closed the door firmly behind him. He came out again at once and stood aside, indicating that I was to enter.

A lieutenant-colonel of medium height whom I did not know was sitting at the commander's oak desk. I had caught sight of him among the officers accompanying the umpire that day. Who on earth could he be? Where was our commanding officer, where was the chief of staff? And why was a lieutenant-colonel sitting at the commanding officer's desk? Surely he wasn't a more important officer than our commander? But of course, he must be more important, otherwise he would not be sitting at that desk.

'Sit down, senior lieutenant,' the lieutenant-colonel said without waiting for any greeting from me.

I sat down, on the very edge of the chair. I knew that there would be some tough talk to follow and that I would have to jump to my feet. So I kept my back dead straight, as though I were on parade.

'Tell me, senior lieutennant, why did you smile when Colonel Yermolayev relieved you of command of the company?'

The lieutenant-colonel's eyes drilled right into me, as if to say: You'd better tell the truth – I can see right through you. I looked at him and the freshly laundered collar on his worn but clean and well-pressed tunic. What was I to reply?

'I don't know, comrade lieutenant-colonel.'

'You were sorry to leave the company?'

'Yes.'

'Your company performed with great skill. Especially at the very end. As for the wall, everybody agrees that it was better to knock it down than to expose the whole regiment to attack. It is not difficult to rebuild a wall . . . .'

'It has already been rebuilt.'

'So listen to me, senior lieutenant. I am Lieutenant-Colonel Kravtsov and I am Chief of Intelligence of the 13th Army. Colonel Yermolayev, who removed you from the company, thinks he is Chief of Intelligence, but he has been relieved of his post although he does not know about it yet. I have already been appointed in his place. We are now going round the divisions. He thinks he is carrying out an inspection, but in fact I am handling all the material and getting to know about the state of intelligence work in the divisions. None of his decisions or orders has any force. He issues instructions every day, but in the evening I submit my papers to the regimental and divisional commanders and all his orders are annulled. He has no idea that this is happening. He doesn't realise that his shout is no more than a rustling in the forest. As far as the Soviet Army and our whole State are concerned he is already a zero, a private person, a failure expelled from the army without a pension. There will shortly be an announcement to that effect. So his order relieving you of your company has no force.'

'Thank you very much, comrade lieutenant-colonel!'

'Don't be in too much of a hurry to thank me. He does not have the right to remove you from command of the company. Therefore *I* am removing you.' And, with a change of tone he said, quietly but with authority: 'I order you to hand over your company!'

I have long been in the habit of meeting the hard blows of fate with a smile. But this blow was so sudden that I couldn't raise a smile. I stood up, saluted and barked out:

'Very good! I am to hand over the company.'

'Sit down.'

I sat.

'There is a difference. Colonel Yermolayev removed you because he considered a company was too much for you. I am removing you because a company is too little for you. I have a job for you: chief of staff of the division's reconnaissance battalion.'

'But I am only a senior lieutenant.'

'I am also only a lieutenant-colonel. But I have been selected and ordered to take over the intelligence work for the whole Army. I am now not only taking over my job; I am also forming my team. Some people I have brought along with me from my previous job. I was Chief of Reconnaissance of the 87th division. But I am now responsible for a field of activity many times bigger and I need a lot of intelligent and capable men on whom I can depend. The headquarters of the reconnaissance battalion is the least I can offer you. I shall also try you out in a more important job. That's if you cope . . . . ' He looked at his watch. 'You've got twenty minutes to get your things together. At 21.30 our bus leaves for Rovno and the headquarters of the 13th Army. You have a seat reserved on it. I'll take you onto my staff in the intelligence department at the headquarters of the 13th Army if you pass the examinations tomorrow.'

I passed the examinations.

Chapter Two

It was two hundred and forty paces from the officers' quarters to the headquarters of the 13th Army. Every morning I walked slowly past the rows of old maple trees and the empty green benches till I reached a tall brick wall. On the other side of the wall in a well-planted garden stood a mansion which had once, a long time ago, been the home of a rich man. He had of course been murdered, because it wasn't fair that some people should have big houses while others had little ones. Before the war the mansion had housed the NKVD, and during the war the Gestapo. It was a very convenient place for them. After the war the house was taken over by the headquarters of one of our numerous armies. That was where I was now serving.

A headquarters is a place where power is concentrated – brutal, inexorable, unyielding power. By comparison with any of our enemies our headquarters are very small and extremely mobile. The staff of an Army consists of seventy generals and officers and a security company. And that's all. No bureaucracy. The staff of an Army must be ready at any moment to get aboard ten armoured personnel carriers and disperse into the grey-green mass of their subordinate troops without losing control of them. It is this invisibility and mobility that makes it invulnerable. But even in peacetime it is protected against any accidents. The first owner of the house had surrounded it and its big garden with a high brick wall, and all subsequent owners had strengthened the wall, making it higher and adding all sorts of defences to it, to discourage people from the slightest desire to climb it.

A guard stood at the green gate and I showed him my pass. He studied it carefully and then saluted: please enter. The building itself was not visible from the checkpoint. There was a pathway leading to it between walls of thick bushes. You couldn't leave the pathway, because in the bushes was an impassable network of barbed wire. The pathway was like a tunnel which turned gradually in the direction of the house, hidden among the chestnuts. The windows of the ground floor had been walled up many years previously. The windows of the first floor were protected by strong ironwork on the outside and solid shutters within. The driveway in front of the main entrance was paved with clean white paving stones and surrounded by thick hedges. If you looked carefully you could see in the bushes, as well as the barbed wire, some grey, rough concrete. These were the machine-gun casemates, connected by underground tunnels with the basement of the staff building where the guard was posted.

From here, from the main courtyard, a pathway led around the house to a new three-storey block built on to the main building. From there you could at last enter the grounds which surrounded the whole of our White House with a mass of greenery.

In daytime you would see only staff officers walking along the paths through the park, and at night-time only guards with their dogs. And right here in the park, quite unnoticable to an outsider, was the entry into the underground command point, constructed deep beneath the surface and protected by thousands of tons of concrete and steel. Under the ground there was working and living accommodation, a communications centre, a restaurant, a hospital, stores and everything necessary for living and working in conditions of complete isolation. But, apart from that underground command point there was yet another one, protected not only by concrete, steel and dogs but also by secrecy. This one was just a spectre. Very few people knew where it was situated.

It was still twenty minutes before the working day was due to begin, and I was strolling along the paths, disturbing the first gold of autumn. Far, far away in the sky a fighter aircraft was making patterns and scaring the cranes circling above fields invisible from where I stood.

Officers were moving in the direction of the White House. It was time for me to move too. Along a little pathway leading into a wide avenue, past a murmuring stream, then around the left wing of the mansion and I found myself again in the central courtyard among the thick bushes under the stern gaze of the machine-gun embrasures beneath the low concrete brows of the gloomy casemates. Again I showed my pass to a saluting guard and entered an echoing white marble hall which had once rung with the sound of spurs, where silk skirts had rustled and ostrich feather fans had hidden languid glances. There were no skirts now. Only occasionally one might catch sight of a girl telegraphist from the communications centre. She would be wearing a skirt of simple cloth, part of a uniform. Khaki, and close-fitting. To attract the colonels, no doubt.

I climbed up the white marble staircase. At the top was a guard and another document check. By no means all the staff colonels were permitted to go up there, and I was only a senior lieutenant. But the guards let me through. Those who saw me from below were surprised. Who was this? What right had he to go up the marble stairs?

I showed my pass once again and entered a darkened corridor, where carpets deadened the sound of footsteps. At the end of the corridor were four doors, and four at the beginning too. At the end were the offices of the Army commander, his first deputy, the chief of staff, and the political god of the 13th Army known as the Member of the Military Council.

The four doors at the beginning of the corridor led to the most important departments of the staff: the First, Second, Eighth and Special. The First was the operations department, dealing with battle planning. The Second was the intelligence department which provided the First department with all information about the enemy. The Eighth department had no name, only a number. Very few people knew what that department did. The Special department, on the other hand, had no number, only a name. What its business was everybody knew.

Our corridor was the most carefully guarded part of the headquarters and only a very limited number of officers were permitted access to it. It was of course used by a number of lieutenants from the Special department and by the generals' adjutants. But the colonels turned to look at me: who on earth was I? I was not from the Special department and I was not an adjutant. I was an officer from the Second department. Here was our black leather-covered door – first on the left. I selected the code number on the console and the door slid open. Beyond it there was another door, made of armour-plate, as in a bank. I pressed the bell button, a vigilant eye peered through the bullet-proof viewing slit and clicked the lock – I was home.

In the past this had been presumably one large room which had later been divided into six not very large offices. The more the merrier, as they say. In one of the offices was the Chief of Intelligence of the 13th Army, my benefactor and protector, still a lieutenant-colonel, Kravtsov. In the five other offices worked the five groups of the department. The first group directed all the intelligence work in lower units – division reconnaissance battalions, regimental recon-naissance companies, supplementary reconnaissance companies, and artillery, engineering and chemical reconnaissance. The fifth group dealt with electronic reconnaissance. It had at its disposal two battalions for direct-finding and radio interception, and apart from that it controlled electronic reconnaissance in all divisions forming part of our 13th Army. The second and third groups were *terra incognita* for me. But after working in the fourth group for a month I was beginning to guess what those totally secret groups were doing. The fact is that our fourth group dealt with the final processing of information arriving from all the other groups in the department. Apart from that, information flowed in from below, from divisional headquarters, from above – from the district HQ – and from the side – from our neighbours, the KBG frontier troops.

There were three men in our groups in peacetime. In time of war there should be ten. There were three desks in the office, where two lieutenant-colonels – an analyst and a forecaster – and I, a senior lieutenant, worked. I had the simplest job of all – troop movements. Naturally the analyst was the senior man in our group.

Previously the officer working on troop movements had also been a lieutenant-colonel. But the new Chief of Intelligence had thrown him out of the department to make room for me. It was a lieutenant-colonel's job according to the establishment, which meant that if I managed to hold it down I would very soon be made a captain and in four years' time I would equally automatically become a major and in another five years a lieutenant-colonel. If after that I succeeded in advancing further, higher ranks would follow automatically. But if I slipped up somewhere, then for every promotion I would have to fight tooth and nail.

25

The lieutenant-colonels were not at all pleased with the new Chief of Intelligence for having put a senior lieutenant at a lieutenant-colonel's desk. My appearance on the scene was a reflection on their authority and experience; but that was not the main thing. Most important for them was the fact that their new boss might put young and eager officers in *their* places. They both eyed me with suspicion and acknowledged my greetings with only slight nods of the head.

In the office of the information group of the reconnaissance department there were three desks, three large safes, bookshelves covering the wall and a map of Europe, also covering a whole wall. Immediately opposite the entrance hung a portrait of a young-looking three-star general. Sometimes, when no one was looking, I smiled at this colonel-general and gave him a wink. But the general never smiled back at me. The expression on his face was cold, severe and serious. His eyes, that mirror of the inner man, were cruel and commanding. At the corners of his lips there was a touch of contempt. There was no inscription beneath the portrait or on the back of it – I checked this when nobody was in the room. Instead of a name there was only a stamp which read 'Military unit 44388' and a stern warning: 'To be kept only in the secure premises of the Aquarium and its subordinate instructions.' I knew the commanders of the Soviet Army pretty well. It was the duty of an officer to know them. But I was quite sure that I had never seen the colonel-general in the portrait in any military publication, including secret ones. All right, general, don't interfere with our work.

On the table in front of me was a pile of messages which had arrrived in the preceding night. My job was to sort them out, enter the changes in the composition and location of the enemy troops in the 'regrouping log' and record them on the big map which was kept in the First department at Army HQ.

I was stumped by the very first message: an echelon of twenty British Chieftain tanks had been observed on a railway bridge across the Rhine near Cologne. The idiots! In which direction was the echelon going? Was it a reinforcement or a reduction in force? Twenty tanks were a mere trifle. But from such crumbs, and only from them, it was possible to form a general idea of what was happening. Both the analyst and the forecaster had copies of the same messages on their desks. And, since they had an absolutely clear picture of what was going on, and since they kept in their heads thousands of figures, dates, and names of people and things, they of course had no need to refer to the previous days' messages to find the key to unravel such a trifling problem. They looked probingly at me and were in no hurry to hint at the answer. I got up from my seat and went to the safe. If I read all the preceding messages the answer would probably be very simple. Four hostile eyes were directed at my back: get on with it, they were saying – you'll find out how lieutenant-colonels earn their living.

Our working day went on to 1700 hours with an hour off for lunch. Anyone who had urgent work to do could stay in the office until 2100 hours. After that all documents had to be handed over to the secret registry and safes and doors had to be sealed. Only the underground command point never slept. At times of heightened tension we would take it in turns to remain at headquarters, one officer from each group. But in case of a major crisis all staff officers would live and work for several days at a time in their offices beneath the ground. The living conditions in the underground command point were much better, but there was no sunlight down there, so that when it was possible we would spend the greater part of our time in our rather cramped offices.

If there were no messages I used to read the 'Intelligence Summary' of the General Staff. I had come to like this bulky 600-page book and I became so engrossed in it that I could repeat many pages from it by heart, even though every one of them would contain as many as a hundred figures and names. When there was no crisis or special alert the lieutenant-colonels would disappear at exactly 1700 hours. Like the dogs in Pavlov's experiments their digestive juices became active at that time, though in their case the saliva was put to a different use as they spat on their military seals before stamping the document cases which then went in the safe. From that moment I was on my own. I would read the 'Intelligence Summary' for the hundredth time. Apart from the general summary there were similar books about armoured equipment, the Navy, the Bundeswehr's mobilisation plans, French nuclear research, the NATO alarm system and goodness knows what else.

'Do you ever get any sleep?'

I had not noticed that lieutenant-colonel Kravtsov had appeared at the door.

'Sometimes, and what about you?'

'Like you – sometimes,' Kravstov said with a laugh. I knew that Kravstov worked very late every night or else was missing for weeks on end visiting units under his control.

'Shall I test you?'

'Yes please, comrade lieutenant-colonel.'

'Where is the 406th tactical fighter training wing of the United States Air Force?'

'In Saragossa, Spain.'

'What does the US Fifth Army Corps consist of?'

'The 3rd armoured division, the 8th mechanised division and the 11th cavalry regiment.'

'Not bad, for a start. But watch out, Suvorov, you'll soon have to pass a test, and if you don't cope with your work you'll be chucked out of headquarters. They won't throw me out, but I'll get a thick ear.'

'I'll do my best, comrade lieutenant-colonel.'

'Now go and get some sleep.'

'I could work for another hour.'

'I said get some sleep. You'd be no use to me with a nervous breakdown.'

A couple of weeks later, when the lieutenant-colonel forecaster was away at

27

district HQ, I had to do his job. In the course of a day and two nights I prepared my first intelligence forecast: two thin typed sheets entitled 'Probable military movements by the 3rd corps of the Bundeswehr in the forthcoming month.' The Chief of Intelligence went through my forecast and ordered it to be passed to the First department. It was treated like an everyday affair. Nobody praised me, but nobody laughed at my work.

A sudden draught swept papers off the desks and the lieutenant-colonels rushed to conceal them with their bodies. They were afraid the papers might blow away. You could get fifteen years for a single mislaid paper. The door of the office opened without a preliminary knock to reveal a lieutenant standing there.

'Good morning, Konstantin Nikolayevich,' the colonels greeted him with a smile. He was a handsome man, tall and broad-shouldered. His finger-nails were pink and polished. A lieutenant on the staff was addressed only by first name and patronymic. It was an enviable position to have – adjutant to the Army chief of staff. Therefore to address him simply as 'comrade lieutenant' would almost amount to an insult. Hence – 'Konstantin Nikolayevich'.

'The movements report,' Konstantin Nikolayevich said casually, without any preliminaries. He could of course have said: 'The chief of staff wants to see the officer dealing with troop movements with a report on changes in the dispositions of the enemy last night.' But there was a simpler way to say it, as Konstantin Nikolayevich had done: short and to the point and with a touch of disdain.

I quickly gathered up the messages into a file cover. The general's adjutant became a little more agreeable and then grinned, and said: 'Haven't you ever been told to smile when you've got a customer on top of you?' The colonels grinned obediently at the adjutant's joke. Wretched staff men, anxious to hang on to their soft jobs. I just couldn't stand it. I had nothing to lose but my chains, so I said:

'Don't be rude, lieutenant.'

The adjutant drew a long face. The lieutenant-colonels fell silent and stared at me in amazement. Fool, upstart, ignoramus. How dare he speak like that to the adjutant? To Konstantin Nikolayevich! You're not in your battalion now, they were thinking. This is the staff. You have to have a feeling for the situation. You are an uncouth country bumpkin and you're likely to bring us trouble!

I walked out of the office, not letting the general's adjutant go in front of me. I would never let him go ahead of me. What if he was an adjutant? A general's lackey. Had he ever seen a soldier in the firing line? When the soldier has got a loaded automatic and you have nothing but a red flag in your hand? Once he feels his weapon in his hands a soldier can easily fall prey to the thought that he might fire a burst of bullets at his commanding officer. In my time I had led my

28

men dozens of times through the firing line. And I had never once detected doubt in the soldiers' eyes: to fire at the target or indulge in some real killing. Had that adjutant ever led soldiers to the firing line? Had he ever been face to face with them in a forest, in open country, in sub-zero temperatures or in the mountains? Had he ever seen troops really angry? Had he ever come across a whole company drunk, with weapons in their hands? The adjutant was making a career on the soft carpets; but he had no need to get at Vitya Suvorov. I would have put up with it if he had been a captain or if he had at least been the same age. But he was a mere schoolboy, at least a year younger than me.

In the corridor the general's adjutant trod heavily on my foot as though by accident. I waited for a chance to get my own back and was ready when it came. I was walking a little ahead of him and to his left. So I jerked my right elbow sharply back and got him in a soft place. The adjutant let out a sort of gurgle and then a groan, gasped for air with an open mouth, bent double and collapsed against the wall. Slowly he straightened himself out. He was taller than me and bigger built. He had huge fists. But he turned out to be weak in the paunch. Perhaps he hadn't been expecting the blow. That was his fault: you should always be on the alert, every minute of the day. Then it does not have such a devastating effect.

The adjutant was slowly straightening himself up but without taking his eyes off my hand. I had two fingers sticking out like a catapult prong. In other countries that meant victory. But for us the gesture means 'I'll poke your eyes out, you bastard.'

He raised himself up slowly by the wall, still keeping his eyes on my projecting fingers. He realised that his highly placed protector could now offer him no protection. We were face to face in an empty corridor. The adjutant was taller than me and broader, but he realised that I no longer had any great ambitions, that nothing mattered to me except victory here and now. He already knew that at the slightest move or even word on his part I would reply with a terrible jab from my fingers in his eyes and would grab him right away by the throat and never let him go.

Without blinking he slowly raised his hands to his throat, felt for his tie and straightened it out. Then he said:

'The chief of staff is waiting . . .'

'. . . for you . . .' I interjected.

'The chief of staff is waiting for *you*.'

I found it difficult to bring myself back to real life. I had already taken leave of it, preparing for a fight to the death. But he did not want to fight. I took several deep breaths and rubbed my hands, numb from the tension. He did not take his eyes off my face. Apparently my expression had changed, so as to suggest to him that I no longer intended to kill him. I turned about and strode off down the corridor. He followed me. I was a senior lieutenant and he was still a simple lieutenant: let him potter along behind.

There were two desks in the outside office, like bastions each defending a door. One door led to the Commander's office, the other to the chief of staff's.

Behind the polished desk at the Commander's door sat his adjutant. He was also a lieutenant, and he also was never addressed by his rank or by his surname – but simply as Arnold Nikolayevich. He too was tall and handsome. His uniform was not made from ordinary officers' material but from general's cloth. He then showed me not the slightest respect either, but looked straight through me. There was a reason for this: my boss, the Chief of Intelligence, Lt-colonel Kravtsov, had been appointed to that important post without the agreement of the Commander of the Army, his deputy or the chief of staff, and had ousted their man from the job. That accounted for the disdain of the Commander and the fault-finding on the part of the chief of staff. It also accounted for a general loathing on the part of all the staff officers, especially those working in 'Olympia' on the first floor, for all the people Kravtsov had brought along with him. We were outsiders, uninvited guests.

The chief of staff, Major-General Shevchenko, asked me sensible questions and listened to me without interrupting. I expected some criticism, but he simply stared me straight in the face. New officers were appearing on the staff. Someone's invisible but powerful hand was pushing them right on to the soft carpets of the first floor. And for some reason nobody was asking the chief of staff's opinion. That could not possibly please him. Power quietly slips away between your fingers, like water; how can you stop it? He swung round towards the window and looked out into the garden, gripping his hands behind his back. His cheeks were bluish in colour and his veins stood out a little. I remained in the doorway, not knowing what to do next.

'Comrade general, may I take my leave?'

He did not reply. He just remained silent. Perhaps he had not heard my question. But he had heard it, and after another short silence he muttered, 'Yes' without turning towards me.

In the outer office the two adjutants greeted me with unfriendly looks. The chief of staff's adjutant had obviously told his colleague all about it. But they had not yet, of course, reported what happened to their protectors, though they would certainly do so in time. But for that they would have to choose a suitable moment, when their bosses were in the right mood to hear such news.

I went towards the door feeling their malevolent looks like guns in the back of my neck. I could distinguish two emotions in me then: relief and disappointment. My posting to the staff was now over, and I could look forward to a limitless white icy emptiness beyond the Arctic circle or else the parched yellow desert of Central Asia, and possibly an officer's court of honour.

The colonels greeted me with deathly silence. They did not of course know what had happened in the corridor, but what had happened already in the office was quite sufficient for them to ignore me. I was an upstart. I had suddenly shot up to a high place without understanding or appreciating what had happened to me; I had not held the job down and had fallen into the abyss. I was now nobody, an un-person. My fate caused them no concern. What interested them more was the question: would my punishment be extended to include my boss whom they hated so much?

I locked my papers in the safe and hurried off to see Lt-colonel Kravtsov and to warn him of the impending unpleasantness.

'You shouldn't pick quarrels with the adjutants,' he said in a helpful tone without appearing to be especially concerned about what had happened. In fact, he appeared immediately to have forgotten what I had told him. 'What do you plan to do this evening?'

'Prepare to hand over my job.'

'But nobody's turning you off the staff.'

'They soon will, though.'

'They can't do it. I brought you here, Suvorov, along with me, and I alone can order you to get out of here. So what do you propose to do this evening?'

'Learn about the 69th group of the US 6th Fleet.'

'All right. But, apart from intellectual effort, you need physical exercise as well. You are an intelligence officer, and you must go through our training course. Do you know what the second group in our department does?'

'Yes.'

'But how could you know?'

'I guessed.'

'So what does it do in your opinion?'

'It's in charge of espionage by secret agents.'

'That's right. And maybe you know what the third group does?' He looked at me sceptically.

'Yes, I do.'

He strode around the room, trying to grasp what I had said. Then he sat himself down suddenly in a chair.

'Sit down.'

I sat down.

'Look here, Suvorov, you have been receiving from the second group little scraps of information for processing, so that you could reasonably guess where they came from. But you haven't been getting anything at all from the third group. . . .'

'From which I concluded that the forces controlled by the third group are brought into action only in wartime, and the rest I guessed.'

'Your guess might have been wrong.'

'But the officers in the third group are a very tough lot, every one of them. . . .'

'So what do you think they do?'

'In wartime they extract information by force . . .'

'. . . and cunning,' he interjected.

'They are saboteurs and terrorists.'

'Do you know what we call the group?'

'No, I couldn't know that.'

'It's called *Spetsnaz*. Special reconnaissance units. It's sabotage and recon-naissance by force. Could you guess how many such troops there are at the disposal of the third group?'

31

'A battalion.'

He jumped up out of his chair.

'Who told you that?'

'I guessed it.'

'But how?'

'By analogy. In every division there is one company doing reconnaissance in depth. It is of course not *Spetsnaz*, but it's very similar. An Army is a stage higher than a division, which means that you should have at your disposal not a company but a battalion, that is one stage higher.'*

'Four times a week you are to turn up in the evening at this address, bringing your sports equipment with you. That's all. You may go.'

'Very well.'

'If a new Army Commander and a new chief of staff arrive and consequently new adjutants, try to be on good terms with them.'

'Do you think the command of our Army is going to change soon?'

'I didn't say that.'

In our information group in the reconnaissance department some slight changes had taken place. The lieutenant-colonel who dealt with the forecasting was suddenly retired into the reserve. He was summoned to appear before a medical commission which discovered something that made it impossible for him to stay in the Army – better for him to take his pension. He hadn't the slightest desire to retire, because every year's service over twenty-five would have produced a substantial increase in his pension. But the doctors were adamant: his health was the most important thing.

A captain from the intelligence unit of the 87th division was appointed as forecaster in place of the lieutenant-colonel.

The chief of staff had to know everything available about the enemy; so every morning, once I sorted out the messages received, I would report to him. He never summoned me by telephone, but simply sent his adjutant for me.

Two weeks had already passed since our row. I was sure that the adjutant had long ago informed his chief about what had happened, in a way that reflected well on himself, of course. But I was still walking around the corridors of the first floor: I had still not been banished. The general's adjutants couldn't quite make this out. They could see that I was a sort of exception to the rule, but they didn't know exactly in what way or why, and

---

* Later, this battalion was reduced to a company. Spare companies have been used to create independent *Spetsnaz* regiments.

consequently they treated me with more respect. I was also puzzled by it. Why on earth should I be an exception?

More changes. The officer in charge of the First department was replaced, and along with him the older men in the group and several leading officers were dismissed. A lieutenant-colonel was appointed in place of the colonel, and he brought along with him a whole crowd of captains and first lieutenants and settled them down at the lieutenant-colonels' desks.

'The Chief of Intelligence of the 13th Army ordered me to do a short course to prepare myself for work in the third group.'

'Yes . . . yes . . . I know . . . come in.' He had a broad grin on his face. His huge hands reminded me of a crab's claws. 'Information officers must work with us and must understand how the little scraps of information are gathered and what is their value. Get changed.'

He was already bare-footed, in a green tracksuit of soft but apparently tough material. His forearms were bare and reminded me of the powerful, unusually clean, hairy arms of the surgeon who, five years previously, had put me together from small pieces.

We were in a spacious sunny sports centre. In the middle of the area were two ordinary chairs looking very small in that vast space.

'Sit down.'

We sat face to face in the middle of the area.

'Put your hands on your knees and relax them completely. Always sit like that. In all circumstances you must be utterly relaxed. Your lower jaw should not touch the upper one. It should hang down slightly. Relax your neck, your legs, your feet. Never cross your legs, because that interferes with your blood circulation. That's the way.'

He stood up and walked round me, inspecting me critically from all sides. Then with his strong hands he felt my neck, the muscles in my back and my grip.

'Never sit drumming your fingers on your desk-top. Only people suffering from nerves do that. Soviet military intelligence doesn't keep such people in its ranks. Now then, you are relaxed enough, let's do some exercises.'

He sat down on a chair, holding on to it with his hand, started rocking back on the back legs, and then suddenly tipped right over backwards along with the chair. And he was still smiling. He jumped up, lifted up the chair and sat down on it, hands on knees.

'Remember – if you fall backwards when sitting on a chair, nothing can happen to you, so long, of course, as there's no wall or hole behind you. To fall backwards while sitting on a chair is as easy and as safe as going down on your knees or walking on all fours. But human nature makes us resist falling backwards. It's only our mind that holds us back. . . . Now hold on to the chair with your hands. . . . I'm not going to be your safety net; you can't hurt yourself anyway. Rock back on the chair. . . . Stop; stop: are you afraid?'

'Of course I'm afraid.'

'Never mind. That's normal. Everybody gets scared. It would be strange if you were not afraid. Everybody is. So hold on to the seat. Start rocking without me telling you. . . .'

I rocked back on the chair, carefully balancing my weight, then gently upset the balance, rocking a bit further, and the chair fell slowly back into the depths. I squeezed myself into the seat and drew my head into my shoulders. The ceiling shot upwards, but the fall dragged out. Time stopped. And suddenly the back of the chair crashed down on the floor. It was only then that I got really scared and at the same moment burst out laughing: nothing at all had happened to me. My head, responding to a reflex a million years old, had moved forward, so that I couldn't possibly hit the back of it. It was my back, pressed tightly to the chair-back, that took the blow. But the area of the back is much greater than the area of the bottom of the feet, so that it is less painful to fall backwards than to jump off a chair on to the floor.

He offered me a hand.

'Can I try again?'

'Of course.' He smiled.

I sat on the chair, grabbed the seat and fell over backwards.

'I'll have another go,' I cried out happily.

'Carry on – enjoy yourself.'

'The Academy of Science has worked out at our request what is the best technique for jumping off fast-moving trains and out of motor-cars and trams. . . . But don't worry about the mathematics. There's one simple rule to remember: from a really fast train you must jump backwards and in the opposite direction to the way the train's moving; you must land with your legs doubled up, trying to keep your balance and not touching the ground with your hands. As you hit the ground you must make a violent effort to push it away and for a few seconds continue to run alongside the train, gradually slowing down. Our men can jump from a train travelling at 70 kilometres an hour. That's the average. But some can do much better than that, jumping off at much higher speeds, going down hill, from bridges, jumping when carrying weapons and with a heavy weight on their backs. Remember, the most important thing is not to touch the ground with your hands. Your legs will carry you along. The leg muscles are exceptionally strong, are very dynamic and have great staying-power. By touching the ground with your hand you may upset the rapid rhythm of the leg movements. That would cause you to fall and die a painful death. We'll have some training at it, first in the gymnasium and later on a real train. We start at a speed of 10 kilometres an hour ...'

A month later we were standing on an open railway bridge and looking down. There was no parapet, and far beneath a cold leaden-coloured river was flowing slowly through the bridge, swirling into snake-like whirls as it met the bridge supports. I had already been through my training and realised that a man could walk along a telegraph wire above a bottomless abyss. It was all a matter of psychological toughening. You had to be convinced that nothing bad was going to happen and then all was well. Circus performers wasted years on elementary matters. They were wrong. They did not have a scientific approach. They based their training on physical exercises and did not pay enough attention to psychology. They did a lot of training, but they didn't like the thought of death, they were afraid of it and tried to avoid it, forgetting that you could derive pleasure not only from another person's death but from your own too. And only people who did not fear death could perform miracles along with the gods.

'Fools say that you mustn't look down,' he shouted. 'But there's great pleasure to be had from looking down at whirlpools.'

I looked down into the depths and they no longer seemed to have that fatal attraction that a snake's jaws have for a frog. The palms of my hands no longer broke out in a cold sweat.

Further changes were announced in the command of the 13th Army. There were two major-generals of artillery in each Army. One was in command of the missile units and the artillery; the other of the anti-aircraft defences. In the 13th both of them had been replaced.

Really sweeping changes had taken place in the Carpathian military district.

The commanding officer of the district, Colonel-General Bisyarin, had died suddenly. It was less than a year since he had been in command of the Carpathian Front in Czechoslovakia. He had been fit and well and had led the four armies of his Front without apparent strain. It was said that he had never been ill. Suddenly he was gone.

Command of the military district was taken over by Lieutenant-General of Tank Forces Obaturov. And immediately, in the staff of the military district, there was a wholesale clear-out of Bisyarin's people and their replacement with Obaturov's. The winds of change swept down into the staffs of the Armies. There were four of them in the district: the 57th Air, the 8th Guards Tank, the

13th and the 38th. Two new generals – the new officer commanding our 13th Army and the new chief of staff – were soon treading the soft carpeting of our corridor.

One day I was responsible for opening the armour-plated door of the reconnaissance department to all visitors. There was a ring at the bell, and through the glass of the spy-hole I saw a strange lieutenant. I quickly realised who it was.

'Password?'

'Omsk'.

'Authority?'

'106.'

'Enter.' – The heavy door moved smoothly aside to let him in.

'Good morning. Comrade senior lieutenant, I have to see the Chief of Intelligence.'

'I will tell him. Just wait a moment please.' I knocked on my boss's door and went straight in.

'Comrade lieutenant-colonel, the new Army Commander's adjutant to see you.'

'Show him in.'

The lieutenant entered.

'Comrade lieutenant-colonel, the Army Commander would like to see you.'

I knew in advance that there would be large-scale exercises, that messages would be pouring down as from the horn of plenty, that the young adjutants would be exhausted and would have red, bloodshot eyes as we spent nights together poring over the Big Map. I knew that after the first exercises the two new adjutants and I would get together, get really drunk and become friends. I would tell them dirty jokes, and they would tell me funny stories concerning the private lives of their protectors. But even now, after our very first meeting, from the way the adjutant addressed me and the way he entered my chief's office, I felt that we were people of the same ilk. The new generals on the Army staff were Obaturov's people. The new heads of departments, including Kravtsov, were Obaturov's people. The new adjutants and the new staff officers were all Obaturov's people. I felt for the first time that I was also a member of that group. And I knew that the new officer commanding the Carpathian military district, Lieutenant-General Obaturov, belonged to some powerful group which was moving fast and irresistibly into positions of power.

All those who had been appointed to the staff and to the other staffs in the district before us were people of a different ilk. Their day was over. Those who were old enough would be thrown out on a pension; the others would land up in the burning deserts. The old group had collapsed from a mighty blow, invisible from outside, and its individual pieces were fated never to be loyal servants of the powerful of this society or to bathe in the warmth of the real power.

I came across the former adjutant of the former chief of staff in the secret registry. He was handing over documents before leaving for somewhere very remote to take command of a platoon. He had been an officer for more than two years but had never had command of any group of soldiers, let alone a bunch of undisciplined, half-drunk and utterly unmanageable soldiers. If he had started his service like that all would have been well. But his service had started with soft carpets. Whatever happened, he ate his fill and lived in comfort. Now all that was over. A man gets accustomed to living on the edge of a precipice. And if he has always lived there it is difficult for him to imagine that there can be any other life. But the lieutenant was swept up to the very top and had now dropped again into the abyss. To the very bottom. And the fall was very painful.

He was smiling at me. But it was a rather canine smile. Once, long ago in the Far East, I saw two dogs trying to attach themselves to a strange pack. But the pack snarled, unwilling to accept strangers into their company. Then one of the dogs attacked its unfortunate comrade and bit it. Their fight continued for a long time while the pack watched patiently for the outcome of the duel. One howled, while the other, weaker one let out terrible yelps, reluctant to part with its life. Once he had killed his comrade, or maybe brother, covered with bites and scars, the victorious dog, tail between his legs, approached the pack, indicating his readiness to submit. The whole pack then set upon him and tore him to pieces.

For some reason the former adjutant reminded me of that dog with his tail between his legs, ready to fight anybody if he could only be accepted into the company of the victors. Fool, I thought, act proud: go to your desert and don't drop your tail until you are attacked.

The examination was long and difficult. I passed it. Without any special distinction – but I passed.

'Well, then,' said Kravtsov, 'it's time to try you out on the real thing. The training starts soon. I'll send you off with a *Spetsnaz* group. As an inspector.'

'I'm ready, comrade lieutenant-colonel.'

'In the normal course of events, inspecting is easy. But *Spetsnaz* is an exception. To inspect a group, you have to jump with it. That's the first thing. The second thing is that you mustn't lag behind the group. These lads have high standards. If the inspector lags behind they won't wait for him. Often, in the early days of a training operation, they make a special effort to break speed records in order to leave the inspector behind and stop him from interfering with their work. There are no punishments, no reprimands for them. We reserve the punishments for inspectors who can't stand the pace.'

'I won't lag behind.'

'We'll see.'

Chapter Three

The most important item in the equipment of a *Spetsnaz* soldier is his footwear. Apart from his parachute, of course.

A storekeeper who, to judge from the scar on his neck, had had long experience in the *Spetsnaz* himself, handed me a pair of boots from the store and I inspected them with interest. They are a form of footwear which is neither a boot nor a shoe, but something in between, a hybrid combining the best features of both. The boots are known officially as J-Bs – Jump-Boots.

The boots are made from thick, soft ox-hide and weight a good deal less they appear to at first sight. There are lots of straps and clasps on each boot; two straps around the heel, one around the sole, and two around the calf. The straps are also very soft. Every boot is the result of thousands of years of experience. Since that was the way our ancestors embarked on campaigns – their feet wrapped in soft leather and tied up with straps –that was the way my boots were made – soft leather and straps.

On the other hand, our ancestors never saw such soles as my boots had. They were thick, broad and soft. But their resilience did not mean that they were not hard-wearing. Each sole was made up of three thick layers, one on top of the other like scales, making the sole both tough and flexible. Similar scale-like layers are used in bullet-proof jackets. But they are not used in the boot soles to protect you from bullets, of course. They are to protect the soles of the feet from the spikes and stakes which are to be encountered in the approaches to specially important targets. With these soles it is even possible to run across fire. And they have one other use: they project a little at the sides and can be used for attaching ski bindings.

The pattern on the soles of our boots is copied from the soles of boots worn by the troops of our probable enemies. Depending on what area we are to operate in we can leave behind us the standard American, French, Spanish or any other footprints.

That is not, however, the main deception. One of the *Spetsnaz* issue boots or jump boots, has the heel at the front and the sole behind. So when a *Spetsnaz* soldier is going in one direction his footprints point in the other. The heels are, of course, made thinner and the soles thicker, so as to be comfortable on the feet and the reversal of heel and sole does not make it difficult to walk. The deception would be revealed almost immediately, of course, were it not that every *Spetsnaz* soldier has normal boots too. An experienced tracker would probably not be deceived, either. He would know that, in vigorous fast walking, the toe leaves a deeper impression than the heel. But do many people look closely at the footprints left by soldiers' feet? Are there many who know that the toe leaves a clearer imprint? Do many people notice that footprints have suddenly appeared pointing the other way round? Are many able to assess what they see at its real value? Who would have thought of having a boot with the heel and the sole reversed? To whom would it occur that if the footprints appeared to be going eastwards it meant that the man who made them was going west? What's more, we are not stupid. *Spetsnaz*, like wolves, do not go around on their own. And like wolves we walk in each other's footprints. You would never know how many men there were in a group – three or a hundred. And when several feet have trodden in one footprint it becomes practically impossible to detect whether the heels have made a deeper impression than the toes.

Only one kind of sock is used with the *Spetsnaz* boots: a very thick sock made of pure wool. Wherever we go, into the permanent frost or the burning desert, we always wear exactly the same kind of socks: very thick, woollen and grey. Such socks keep your feet warm, protect the foot from perspiration, do not rub and do not wear into holes. Each *Spetsnaz* soldier has two pairs of socks. Whether for a day or a month, just two pairs. It's up to him to make do.

As for the rest of a *Spetsnaz* soldier's clothing, his underwear is made of thin linen. It should be new but already used a little and laundered at least once. Over the thin underwear he wears a vest made of a thick string, so that there is always a layer of air about a centimetre deep between the underwear and the outer garments. This was cleverly thought out. If it's very hot and you are running with sweat and your whole body is burning, the string vest is your salvation. Your clothes do not cling to your body and there is excellent ventilation. When it's cold the air pocket protects the body like a feather duvet, and moreover, weighs nothing. The string vest has yet another purpose. If a mosquito gets its nose through your clothes it reaches empty space and not the body. Only in very difficult circumstances does a *Spetsnaz* soldier allow himself to be driven out into the open. He spends his time in forests and marshes. He may lie for hours in a burning hot marsh or in fierce stinging nettles with clouds of mosquitoes buzzing around him. Only the string vest can save him then. Over it he wears trousers and a tunic of green cotton material. All seams are treble-stitched. The tunic and trousers are soft but hard-wearing. At the elbows, knees and shoulders the material is trebled for greater strength.

On his head a *Spetsnaz* soldier wears a helmet. In winter this is made of fur with a silk lining, in summer from cotton. It consists of two parts: the helmet proper and its mask. The helmet must not leave his head in any circumstances, even in the course of a parachute jump. It must have no clasps, straps or projections on the outside, because at the time of the jump it is right next to the parachute. There must be nothing on the helmet to interfere with the opening of the parachute's canopy and cords. Consequently the helmet worn for a drop is made exactly to the shape of a man's head, covering his head, neck and chin and leaving exposed only the eyes, nose and mouth. During operations, or when the weather is particularly bad, the mask is pulled down over the eyes, nose and mouth for the sake of camouflage.

The saboteur also wears an outer garment like an anorak. It is thick, warm, light and waterproof. In it you can lie in a marsh without getting wet or sleep in the snow without freezing. It comes down to the middle of the thighs so as not to interfere with walking, and if need be you could sit for days on a patch of ice, as it provides something to sit on. It is very full at the bottom, which is important when running or walking fast. But if necessary the lower part can be pulled in tightly round the legs and so keep the warmth in. The *Spetsnaz* used to have similar trousers, padded and warm. But that was a mistake. When you have to walk for days on end without stopping such trousers are a nuisance. They upset the ventilation. Our wise ancestors never wore fur-lined trousers. Instead they had fur coats reaching down to their heels. And they were right, because fur trousers make you sweat but a long coat doesn't. We have now learnt this lesson, and a *Spetsnaz* soldier has not only a top coat, but a long skirt covering his body almost down to the heels which he can attach to it. In this way he can keep warm, but is never too hot. The skirt is easily unbuttoned and rolled up so that it does not take up much space in the man's kit.

In the old days the top coat was reversible. One side was white and the other grey and green in patches. But that was also a mistake. The coat had to be soft inside, like a woman's skin, but on the outside it had to be as rough as rhinoceros hide. That is why the top coats are no longer reversible. They are soft inside and rough on the outside. And they are light grey in colour, like last year's grass or dirty snow. It's a very well-chosen colour. But in case of great need a white camouflage smock can be worn over the coat.

The whole of a *Spetsnaz* soldier's equipment is carried in his special field back-pack. Like all his clothes and other equipment it is light grey in colour. It is not large, is rectangular in shape, and is made from a very tightly woven material. In order that it should not drag the shoulders back it is made very flat, but wide and long. The fastenings are arranged so that it can be attached to the body in different places. It can be carried on the chest, or it can be carried high on the back, or it can be dropped right down to the man's backside and be suspended on his belt, thus freeing his sore shoulders for a while.

Wherever a *Spetsnaz* soldier has to go he takes only one flask of water with him – 810 grams. Apart from that he has a little bottle of small brown disinfecting tablets. You throw one of the tablets into water polluted with oil, dysentry bacillae and soap suds, and in one minute all the filth falls to the bottom and you can pour off the top and drink it. Pure water produced in this way has a revolting taste and a strong smell of chlorine. But a *Spetsnaz* man will drink it. Anyone who knows what real thirst is like will drink this treated water with the greatest of pleasure.

When a *Spetsnaz* soldier sets out, whether for a week or a month, the duration of the operation makes no difference. He always takes with him exactly the same quantity of food – 2,765 grams. It frequently happens that in the course of an operation, food, water and ammunition are dropped from aircraft. But it may not happen, and then he has to make out as best he can. Nearly three kilograms of food is a great deal, bearing in mind the unusually high calorie content of the specially developed and prepared food. But if it's not enough, then he will have to obtain food independently. He might kill a deer or a wild boar; he may catch fish; eat berries, mushrooms, hedgehogs, frogs, snakes, snails and earthworms; he can cook up birch bark and acorns .... There's plenty a hungry man can eat, especially if he is equipped with the concentrated experience of many centuries.

Apart from food, the *Spetsnaz* soldier carries in his back-pack four boxes of special matches which are not affected by the wet, and will light in any wind or the heaviest downpour. He has a hundred tablets of dry spirit. He is not allowed to light any fires, so he keeps warm and cooks his food by the flame from a tablet. The flame is exactly the same as a candle flame, only more dependable in a wind. Also in his back-pack are twenty other tablets – medicinal ones to deal with every kind of illness and poisoning. There is also one towel, a toothbrush and paste, a safety razor, a tube of liquid soap, a fish-hook and line, and a needle and cotton. A *Spetsnaz* soldier has no need to take a comb with him, because before he jumps his head is shaved bald, so that his head perspires less and wet hair cannot get into his eyes. The hair grows again in the course of a month, but not long enough to justify wasting space on a comb. He takes quite a lot with him as it is.

As for weapons, there are two possibilities: the full complement, or a lightweight issue.

The full complement consists of a Kalashnikov automatic AKMS and 300 rounds. Some automatics are equipped with the PBS – a silencer and flame suppressor—and the NSP-3 – a night gunsight dimmer. During a parachute drop the automatic is kept in its case so as not to interfere with the proper opening of the parachute. In order that he should not be defenceless immediately after landing each man has a P-8 silenced pistol and 32 rounds to go with it. Apart from that he carries on his right calf a huge knife for cutting parachute lines, and on his left calf four spare blades. The *Spetsnaz* knife is no ordinary knife. It has a powerful spring in it so that when you remove the safety catch and press the release button the knife blade shoots out with a terrible hiss, forcing the hand holding the empty handle smartly back. The heavy blade can carry 25 metres. If it lands in a tree it is not always possible to pull it out again, in which case the soldier puts a spare blade into the empty handle, leaning on it with all the weight of his body to compress the powerful spring. He can then put the safety catch on and use the knife again as an ordinary knife: for slicing people or bread, as a file or as a wire-cutter. If a *Spetsnaz* soldier is carrying the full complement of weapons, he then has in his pack in addition to everything else six grenades, some plastic explosive, and directional mines or some other heavy weapon.

The lighter complement of weapons is carried by officers and radio operators. It includes an automatic with 120 cartridges, a noiseless pistol and a knife. I was issued with all this in the store by the highly experienced quartermaster. The pistol I was given was a real one, but the automatic was only for training. I was going out with a *Spetsnaz* group as an umpire, and since I was only an observer I had no need to shoot. But I was also an intelligence officer and had to experience the weight of an automatic and its ammunition. So I carried a training weapon. It was the same as the ones used in action except that it was worn out and had been written off. An opening had been bored in the cartridge chamber of the barrel and a warning engraved: 'For training purposes only.'

I slung the automatic over my shoulder. It was many years since I had had to carry a training automatic with a hole in the chamber. The rawest of privates and cadets at military colleges begin their service with these weapons. Anyone carrying one in the Army usually finds himself the butt of friendly jokes. I did not of course feel myself to be raw or inexperienced. But I was nevertheless completely new to the *Spetsnaz* forces. So, having been issued with an automatic with a hole in it, I decided to find out if I was being taken for a greenhorn. Were the men trying out one of their old Army tricks on me? I quickly took the pack from my shoulder and opened the side pocket. I found what I was looking for. There was a spoon, as there should have been, but like the automatic, it had a hole drilled in it and the same inscription: 'For training purposes only'.

'Sorry, comrade senior lieutenant,' said the *Spetsnaz* veteran looking slightly sheepish, 'we didn't check it properly.'

He was disappointed to find that it was not my first day in the Army and that I knew the old tricks and had my wits about me. He summoned his assistant, a very young private, and told him off on the spot for being so careless. We both understood that it had nothing to do with the young private and that it was the sergeant himself who had slipped me the spoon. He ordered the spoon thrown away at once. I knew, of course, that it would not be thrown away. It would be used again on many generations of *Spetsnaz* recruits. But rules are rules. The sergeant had to give the necessary instructions, and the private had to be punished. The sergeant quickly found another spoon and gave it to me. He reverted to his serious, businesslike manner:

'Good luck, comrade senior lieutenant.'

'Thank you, sergeant.'

Everyone in the Soviet Army folds his own parachute. This applies even to generals. It makes sense: if your parachute fails to open all the responsibility lies with you, even if you're dead. No living person bears any responsibility.

All the parachutes are kept in the stores. They are folded, marked and always ready for use. Each parachute is signed on the silk with the man's name and the words: 'I folded this parachute myself.'

But when we are not roused by a night alarm, but are going on an exercise with time for proper preparations, then all the parachutes are unpacked and refolded. And again everyone signs: 'I folded this parachute myself.'

The folding procedure is carried out in the conditions in which the jump will have to be made. We were to jump in sub-zero temperatures, so the folding was also done below zero, at six in the morning.

The whole battalion was folding parachutes that day, on a huge parade ground surrounded by a tall fence to defeat the curiosity of other troops.

The 'parachute tables' had been prepared. They were not really tables but long sheets of tarpaulin spread out on the concrete and held down with special spikes. We took it in turns. First I would help to fold someone else's parachute. Then we would fold my parachute, reversing the roles. Next we would fold his spare one, with him in charge, then mine with me in charge. Some of us would jump with one rather than two parachutes. But everyone prepared both his parachutes, even in a hard frost.

Officers of the intelligence department of the Army were packing their parachutes along with the battalion. We were acting as observers and would have to spend weeks along with the *Spetsnaz* plodding through the snow . . . .

We then went off to our warm barracks, leaving our parachutes under heavy guard in the cold. If they had been brought into the warm premises invisible drops of moisture would have condensed on the cold material, and when next day they were taken out into the frost again the drops would turn into minute pieces of ice, making the layers of fabric stick hard together. That would be certain death. It was perfectly simple, and even the youngest privates knew it. Yet such things happen, and a whole group of soldiers could perish in one go. A whole platoon, a whole company. There are hundreds of mistakes that can be made in packing and storing parachutes. The price is always the same: your life. With a hand stiff from the cold I had signed my name on the silk stripes of my two parachutes: 'Senior Lieutenant Suvorov. I folded this parachute myself.' If I smashed myself up they would always be able to find the culprit.

We were warming ourselves in the comfort of the barracks. Then we would have a late supper, and after that the final preparations. Everybody was already shaved bald. Everyone had been to the baths and taken a steam bath. The men needed to warm themselves through, because it would be some time before they came across warm water again. Long after midnight everyone was asleep. They had to store up sleep for many weeks ahead. They all needed to have ten hours. All the barrack windows were blacked out so that nobody should be awakened early. Everyone needed deep sleep. For that there is a little secret. You lie on your back, stretch out and relax the whole body. Then you shut your eyes and look upwards beneath your eyelids. That is the normal position of the eyes during sleep. In such a position a person will drop off to sleep quickly, easily and deeply. We were to be wakened very late. And it wouldn't be the usual, 'Everybody out! On parade in thirty seconds!' No, a few privates and sergeants who were not going on the exercise and who had been guarding the company's weapons and parachutes, would come in quietly and wake each one gently: 'Come on, Kolya, time to get up.' 'Time to rise, comrade senior lieutenant.' Time, time. Get up, lads. It's time for us to move.

The forty-third *Spetsnaz* group of the 296th independent reconnaissance battalion of the *Spetsnaz* consisted of twelve men. I, as the intelligence officer, made the thirteenth. I was going as an umpire, checking on the performance of the group. I had the easiest job. I didn't have to take any decisions. My job was to put questions to the troops, to the commanding officer or to his deputy, just when they least expected them. I had with me a list of a hundred questions, many of which I still didn't know the exact answer to. My job was to put the question and record the reply. Officers of the third group headed by lieutenant-colonel Kravtsov would later go through the replies and decide who got it wrong and who got it right.

A *Spetsnaz* group takes with it two P351-M radio sets, a scrambling apparatus and an instrument for the high-speed transmission of signals.

That night we had to carry out a large-scale operation to put out of action the radar stations of the 8th Guards Tank Army, against which we were going into action. Simultaneously a massive missile and air attack was to be carried out on its command posts and troop concentrations, in the course of which twenty-eight leading *Spetsnaz* groups from our battalion were to be dropped. The groups had various tasks and were of differing composition, from three to forty men. Some were led by sergeants, others by officers. On subsequent nights further groups would be dropped, in a variety of districts, by different routes and from different heights. We were to be dropped today from a very low level, about a hundred metres. Each of us had only one parachute, which would open up explosively with the help of a gas canister. As such a height a second parachute was not necessary.

Have you ever seen animal fear in people's eyes? I have – when they were preparing to be dropped from a low level with the gas-assisted parachute release. Before the take-off we had all been weighed, along with what was hanging on us. And there we were, sitting in the plane in accordance with our weight. The heaviest had to jump first, then progressively lighter men down to the very lightest. That was so that the heaviest should not fall on to the canopies of the lighter ones and so collapse their parachutes. First to go was the big high cheek-boned radio operator whose name I did not know. He was known in the group by the nickname of Bald Tarzan: a great, sullen hulk of a man. There were bigger people in the group, but he had been weighed along with his radio set and was consequently the heaviest; so he jumped first. After him went another radio operator known as Brother Yevlampius. Third in weight was Genghis Khan, the group's cipher clerk. These three who went first had a very difficult jump to make. Each had to take with him a container suspended on a fifteen-metre rope. Each had to jump clutching the container to his chest and then, when the parachute opened, to let it drop down beneath him. The container would drop along with the paratrooper but fifteen metres below him. In such an operation the container hits the ground first, after which it becomes a little easier for the paratrooper, and in the last fractions of a second his speed reduces a little. He lands right alongside the container. Because of the speed and the wind he is carried a little to one side and practically never lands on his container. But that doesn't make it any easier – the jump with a container is a very risky business, especially at low levels. The fourth to jump was the deputy commander of the group, Sergeant Drozdov, the biggest man in the group. He was known as the Fist and, looking at his huge hand, I realised that you couldn't think of a better nickname. A huge man – tremendous. Fancy nature producing such an extraordinary person! After the Fist went Lieutenant Yeliseyev, the group's commander: also a very big man, although not as big as his deputy. The lieutenant is known by the number of the group – 43-I. He also has some nickname, of course, but who would dare to call an officer by his nickname in front of another officer? Next to the commander sat the ordinary paratroopers, broad-shouldered and of powerful physique: the Whip, the Vampire, the Smoothing Iron, Nicholas the Third, Negative, Chopin, Karl de la Duchesse. They also have some name for me, of course, but officially I have no nickname, only number 43-C, standing for control.

I was the smallest and the lightest in the 43rd sabotage group. Consequently I was tossed out of the plane last. That meant that I was sitting right next to the hatch. The last one to jump also took the job of despatcher who checked each one at the last moment and had the right if need arose to call a halt to the jump at any moment. It was a very tough job, if only because he sat at the very tail end and all had their faces turned to him. It was as though he was on a stage and everyone was looking at him. Wherever I looked the eyes of a man about to jump were staring at me – wild eyes, all of them, except perhaps the commander's. He seemed to be dozing quietly, completely relaxed. But all the other eyes had a faint glint of craziness about it. It's fine to jump from three thousand metres – really beautiful! But this was only a hundred. All sorts of dodges have been thought up for suppressing fear, but you can't really get away from it. It was sitting right next to us.

My ears popped as the plane went into a sudden dive. The tops of trees flashed past. I had a rotten part to play: they all had their release lines attached to the central rail and I alone had it loose on my chest. I had to let them all go past me and at the last moment to hook my line on above my head. But what if I missed? What if in the confusion of jumping I didn't manage to clip it on? It would be too late then to open the parachute by hand: the ground would be coming up at me. I suddenly imagined myself falling without a parachute, my arms and legs spread out like a cat. I would let out such a shout! I could just imagine howling in the face of death, and it made me laugh. The parachutists look at my sympathetically: the umpire was having hysterics. But with me it was not hysteria: it was simply funny.

The blue light above the baggage hatch flickered nervously.

'Stand! Get down!'

The first paratrooper, Bald Tarzan, crouched down with his right leg forward to steady himself. Brother Yevlampius leant heavily on him with his whole body. The third man lay on the back of the second man, and so the whole group formed a single unit to await the signal to jump. When the signal came those behind leant on those in front and the whole lot went out through the wide hatch almost at the same time. It was all right for them. But no one was going to give me a push.

The huge doors of the hatch moved aside with only a slight noise. I felt the icy-cold wind in my face. There was no moon that night, but the snow was dazzingly bright. Things were as clear as daylight. There was the ground underneath; the bushes and undergrowth seemed to have gone mad, rushing past in a wild gallop. We were off.

Come on men, get going!

Mankind had devised nothing worse than this. Wild eyes flashed past me. A siren howled like a dying animal. Its howl hurt my ears, driving fear deep inside me. Faces were distorted. Everyone was shouting the frightful words: 'We're off!' There was no getting out of the way, no way of resisting the pressure from behind. The ones in front had landed in a freezing mist. The wind was tipping everyone upside down. Away! Those coming behind, swept along by some herd instinct, landed in a black swirl of snow. I reached upwards and floated out into the sort of freezing fog that decent people don't go into. Devils and witches on a broomstick, and Viktor Suvorov with his parachute.

In a low-level jump everthing happens at once: head down, frost whipping your face till it burns, legs in the air, wind in your chest under your fur jacket, the shock to your legs as you land, the rough lines of the parachute across your face again, gloves and sleeves full of snow to the elbows and beginning to melt. Quite sickening.

We buried the parachutes in the snow and scattered some evil smelling stuff around them to keep the dogs off. The whole of the local police force, the KGB and units of the interior ministry were all involved in the exercise. They had all been thrown into action against our unfortunate groups. But we had our hands tied. If it had been a real war we would have seized a few personnel carriers or cars and skirted the district. But it wasn't a real war, and we were not allowed to commandeer transport. There was a draconian order: just on our feet, away from the dogs.

We had short, wide skis, with real fox-fur on the underside. They were easy to drop by parachute. They would slide forward but not slip back: the fur prevented them from going back. Skis like that often left no trace, especially on tightly packed snow. They were so wide that they did not sink in. They could also be used to make a little hide-away in the snow, with the fur to the inside, so that you could take it in turn to sleep. But most important was that they should not get iced up or covered with a sheet of frozen snow.

By the morning we were completely exhausted. We had marched for three hours away from the dropping zone and had concealed our tracks. Tunics wet through, faces red, sweat running down our bodies. Our hearts were beating fit to burst. Our tongues were hanging out like dogs' in the heat. It was always like that at the beginning. By the fourth or fifth day we would be used to it and would be walking like machines. But the first day was always very hard. The first night and the two following days were awful. After that it would get better.

'Commander – there are dogs barking in the village. Not a good sign. Means there are strangers there.'

That was quite evident. Who on earth would disturb the village dogs in such a remote spot and so early in the morning?

'We'll go round it. Take to the left.'

'To the left there's a KGB ambush. Over there in that little wood. Look, commander, birds are circling over the wood.'

He was right. Who had disturbed them in such a hard frost? Birds should now be perched, silent and still, on the branches, covered in hoar frost. Of course we couldn't go that way, so there was nothing for it but to take the path through the gullies and the fallen trees where ordinary people wouldn't go. That way was only for wolves, and for *Spetsnaz* paratroopers.

'Ready? On your way then.'

The pace was cruel – eight kilometres an hour.

Evening. Frost even harder. Sixty-seven kilometres in a day. Only two breaks. It was time to lie down again in the snow.

'No way, you scroungers,' the commander said, encouragingly. 'You should have slept yesterday.' He was in a bad temper. The group wasn't keeping up the pace. The men were also in a bad mood. It was getting dark, and that was bad too. In the daytime the group could occasionally take cover in the snow, in the undergrowth or marshland, and rest a while. But at night that never happened. The night-time was made for work. Like prostitutes, we were night-birds. And, if you didn't get a rest in the daytime, you wouldn't get one at night.

'Don't put snow in your mouths!' The commander was very stern. 'Or I'll flatten you!'

He wasn't talking to me. His threats were directed at Genghis Khan and Smoothing Iron. My position put restraints on me. I was an umpire. Nobody was allowed to put snow in his mouth, but particularly an umpire. If I hadn't been an umpire I would certainly have swallowed some of the white slush on the quiet. I would probably have stuffed handfuls of it into my mouth. Sweat was pouring off my brow. It was a good thing my head was shaven, otherwise my hair would have been all stuck together. Our tunics were steaming on our backs. Everything was soaked with sweat and then caught by the frost. Our outer jackets had gone as stiff as boards. Orange rings danced before our eyes. The group was not maintaining the right pace. Don't eat the snow! If you do, I'll flatten you! Better look down at the points of your skis. If you look far ahead you simply pass out. But if you look down you are hypnotised, you carry on mechanically and the ever-retreating horizon doesn't drive you mad.

'Come on, you lazy skunks!' the commander shouted savagely. 'Look out ahead! We're running into an ambush! Negative didn't notice the light on the left. Watch yourself, Negative, or I'll knock your teeth out with my ski stick!'

The group knew that their commander was not given to making jokes. He would do it.

'Keep going, rabble!'

The sun rose blood-red across the world. Its ragged, impudent rays skipped across the tips of the fir trees through a freezing mist. There was a hard crisp frost in the forest clearings.

We were resting in a fir plantation for the second night running, and waiting for the return of a patrol we had sent on ahead. All our faces were white, bloodless, corpse-like, and our legs were throbbing. In this situation it was best to put them up so that the blood drained out of them. The radio operators lay in the snow with their feet resting on their containers, and others had also managed to get their feet up somehow. It was now more than twenty-four hours since we had been dropped, and we had been on the move all the time, stopping only every three or four hours for fifteen or twenty minutes. Two men guarded the stopping place and two others went ahead, while the rest lay down and went straight to sleep. Karl de la Duchesse lay there with his head thrown back and steam rising slowly from his unbuttoned tunic. A snowflake descended gently on his exposed throat and slowly melted. My eyelids were sticking together, and felt as if they had grit under them. I would have liked to relax, close my eyes and not open them for a few hours.

The group commander was rubbing his chin – a bad sign. He looked very grim. So did his deputy, the Fist. Five *Spetsnaz* groups were approaching the communications centre of the Tank Army from various directions at the same time. Our orders were quite straightforward: whoever reached the communications centre before three in the morning would attack it at 3.40. Those who did not arrive by the agreed time would not go into battle but would go round the centre in a big arc and carry on to the next objective. Our group had not arrived on time. That was why the commander was looking grim. In the distance we could hear explosions and long bursts of automatic fire. That meant that they were close, that they had taken an attack head-on. Face to face.

At least three groups had made it. But even if only one group got there in time, if it managed to dispose of the guard and smash its way into the communications centre at the end of a cold uncomfortable night, the operation would still be counted a total success. One group could do a great deal against a communications centre set up in nice warm cabins, against bespectacled, overweight signals troops, both men and women, and against dissolute telephone operators also of both sexes eaten up by idleness and lechery.

One felt sorry for the commander because not all his troops had managed to reach that tempting target. he was confident that the group belonging to the lieutenant we called 'Angry' had arrived dead on time. And sergeant Akl had probably brought his men in in good time, too. Akl – that was Akula, the Shark. The sergeant's teeth were sharp and strong but uneven, as if they were into two rows. That was why he was called the Shark. But perhaps not only because of that. Our commander ground his teeth now. It was obvious that he wasn't going to let the group relax today. Keep going, rabble.

We were sleeping. It was the eleventh day after the drop. In daylight we couldn't stick our heads out: the sky was full of helicopters. All the roads were cordoned off, and there was an ambush at the edge of every wood. We came across a lot of phoney objectives: missile batteries, communication centres and command posts. The *Spetsnaz* groups attacked them, but got caught in the trap. The battalion had already lost dozens of its groups. We didn't know how many. Supplies were dropped to us every night: ammunition, explosives, food and sometimes liquor. Such concern indicated only one thing: there were only a few of us left. In the last few days our group had come across a radio-relay link which the staff had not known about before. By using directional receivers and transmitting aerials, the group had detected an important communications centre and a command post in the rear. On the fifth day of the exercise the group had gone on the air for the first time to announce its discovery. For that it received congratulations from the commanding officer of the 13th Army and an order to leave that area. They were probably softening it up with missiles or aircraft. On the seventh day the group linked up with four others, thus forming a unit under a captain known unkindly as the Useless Extra. The whole unit then made a successful attack on an aerodrome in full daylight just as a fighter squadron was taking off. The unit got away without losses and dispersed into small groups. For the time being our 43rd group did not exist, but divided into two: the 431st and the 432nd. Then they were reunited. But it was still not possible to take effective action, because of the helicopters in the sky, the roadblocks on every side, the ambushes in the woods and the traps set near the targets. None the less we were doing our job: the Eighth Guards Tank Army was almost completely paralysed, and instead of engaging in battle it was trying to catch us behind the lines.

Daylight was fading. Nobody had bothered us during the day and we had

had a rest. Our group had so far not been caught because our commander was as cunning as a snake. That, presumably, was why they called him the Snake. He had found an ammunition store belonging to our opponents, and that was where we spent our days. It served as our base, and we were able to keep all our heavy equipment there. At night some members of the group, travelling light, would carry out daring raids far from the base and then return by morning. All the groups which had taken cover in the dense forest had been destroyed long ago. But not us, so far. It was difficult for our opponents to believe that our base was hidden under their very noses. Now the helicopters did not bother us, and as for the ambushes and roadblocks, you simply had to be very careful.

'Are you ready, men?'

The group was ready, skis adjusted and belts tightened.

'Jump about a bit.'

Before setting out you always had to jump up and down, to make sure that nothing rattled or clattered.

'Time to go. Carry on.'

'Listen, Chopin, just imagine we're fighting a real war. The deputy commander is killed and the commander himself is wounded in the leg. If we take him along with us we're all finished; if we abandon him it will also be the end of the group. The enemy will make him talk, even if they have to cut his liver out. There's no provision for evacuating the wounded in *Spetsnaz*. So just imagine, Chopin, that you have taken over command of the group – what are you going to do with the wounded commander?'

Chopin took out of the little pocket on the sleeve of his tunic a disposable syringe. It was known as 'Blissful death'.

'That's right, Chopin, absolutely right. In wartime the only way we have of surviving is to kill off our wounded ourselves.

And I entered another good mark in the umpire's register.

It was the seventeenth day after the drop. There were only five or six groups still operating, including ours. The Shark's group and Angry's group had been captured a long time ago. The commander of the 43rd knew this through some special sense. Angry and the Shark were both his friends and his rivals. Lieutenant Snake was probably thinking about them now and smiling quietly to himself.

'Ready? Jump about. Time to go. Off you go, men.'

He no longer called his soldiers 'rabble'.

Chapter Four

It was a wonderful feeling to walk on thick red carpets after being away for twenty-three days. I was no longer used to quiet or carpets or warmth. In fact, I had returned to the wild, which is something human beings do very quickly, slipping easily back into the animal world. But it was quiet and agreeable in the corridors of HQ and the people there were well fed, well turned out and cleanly shaved. No place there for the hoarse wheezing voice of the commander or the impatient yelping of dogs about to be let off the leash.

Our 43rd group was among the last to be captured. It was surrounded and driven into a ravine. Just like real war. And there were real dogs, those four-legged friends of man that did not understand the difference between a real hunt and an exercise. . . . It was all one to them.

One soldier, known as the Whip for his toughness and resilience, was so thin and agile that he managed to slip out of the trap. He was the first to be separated from the group and driven towards the river on which the ice was already breaking up. They thought they would surround him on the river bank. But he threw away his tunic and his automatic and swam between the chunks of ice. They didn't bother to send a helicopter after one man, and the dogs wouldn't take to the water – they were too smart. Four days later Whiplash arrived back at his battalion's barracks, dressed in a dark grey policeman's greatcoat that he had stolen and thinner than ever.

For that the Whip was promoted to the rank of sergeant and awarded fifteen days' leave. He was by no means the only such man in the battalion. One by one they made their way back to the battalion on broken skis and with their tunics torn to bits, and sometimes with bleeding wounds.

When we were captured, they took us off to a barracks of an MVD regiment, where we were greeted like old friends. They gave us a bath and some food and let us sleep as long as we liked. One complete barrack building had been made available for the captured groups and the regiment's medical section was dealing only with us.

In the bath house the MVD troops eyed us with admiration and some alarm: we were just skeletons.

'You've hit on a pretty tough service, my friends.'

We did not argue. It was tough. But each year in *Spetsnaz* counted as eighteen months' service. If you served ten years you were credited with fifteen. Similarly you received half as much pay again, and you were paid for parachute jumps and for every day on exercises. And we could soon put on some weight. So I slept it all off and had a good rest. And now I was treading the plush carpets again. The other staff officers greeted me with jokes:

'Tell me, Viktor, how did you manage to lose so much weight?'

'Look at our spy – where did he get that sun tan?'

My face was tanned from the frost, the wind and the merciless winter sun. My lips were black and cracked. My nose had peeled.

'How about coming skiing on Sunday, Viktor!'

That was a cruel joke that I found difficult to take. Indeed, ever since serving in the *Spetsnaz*, what I hate most of all in the world is people who, of their own free will, put on skis simply because they've nothing better to do.

I was on my way to see the Chief of Intelligence.

'May I enter? Comrade Lt-colonel. . . . Excuse me. . . .'

Kravtsov now had not two, but three stars on his epaulettes.

'Comrade colonel – senior lieutenant Suvorov reporting for duty on return from manoeuvres.'

'Greetings.'

'Permit me to congratulate you.'

'Thank you. Sit down.' He eyed my burnt cheekbones. 'They certainly trimmed you down a bit. Have you slept it off?'

'Yes.'

'There's a lot of work to do. The world has changed a lot in your absence. Try to bring yourself up to date as quickly as possible. Have you forgotten everything on the exercise?'

'I tried to go over what I know in my head.'

'Shall I test you?'

'Sure.'

'Spangdahlem.'

'Spangdahlem is a US Air Force base in Western Germany, 25 kilometres north of Trier. The 52nd tactical fighter wing is permanently based there. There are 72 F-4 fighters. One runway, 3,050 metres long, 45 metres wide. The wing consists of. . . .'

'Okay. Off you go.'

The world changes at a breathtaking speed. I had not had any access to information for twenty-three days, and in front of me were bulging folders with intelligence summaries, orders and ciphered messages. In twenty-three days, the world had changed out of all recognition. I realised that the Chief of Intelligence had spared my feelings and had asked me an easy question about an unmoving object, an air base. If he had asked me about the 6th Panzer Grenadier division of the Bundeswehr, for example, I would certainly have been in a very tricky situation. You have to follow the situation continually, or else you find yourself peddling out-of-date information.

So I went through it all: 'Top Secret—Agents of the Belorussian military district have noticed a strengthening of the guard over the launching sites for Pershing missiles in Western Germany'.... 'Top Secret—The 5th department of the Intelligence directorate of the Baltic Fleet has recorded a complete replacement of the coding system in governmental and military communications channels in Denmark'.... 'Top Secret—Agents of the General Staff's Intelligence network have discovered'.... 'Top Secret—Agents of the 11th Guards Army of the Baltic military district in Western Germany have observed work on the building of silos for nuclear mines'.... 'Top Secret—I order the Chief of the Second Chief Directorate of the General Staff, Chiefs of Intelligence of GSFG, SGV, ZGV,* of the Baltic, Belorussian and Carpathian military districts to give special attention to the collection of information about the stationing of nuclear mines on the territory of the German Federal Republic: Chief of the General Staff Army-General Kulikov.'

Twenty-three days ago no one had heard anything about nuclear mines. But now a tremendous effort was being made through the network of agents to discover what this mysterious self-defence system in the West amounted to. The Soviet Army was also looking different: 'Secret—Results of experimental exercises carried out by the 8th Air Assault brigade of the Trans-Baikal military district' ... there were no such brigades only 23 days ago.... 'Top Secret—I order you to take into your armament ATGW known as "Malyutka – M" with a guiding system based on two fixed points: Minister of Defence Marshal of the Soviet Union A. Grechko'.... 'For officers of *Spetsnaz* only – Inquiry into the circumstances in which foreign trainees died in the Odessa centre for training of *Spetsnaz* ... in the course of training exercises with 'puppets' ... I order you to increase supervision and security....Give special attention to....'

I read that last order three times over. It made it quite clear how one had to deal with a 'puppet' and how it was to be looked after and preserved. But it was not clear what exactly a 'puppet' was.

It was not easy to train foreign fighters for *Spetsnaz*. We – members of Soviet *Spetsnaz* – would go into action in wartime, but the foreigners were in action already all over the world. They went fearlessly to their deaths for their glorious ideals, never suspecting that they were actually fighting for our *Spetsnaz*. They were amazing people! We trained them, spent millions on their upkeep and risked the reputation of our state for them, yet they continued to believe they were independent. It was very difficult to deal with such people. As they came to us for training they brought with them the West's amazing air of unconcern. They were an naïve as children and as magnanimous as heroes of a novel. Their hearts were full of fire, their heads packed with prejudices. It was said that some of them reckoned you shouldn't kill people during a

* The Soviet forces in Germany, Poland and Czechoslovakia.

wedding; others that you shouldn't kill during a funeral. Extraordinary people! That's what cemeteries were for – to have corpses in them!

The *Spetsnaz* Training Centre soon knocked this romantic nonsense out of them. They were also torn to bits by dogs and forced to run through fire. They were taught not to fear heights, the sight of blood, high speeds and, above all, death. These men often demonstrate to the world their contempt for death – and for other people's lives – when they make a lightning raid to seize an aircraft or an embassy. It is the *Spetsnaz* Centre which has taught them to kill – skilfully, calmly and with relish. But what did they have in their training concealed behind the term 'puppet'?

The Soviet system of preserving secrets has been well thought out, refined and perfected. We keep our secrets by destroying anyone capable of talking too much and by the total concealment of a colossal quantity of factual information. Often not very secret. We keep our secrets by a special system of personnel selection, a system of special passes, and a system of vertical and horizontal barriers to prevent access to secrets. We keep our secrets by means of dogs, security guards, special signals, safes and seals and steel doors and an all-embracing censorship. In addition we keep them by means of a special language or jargon. Even if someone were to get into our safes he wouldn't understand very much of what he found there.

When we are talking about our enemies, we use the normal words which everyone understands: missile, nuclear warhead, chemical weapon, commando, spy. But if we are talking about our own affairs the same things have different names: the goods, CG, special weapon, *Spetsnaz*, special source. Many terms have a variety of meanings. *Chistka*, or 'purge', may mean in some circumstances expulsion from the Party, but in others the destruction of millions of people. A commonly used word may have a great many synonyms in the jargon. Soviet commando troops may be known by the general term of *Spetsnaz* but also as 'deep reconnaissance', 'tourists', 'nosey parkers', or 'raiders'. So what does the word 'puppet' conceal in our language? Do they use 'puppets' also in training Soviet troops, or are they only for foreign trainees? Did the 'puppets' exist previously, or have they been recently introduced, like the air assault brigades?

I closed the folder, firmly determined to find out the meaning of this strange term. There was only one way to do it: to give the impression that I knew what it was all about, and then in the course of casual conversation someone who really did know might let out a little more than was allowed. And one crumb was often enough to guess the answer.

The 296th independent reconnaissance battalion of *Spetsnaz* had been hidden skilfully and with a certain taste. The 13th Army had a signal regiment which took care of communications for the HQ and command posts. Secrets of great importance to the state passed through the regiment, which was therefore specially guarded. But there was a special area within the regiment's territory in which our reconnaissance battalion lived. All the paratroopers wore the uniform of communications troops. All the vehicles in the battalion were closed vans, the same as those used by the signals troops, so that an outsider would see simply a signals regiment and nothing more. What is more, even within the regiment the majority of the officers and men believed that there were three of the usual signals battalions and one unusual one, especially secret, which probably handled governmental traffic.

Within the *Spetsnaz* battalion itself there were quite a few secrets. Many of the men believed that there were three parachute companies made up of ordinary, though strong and tough, soldiers. It was only later that I found out that there was more to it than that. Apart from the three companies there existed another special platoon made up of professionals. It was stationed in another place, far away from the battalion and intended for carrying out especially difficult tasks. I discovered its existence only because, as an information officer, I had to instruct those people in problems of my own trade: the correct and rapid detection of important targets on enemy territory. The first time I travelled to the special platoon I was a little alarmed. Colonel Kravtsov drove me there personally and introduced me.

'See if you can guess what kind of camouflage we have thought up for this platoon.'

'That's beyond my abilities, comrade colonel. I've got no facts to base any guess on.'

'But try all the same. It's an intelligence test for you. Form an idea of them, which is what your imagination is for, and try and hide them, imagining yourself to be Chief of Intelligence in the 13th Army.'

'They must have a very accurate idea of the territory in which they will have to operate, and therefore they must frequently travel abroad. They must be in first-class training . . . I would be inclined, comrade colonal, to attach them to a sports team. That would provide the camouflage and the opportunity to travel abroad. . . .'

'Correct . . .' he laughed. 'All very simple. They form a team in the army's sports organisation – parachutists, runners, sharp-shooters, boxers, wrestlers. Every army and flotilla has such a team. Every military district, fleet and group of troops has even stronger and even better trained sports teams. We do not spare resources when it comes to sport. But where would you hide your sportsmen's training centre?'

'In Dubrovice.'

He was a good intelligence officer, and so he kept control of himself. There was only a slight sound from his teeth and the veins on his cheeks twitched a little.

'Why in Dubrovice?'

'In our much loved 13th Army there is only one penal battalion and that's in Dubrovice, in the military prison. Young soldiers from our division have often fetched up there. The fences are high, the dogs fierce and there are many rows of barbed wire. All you have to do is to cut off a section of the camp inside and you can put any secret body you like inside it. People who have to go there can be taken in prison vans and nobody would be any the wiser. . . .'

'In our 13th Army there are quite a few well guarded places. The APRTB,* for example. . . .'

'But in the APRTB, comrade colonel, there is nowhere to hide a 'puppet'. . . .'

He gave me a long, searching look, but said nothing.

It is only on autumn nights that there are so many stars. Only on a cold September night can you see them so clearly, looking like silver studs on black velvet.

How many of them there are looking at us out of the cold dark emptiness! When you are looking at the Great Bear, not far from the bright star at the bend in the handle you can make out a very small star. Perhaps it is by no means as small as all that, but simply very far away. It may be a tremendous heavenly body with dozens of huge planets round it. Maybe it is a galaxy with millions of other bodies. . . .

We are of course not alone in the universe. There are millions of planets in outer space like our own. What grounds have we for considering ourselves an exception? We are no exception. We are like all the others. Only the shape and colour of our eyes may be different. The inhabitants of some planets have blue eyes, like Colonel Kravtsov's, while others have green eyes, triangular with a tint of emerald. But that is, apparently, where the differences end. In all other respects we are identical – all of us animals. There are of course different kinds of beasts: thinking, civilised ones and those that do not think. The first distinguish themselves from the second by the fact that they endeavour to camouflage their animal nature. When we have plenty of food, warmth and female company we can allow ourselves to be kindly and sympathetic. But the moment nature or fate faces us with the question point-blank – who is to die and who is to survive?—we immediately plunge our yellow fangs into the throat of our neighbour, brother or mother.

We are all animals. I certainly am, and I make no effort to conceal it. And the inhabitant of the twelfth planet of the orange body lost in the depths of the galaxy without a name – he is also an animal and also tries to appear good and kindly. The Chief of Intelligence in the 13th Army Colonel Kravtsov is also an animal. He is a wild beast such as you rarely come across. There he sits at the camp fire stirring the embers with a stick. Not very tall, very trim, with a handsome young face, slightly disdainful. He has a broad, engaging smile,

* APRTB – the Russian initials standing for Army Mobile Missile-Technical Base, a unit included in all-arm and tank armies which handles the transportation, protection and technical servicing of missiles for the missile brigade of an Army and for missile battalions of divisions forming part of that Army.

though the corners of his mouth are always turned down – a mark of his capacity for restraint and precise calculation. His look is devastating and penetrating, forcing anyone who meets it to blink and turn away. He has delicate hands, not proletarian ones. His colonel's epaulettes suit him well. People of his kind sometimes have the strangest habits. Some, I have heard, collect rusty kopeks. I wonder what our colonel amuses himself with? For me and the rest of us he is a puzzle. We know surprisingly little about him, while he knows all there is to know about all of us. He's an animal. Small, bloodthirsty and deadly dangerous. He knows where he's going and never turns aside from his path. I know what his guiding star is. It is called Power.

As he sat at the camp-fire the red flames played upon his manly features. His dark, clean profile. Shades of red. Nothing more. No sudden change of mind. No compromises. If I made just one mistake he would get rid of me, crush me. If I were to deceive him he would be able to tell by my eyes – his intellect was that powerful.

'Suvorov, did you want to ask something?'

We were alone by the camp-fire in a little ravine in the endless steppe. Our vehicle was hidden far away in the undergrowth and the driver had been given permission to sleep. We had a long autumn night ahead of us.

'Yes, comrade colonel, I have long wanted to ask you. . . . You have under your command hundreds of intelligent, promising officers with excellent training and refined manners. . . .But I am a peasant, I haven't read many of the books you talk about . . . it's difficult for me in your company . . . I am not interested in the writers and artists whom you admire. . . . So why did you choose me?'

He spent a long time fiddling with the kettle, apparently debating whether to give me the usual reply, commenting on my diligence and originality of mind, or to tell me the tuth. He was cooking up a murderous drink – a mixture of coffee and cognac. If you drank it you didn't sleep for twenty-four hours.

'I will tell you the truth, Viktor, because you are capable of understanding it yourself, because you are difficult to deceive, and because you ought to know it. Our world is very cruel. You can survive in it only by scrambling upwards. If you stop you slide down and you will be trampled underfoot by those who are climbing up over your bones. Our world is a bloody uncompromising battle between two political systems, but at the same time it is a struggle between individuals, and in that struggle everyone needs help and support. I need helpers who are ready for anything, ready to risk their lives in the cause of victory. But I don't need helpers who will betray me at the most difficult moment. To achieve that there is only one way: to choose helpers from the very lowest level. You owe everything to me, and if I'm kicked out you will be kicked out too. If I lose everything so will you. I pulled you up, I picked you out of the crowd, not because of your ability but because you are one of the crowd. Nobody needs you. If something happens to me you will find yourself again in the crowd, without any of your power and privileges. This way of choosing assistants and bodyguards is as old as the hills. It has been used by all rulers. If you betray me you will lose everything. That is exactly how I was picked up out of the dust. My protector is on the way up and is dragging me along with him, counting on my support in every situation. If he bites the dust, who will need me?'

'Your protector is Lieutenant-general Obaturov?'

'Yes. He took me into his group when he was a major and I was a lieutenant . . . not a very successful one.'

'But he is also working for someone. He is also being pulled upwards?'

'Of course. Only that is none of your business. Rest assured that you are in the right group and that General Obaturov has extremely powerful protectors in the General Staff. But listen, Suvorov, I know you pretty well now, and I have the feeling that that was not the question that was bothering you. What's the matter?'

'Tell me about the Aquarium.'

'You know about that too? You couldn't have heard that word used, which means that you have seen it somewhere. Let me think and I'll tell you where you might have seen it.'

'On the back of the portrait.'

'So that's it. Let me advise you, Suvorov, never to ask anybody about it. The Aquarium takes too serious a view of its secrets. You only have to ask that question to find yourself hanging on a hook. No, I'm not joking. By the neck or by the ribs, and upside down. If I were to tell you about the Aquarium, you might tell someone else and he might do the same. Then the time might come when things began to move in the opposite direction. One man is arrested, they find out from him where he heard that word, he names you, and you point the finger at me.'

'Do you believe that if they were to torture me I would give you away?'

'I have no doubt about it at all, and you shouldn't either. Some fools say that there are people so strong-willed that they can stand being tortured and others so weak that they can't take it. That's nonsense. There are good interrogators and bad ones. In the Aquarium the interrogators are good. . . . If you are put on the 'conveyor' you will confess to everything, including things that never happened. But . . . but I am confident, Viktor, that you and I will not land up on the conveyor, and for that reason I'm going to tell you a little about the Aquarium.'

'What sort of fish are there swimming there?'

'There's only one kind there – piranhas.'

'Have you ever worked in the Aquarium?'

'No, I was never accorded that honour. Maybe in the future. . . . The people there probably think that my teeth are not yet sharp enough. So listen. The Aquarium is the central building of the 2nd Chief Directorate of the General Staff, that is, of the Chief Intelligence Directorate, the GRU. Military intelligence has existed under various names ever since October 21, 1918. The Red Army was then already a huge and powerful force, administered by the general staff – the brains of the Army. But the staff reacted too slowly and uncertainly because the organism it commanded was blind and deaf. Information about the enemy was provided by the Cheka. It was just as if the brain was receiving information, not from its own eyes and ears but from the lips of another person. What is more, the Cheka people always looked upon reports to the Army as something of secondary importance. It couldn't be otherwise: the secret police has its own priorities; the general staff has different ones. And however much information the general staff received from elsewhere it would never be enough. Just imagine, if there were some major failure, who was going to be held responsible? The general staff could always say that information about the enemy was insufficient and that that was the cause of the failure. And they would always be in the right, because however much information was collected the chief of the general staff would always be able to ask another million questions to which there is no answer. That is why it was decided to hand over military intelligence to the general staff and to let the CGS handle it, so that if there was not enough information about the enemy it would be the fault of the general staff itself.'

'And the KGB never tried to take control of the GRU?'

'It was always trying, and it's still trying. Yezhov once succeeded in doing it: he was at the same time head of the NKVD and of military intelligence. Because of that it became necessary to destroy him immediately. He had too much power in his hands. He had established a monopoly over all secret work, and that was a very alarming monopoly for the top leadership. As long as there are at least two secret organisations fighting each other behind the scenes there is no need to fear a conspiracy within one of them. So long as there are two organisations the quality of the work is maintained because of the competition. The day one organisation swallows the other will mark the end of the Politburo. But the Politburo won't let that happen. The scope of the KGB's activity is limited by the activity of hostile organisations. Within the country the MVD does very good work. The MVD and the KGB are ready to gobble each other up. Apart from that there is yet another secret police operating within the country – the People's Control. Stalin became dictator after having been head of that very organisation.'

I remained silent, chewing over the significance of what had been said. The long night was still ahead. Some thirty metres away from us, hidden in an osier bed, was a big inflated model of a 'Pershing' missile – an exact copy of the American original. On the previous night a complete *Spetsnaz* battalion had been dropped in small groups far away from this place. It was a competition. They had to cover 307 kilometres with five control points along the route: missiles, radar, HQ. The group which first covered the route, having found all the targets and reported their exact position, were to be given leave and each soldier was to be presented with a gold watch. All the privates in the winning group would be made corporals, and the sergeants would be made senior sergeants. Staff officers of the intelligence department were keeping watch over the progress of the groups. Kravtsov himself usually followed the competition from a helicopter. But on this occasion he had decided for some reason to be at one of the control points and had taken me as his assistant.

'Sounds as if someone's coming.'

'We'll talk later.'

There was the sound of gravel being trodden underfoot and of stones rolling downhill, and a huge shadow crept like a snake down through the ravine. In the darkness the camp-fire nearly blinded the broad-shouldered paratrooper. He looked closely into our faces and, recognising Kravtsov, reported: 'Comrade colonel: the 29th group of the 2nd *Spetsnaz* company. Sergeant Polishchuk in command.'

'Greetings, sergeant.'

The sergeant turned to his group and gave a quiet whistle. There was the sound of paratroopers sliding down the hillside. Two of them took up position on a ridge as look-outs and defence. The radio operator quickly put up his aerials. Two others spread out a groundsheet beneath which the group's cipher clerk would perform his mysteries. Ordinary mortals were not allowed to know how he prepared his messages for transmission, and for that reason he always worked under cover of a groundsheet. In war conditions the group commander answers with his life for the safety of the codes and the cipher clerk. If the group runs into danger the commander has to kill the cipher clerk and destroy the codes and cipher machine. If he doesn't do it not only he but the whole group answer with their lives.

Now the message was ready. We could all see what it was: an ordinary photographic film with a few rows of little holes punched in it. The message was put into the radio transmitter, but the set was not yet switched on or tuned. The radio operator looked at his chronometer. then he pressed a knob. The radio set switched on, tuned itself automatically, drew the piece of film into its interior and immediately spat it out the other side. A few little lamps on the set immediately went out. The whole transmission had not lasted more than a second. In effect the radio shoots its charge of information out like a gun.

The cipher clerk put a match to the film which disappeared in a flash, hissing fiercely. The film appeared to be quite ordinary. It burnt up as quickly as the radio had transmitted the ciphered message.

'Ready? Jump about. Time to go. Quick march.'

Sergeant Polishchuk was a very demanding commander. He would be very tough with his group and drive them on without stopping. Because you can count your chickens only at the finishing post. All was going well for the moment. But what if the group collapsed in the first couple of hundred kilometres? The group commanders were given considerable powers. That was the point of the competition. They could halt the group if they wished, or let them sleep, or let them rest every ten minutes. But if you fetched up among the last groups you lost your sergeant's stripes and were reduced to the ranks. There were plenty of takers for your sergeant's position.

'Comrade colonel, the 11th group of the 1st company. Commander Sergeant Stolyar.'

'Greetings, sergeant. Carry on and pay no attention to our presence here.'

'Very good. Rhinoceros and Ugly Duckling – keep an eye open!'

'Okay.'

'Blevantin!'

'Here, sergeant.'

'Contact HQ.'

'Very good.'

'Ready? Jump. Time to be off. Quick march!'

The groups started arriving in a stream. It was always like that with competitions. A few groups would dash on far ahead of the others; they would be followed by the main body at short intervals or no interval at all; and finally the laggards, the ones who had got lost or were already exhausted, would arrive. Some of them would take a rest by our camp-fire for a whole hour. Others would stay for two. Some would stop simply to establish contact, transmit their message and carry on further. Alongside us several groups were preparing a simple supper. It was forbidden to light a fire during exercises, so the paratroopers cooked their food over a spirit fire. But on competitions you could light a fire. The most important points in competitions were precise orientation, speed, map reading and communications. The rest was less important.

The smell of cooking reached us from the camp-fire. The paratroopers were cooking a chicken. They had their own special way of doing it. They would clean it out, chop off the head and claws, but leave the feathers. Then they would cover it with a coating of wet clay and put it into the fire. Hence the smell. It would soon be ready to eat. A paratrooper carries no utensils, so that he has to cook in clay. When the bird is ready they crack off the clay and with it all the feathers, leaving the chicken in its own fat, ready for the table.

'Comrade colonel, be our guest.'

'Thank you. And where did you get the chicken from?'

'It's a wild one, comrade colonel. A stray.'

In the course of competitions the *Spetsnaz* troops may come across a 'wild' pig, pullet or cockerel. Sometimes they find 'wild' potatoes, 'wild' tomatoes and cucumbers, or 'wild' corn. Another group was cooking up some corn in a huge saucepan.

'Where did you get that saucepan?'

'Well, it's like this: it was lying at the roadside. We reckoned we shouldn't let it be wasted. Try our corn! It's very good.'

It was Kravtsov's rule to accept invitations from his men as gratefully as he accepted them from the chief of staff of the District or the C-in-C himself. He made no distinctions. The atmosphere around the fire was relaxed.

The colonel was a great one for jokes. The dirtier the better. For him the

Spetsnaz soldiers were wild men, capable of great deeds and respecting few other men. They were ready to obey any officer put in charge of them, but they did not respect every one, and a *Spetsnaz* soldier, with his animal cunning, had thousands of ways of letting his commander know whether he respected him or not. So why did they respect Kravtsov? Because he did not conceal or try to conceal his animal nature. The troops were convinced that human nature was basically vicious and incorrigible. They had good reason. Every day they risked their lives and every day they had an opportunity to observe people on the brink of death. So they divided everybody into the good and the bad. A good person in their eyes was one who did not conceal the animal seated within him. But a person who tried to *appear* good was dangerous. The most dangerous were those who not only paraded their good qualities but who also believed within themselves they were indeed good people. The most loathsome disgusting criminal might kill a man, ten men or even a hundred. But a criminal will never kill people by the million. Millions are killed only by those who consider themselves good. People like Robespierre do not grow out of criminals but out of the most worthy and most humane types. The guillotine was invented, not by criminals but by humanists. The most monstrous crimes in the history of mankind were committed by people who did not drink vodka, did not smoke, were not unfaithful to their wives and fed squirrels from the palms of their hands.

The men whose corn we were then eating were quite sure that a human being could be good only up to a certain point. When life gets difficult good people become bad and it can happen at the most awkward moment. If you don't want to be caught napping it is better not to have anything to do with good people. Better have dealings with those who are now seen to be bad. You will at least know what to expect from them when your luck turns. In that sense Colonel Kravtsov was one of them. For example, if a shapely girl came down the street, with buttocks bouncing around like melons in a bag, the *Spetsnaz* soldiers would at least rape her visually, if in no other way. But Colonel Kravtsov did the same, quite unashamedly, and they respected him for it. The dangerous man is the one who does not stare after women and who tries to give the impression that he is not interested in such things. It's among those people that you find secret sadists and murderers.

Kravtsov was fond of the female sex and made no secret of it. He was also fond of power, and why should he conceal his feelings? He was very fond of power – any power. I felt it when I first saw him hitting a 'puppet'. It was the apotheosis of might and merciless power.

What we call a 'puppet' is actually a man. A special kind of man for training purposes. For example, you can hit him. But, unlike your partner in a match or your instructor, a 'puppet' also puts up a fight and may even kill you. That's the whole point of using them. Our work is very risky and exceptionally responsible. Just imagine that in time of war a group of *Spetsnaz* who have the task of slitting the throats of some sleeping enemy soldiers hesitate because they are not used to killing or simply because they suddenly experience feelings of compassion, charity or humanity. They wouldn't carry out their task and they might perish themselves and wreck a most important operation which might cost the lives of thousands of our soldiers. To prevent that happening, they invented the 'puppets'. They invented them a long time ago and have been using them in various organisations for more than half a century. In the Cheka they are called 'gladiators', in the NKVD 'volunteers' and in Smersh 'Robinsons'.

A 'puppet' is a criminal who has been condemned to death. Those who are weak, old, sick, especially dangerous or who know too much are executed immediately after sentence has been passed. But others have their life extended by the state and are used for a variety of purposes. The whole of our nuclear industry has been built by such prisoners and is maintained by them. And the longer the sentence a man gets, the more dangerous the work. A person condemned to death is given the most dangerous work. But it is not only there that such people are employed. They are also used as training material. It suits everybody. They get their lives prolonged, and we have an opportunity for real-life training.

There used to be enough 'gladiators', 'volunteers' and 'Robinsons' for everybody. Now there's a shortage. Today the number of death sentences passed in the whole country is not more than two or three thousand a year. Half the people sentenced are disposed of without being put to any useful purpose. At the same time the number of organisations that have a use for people in death row is considerable: the VPK (the armaments industry), the GCh service (for fitting and servicing warheads), the Fleet (for replacing the active zones of the reactors in nuclear-powered submarines), the KGB, the MVD, the GRU, and *Spetsnaz*.

Because we got only a few 'puppets' sent to us, they had to be kept in use for a long time. This meant that by no means all *Spetsnaz* could have training fights with 'puppets', but only specially selected people: certain foreigners, and professionals, who are kept on the strength of *Spetsnaz* and who are being prepared for the most important tasks.

A fight with a 'puppet' – very often a very tough criminal – is a serious and very risky business. You can hit him to your heart's content but you mustn't break any bones. But you must also be careful. He doesn't stick to our rules. He fights back. An animal rage burns within him. Sometimes he hides it in an effort to prolong his wretched life, sometimes he loses control of himself. Hit him, make the most of it! It's not a phoney fight, not a form of onanism. It's a real fight, involving a real risk.

The colonel doesn't have to take any risks, but every time he visits the penal battalion where our special training centre is hidden away, he puts on a tracksuit and visits the training room.

A little water, nearly half a tin of cofffee, a good portion of brandy, and over the camp-fire. It needs to be cooked for a long time. The moment it comes to the boil you take it away and then bring it back to the fire. The resultant liquid will make you want to leap in the air and kick out like a young goat. It puts life into you. The fumes tickle your nose, the smell intoxicates like the smell of gunfire.

A grey sky. The dawn is coming. We are once again alone.

'Has the KGB spilled a lot of our blood?'

'Are you thinking of the whole Army or just military intelligence?'

'Both the Army and the GRU.'

'A lot.'

I again remain silent, taking little sips at the drink which makes my whole insides burn as if from pepper.

'Why did it happen?'

'Because we were too naïve. We were serving our country, but the Chekists were serving themselves.'

'Could it happen again in the future?'

'Yes, if we are as naïve as we were.'

He keeps fingering his hot mug in his hands. It seems to me as if he is balancing my fate on the palm of his hands. It is no accident that he has brought me to this place. He wants to talk to me alone. It is presumably up to me to say something – something he expects from me.

'We shouldn't allow it to happen again. For the sake of our country we don't have the right to permit the KGB to be all-powerful.' I suddenly felt that I have hit on the right key. 'Before the war the Chekists destroyed our generals and our military intelligence and by so doing very nearly brought the Soviet state to its knees. For the sake of our motherland we have a duty not to permit it to happen again!'.

'What would you do in my position? Or in the position of General Obaturov? Or General Ogarkov?'

'I would maintain close contact with a group. And I would consider a blow struck at one of our organisation as a blow at all of us. We need solidarity.'

'Well, let's assume that we have solidarity. Let's assume that we are supporting each other. Then the KGB or the Party strikes at one of us. How would you reply to that? Does everyone resign?'

I stare into the fire. What reply *can* one make? A military conspiracy is out of the question. We have to strike back at our enemies, but the blows have to be struck out of the blue by unknown people.

'I think, comrade colonel, we would have to take action, not against the whole of the KGB, but against particular individuals, the most dangerous ones. . . .'

'But if I do that in the Carpathian military district everyone will know that's it's my work. They would soon get their hands on me. . . .'

64

'It's solidarity we need,' I said in an eager whisper. 'If they hit our people in Siberia the reply must come in another place.'

'What sort of reply?'

'I don't know. In my view, comrade colonel, we must devise some dirty tricks for the benefit of the enemy so that the Chekists are removed from their jobs by other Chekists. They also have different groups squabbling among themselves.'

'All right then, Suvorov, just remember for the rest of your days that this conversation never took place. You've knocked yourself out with those coffee grounds and you've been imagining things. Get it into your head once and for all, if you ever come to be arrested, that it's better for you to remain a single enemy, a loner. If anyone should suspect that you are involved in some conspiracy they will torture you mercilessly in an effort to extract from you the names of your fellow conspirators. I haven't had anything to say to you. It's just that you told me all sorts of nonsense. And now listen carefully.'

His voice changes completely and so does the expression on his face.

'In a week's time you will be picked out to take over control of a *Spetsnaz* group. You will be posted to the Storozhenets training camp. On the second day of the operation your group will split in two. From that moment you will disappear. You will make your way alone to Kishinev. You can go by night using freight trains. In Kishinev there is a teachers' training college which has long been famous for its strong nationalism. Here is the slogan which you will write on the wall of the college at night.'

He hands me a scrap of cigarette paper.

'You don't speak Moldavian, so you must learn these letters off by heart like hieroglyphics. Do it now. Try and write it down. That's it. Once more. Now throw it all into the fire. Remember: you thought it all up yourself. If you get stopped anywhere say you got separated from your group. But nobody will be following our groups just now.'

'What size should the letters be?'

'Fifteen to twenty centimetres will be enough to get rid of the chairman of the KGB in Moldavia. It's not in our military district but in the Odessa district. Maybe they will suspect the military, but the *Spetsnaz* commander of the Odessa district is a bitter enemy of the chairman of the Moldavia KGB and it will be impossible to implicate him.'

'Do you think one slogan will be sufficient to bring down such an important guy?'

'This is a rather special case. There have already been meetings taking place in the college and underground groups and leaflets. A lot of people have been arrested and hundreds expelled. They're all scared stiff, and yet the whole thing suddenly flares up again. It'll be tough on the KGB boys. And I repeat: you were on your own, you thought it all up yourself. You saw the slogan on a wall and learnt it off by heart without knowing what it meant. You haven't forgotten?'

'No.'

We were dropped from three thousand metres. On the second day of the operation the group was divided into two parts. The officers in command of the newly formed smaller groups knew that from that moment they were acting without direct control from above.

Five days later I reported back to Army headquarters. The staff received me with a lot of cheerful banter. I went straight to the Chief of Intelligence. I reported that I had lost my bearings and was not able for a long time to find the right course back. With a slight nod of the head and a barely noticable smile I indicated that the job had been done. A nice clean job.

With a little nod he replied that he had understood. But he did not smile.

Three weeks went past. I studied the newspapers carefully. They don't like writing about dismissals in our press, so they write about new appointments. Of course, they were hardly likely to report appointments within the KGB. But there could also be some reshuffling of officials in the Party machine. And that might be evidence of some deeper changes. Articles might appear with hints of what was going on, such as 'Strengthen proletarian internationalism.' But so far there had been nothing either in the national or in the local press about the need for greater attention to the problem of nationalism.

He laid his hand on my shoulder. He always came up to you from behind, silently:

'You're wasting your time. Nothing's going to happen.'

'Why?'

'Because what you wrote on the wall will do nobody any harm. It was a completely neutral sentence.'

'Then why did I do it?'

'So that I could be sure of you.'

'I was under observation all the time?'

'You'll be under observation all your life. To make sure that you shouldn't have any silly ideas and you don't rush off to tell tales to people who shouldn't know, you will never know exactly whether you are engaged on a genuine operation or whether it is a carefully prepared trial with dozens of traps in it. If it turns out you've talked too much, then. . . . Don't be offended: you chose this path yourself. I am treated in exactly the same way. It is better to put a person to the test than to trust him blindly.'

He looked at me enquiringly, then poured each of us half a glass of iced vodka and silently nodded at one of them. I raised the glass to my lips and drank it in silence. Vodka has to be drunk by the glass. It is only then that it reveals its magical properties.

'Suvorov, I have been studying you for a long time and trying to understand you. In my view you are a born criminal, although you've had no training in criminal ways. Don't start objecting – I know people better than you. I can see right through you. Drink up.'

'Good health.'

'Have a bit of cucumber.'

The expression on his face was grim. He had clearly managed to drink a good deal before my arrival. Which meant he had reason to drink, probably a good reason. When things were going badly he never drank. If he had some success, then he would drink. But when he had drunk he always became serious, even gloomy. It's exactly the same with me. He had apparently noticed that some time ago and, by some other, barely noticable signs, he had formed an idea of my character by reference to his own. I objected rather feebly, secretly admiring the sharpness of his perception.

'If you, you rogue, were to get mixed up with real criminals you would feel entirely at home with them. And they would take you for one of them. And in a few years you would enjoy real authority in the gang. Drink up.'

He had had a lot of vodka. He had opened a fresh bottle for me, which meant that he had already drunk a bottle with someone else before I arrived. Maybe he had had other visitors. The shaking of the fork he held in his hand gave the game away. But his brain was utterly unaffected by alcohol.

'There's one thing I can't understand about you, Suvorov: you don't seem to find any pleasure in tormenting others. We have great possibilities for getting pleasure out of our own strength. You can torment a "puppet" to your heart's content. But you seem to reject that pleasure. Why?'

'Because it doesn't give me any pleasure.'

'That's a pity.'

'Is it bad for our profession?'

'On the whole no. There's an astronomical number of prostitutes in the world, but only very few of them get any pleasure out of their situation. For the majority of them it's simply a very tough job and nothing else. Irrespective of whether she likes the work or not, her standard of living depends on her attitude to her work, on her sense of responsibility and on her diligence. You don't necessarily have to like your profession, but you have to make an effort and show that you can work hard. What are you grinning about?'

'That's an interesting turn of phrase: "a hardworking prostitute".'

'It's nothing to laugh about. We are no better than prostitutes. We do a not very clean job for somebody else's satisfaction. We are very well paid for our hard work. You don't particularly like your profession, but you're hard-working and that's good enough for me. Pour yourself another. You know best how much you can take.'

'What about you?'

'Only a little, really. Two fingers. Enough. Now, this is why I got you here. You can only survive on this stinking planet if you get other people by the throat. Our system enables us to do this. You can hang on to power by scrambling upwards, but only in a group. The group pushes one person upwards, and once he has got a bit higher he helps the whole group. There's a Brezhnev group and a Kosygin group, there are groups in all the ministries and departments; everyone who is scrambling upwards has a group. Soon you will be getting your own group together, but remaining a member of my group.'

Suddenly he grabbed me by my collar: 'If you betray me you'll be sorry!'

'I shall not betray you.'

'I know.' There was a grim look in his eyes. 'You can betray whomever you wish, but not me. Don't even think about it. I know you're not thinking about it. I can tell by the look in your satanical eyes. Drink up and let's be going. It's already late. Be at your desk by seven o'clock tomorrow morning. Get all your secret documents ready to hand over by nine. I have been made Head of Intelligence of the Carpathian military district. I am going to take with me into the Intelligence Directorate of the district's HQ the majority of those people I brought here with me. Not all of them. But I'm going to pull you up with me. Don't forget.'

I just didn't know what was the matter with me. Something was wrong. I would wake up in the night and stare for ages at the ceiling. If they were to send me somewhere to die for some cause or other I would become a hero. I would not mind giving up my life – I had no further use for it. I would then lapse into a short restless sleep. I would feel as though I was being carried somewhere, flying high above the earth. Away from Kravtsov. Away from *Spetsnaz*. Away from the tough fighting. I was ready to fight, to strangle people. But what was the point of it all? Fighting for power is not at all the same as fighting for one's country. But would fighting for my country really console me? I had already been defending my country's interests in Czechoslovakia – not a very pleasant business, to tell you the truth. I flew ever higher in my dreams. From unattainable ringing heights I looked down on my unfortunate country, my mother-country. It was really very sick, but I couldn't make out what it was suffering from. Sheer madness, perhaps, or schizophrenia. And I didn't know how I could help. Somebody had to be killed, but I didn't know who. Where was I flying to? To God, perhaps? But there was no god. All the same – the Lord preserve me.

Chapter Five

Lvov is the most difficult city in the world in which to find your way about. It was built like that many centuries ago, so that the enemy should never be able to find the city centre. And nature has done everything to help the builders: hills, ravines and a river weaving in between them. The back streets of Lvov double back in spirals and land the unwelcome visitor at the river's edge, or down a steep slope, or in a dead-end. I am apparently also an enemy as far as the city is concerned. I just cannot find its centre. The domes of the cathedral can just be seen through the chestnuts. So it's close by. Just round a couple of houses . . . . But the side street leads me upwards, the dives down to a bridge, makes two sharp turns, and I can no longer see the cathedral. In fact I have difficulty in making out in which direction it now lies. So I turn back and start again from the beginning. But that doesn't work either. The side street takes me into a dense web of winding and uneven but amazingly clean streets, and finally brings me out onto a noisy main street with strangely small trams that look like toys. I can't find my way on my own, and all my training in underground work is of no assistance. Taxi! Hey – taxi! To the district HQ! The Pentagon? Yes, that's it, to the Pentagon.

The huge blocks that house the headquarters of the Carpathian Military District have only recently been built. The city refers to the glass monstrosities as the 'Pentagon'.

The Lvov Pentagon is an extremely impressive organisation which over-whelms a new arrival with its wealth of security, its colonels' epaulettes and general's braid.

But in reality things are not quite so complicated as appears on the first day. The headquarters of the military district is a body which has at its disposal territory the size of Western Germany with a population of seventeen millions. The district HQ is responsible for the preservation of the Soviet régime in that territory and for the mobilisation of the population, the industry and the transport in the event of war. Apart from that, the district HQ has under its command four Armies: an air army, a tank army and two all-arm armies. On the eve of war the district HQ becomes the HQ of a Front and will command the armies in battle.

The organisational structure of a district HQ is exactly the same as the structure of an Army HQ, the only difference being that everything is on a higher level. The HQ does not consist of departments but of directorates, and the directorates are in their turn divided into departments, and the departments into groups. Once you know the structure of an Army HQ it is easy enough to make yourself at home in a district HQ.

All was clear. Everything was reasonable and logical. We young new arrivals were once again trying to check our knowledge of everything and poke our noses into every corner: what's that and why do they do that?

The former Chief of Intelligence in the Carpathian military district, Major-general Berestov, had been removed and along with him his whole crew had departed: the older ones to take their pensions, the younger ones to Siberia, to Novaya Zemlya, to Turkestan. The new Chief of Intelligence was Colonel Kravtsov and we, Kravtsov's people, were strolling unceremoniously around the wide corridors of the Lvov Pentagon. Everything had been carefully planned and provided for. Our Second directorate took up a whole floor in an internal block of the colossal complex of buildings. One disadvantage was that all our windows looked out on a huge empty concrete courtyard, probably for reasons of security. The lack of a decent view from the windows was about the only inconvenience, the rest suited us very well. We liked the sensible arrangement of the building, the vast windows and the spacious offices. But what pleased us most was the departure of our predecessors who had until recently controlled all the intelligence work in the district, including our 13th Army. Now fate had swept all those fellows away into the distant corners of the empire. Power is a very tender, fragile thing. You have to hold tightly on to it. And carefully.

Our whole crew, myself included, were quick to find our feet in our new surroundings. Our work was still the same, only on a larger scale. It was more interesting there. I was already known to the others and was met with smiles in the staff. I had already established good relations with the fellows in the 'Inquisition' – the group of translators – and I was already hearing tales told by the cipher officers at the signals centre and the operators at the radio monitoring centre. But there were also people who knew me beyond the limits of the Second directorate. Above all in war planning – that was the First directorate. But war planning could not exist without our prognoses. They were not allowed to enter our directorate and for that reason they invited us to theirs.

'Vitya, what is the enemy in Bitburg planning to do in the next week?'

Bitburg was an American air base in Western Germany, and to answer the question I would have to delve into my papers. Ten minutes later I would already be in the First Directorate:

'Activity on the airfield is within normal limits, with one exception: on Wednesday three C-141 transport planes are arriving from the United States.'

When we delivered such prognoses the operators would smile, as much as to say: That guy's doing a good job!

The operators did not have the right to know where we received our information from. But operators are only human and they also read spy stories, and therefore they probably thought that Kravtsov had a super-spy in some NATO headquarters. Among themselves they referred to the super-spy as 'that guy'. Officers in war planning are also very full of praise and satisfaction for 'that guy'. Kravtsov does in fact have people he has recruited in various places. Every military district recruits foreigners both for obtaining information and for *Spetsnaz* activities. Only in this particular case 'that guy' had nothing to do with it. Whatever was received from his secret network of agents Kravtsov kept in his safe and showed to only a very few people. And the information we provided for the war planners had a far more prosaic provenance. It was actually obtained from what are known as activity charts. This way of obtaining information amounted to careful monitoring of the enemy's radio and radar stations. Every radio station and every radar installation was carefully documented: its type, its function, where it was situated, to whom it belonged and on what frequencies it operated. A great many messages were deciphered by our Fifth department. But there were some radio stations whose messages took years to decipher. Those were the very ones which were our principal concern, because they were the most important ones. But whether we could understand what they were saying or not, an activity chart was kept for such stations and every time they went on the air they were recorded. Every station had its own character, its own handwriting. Some stations worked in the daytime, others at night, still others had days off, while others did not. If every transmission was recorded and studied it soon became possible even to forecast what it was going to do.

In addition, the activity of the radio stations was compared with the activity of the enemy's forces. We obtained priceless information from the men who drove Soviet trucks abroad, from the stewards on Soviet trains, from Aeroflot crews, from our sportsmen, and of course from our network of agents. This sort of information was very scrappy and disconnected: 'Division activated by alarm', 'Missile battery departed in unknown direction', 'Mass take-off of all aircraft'. Our computer compared these scraps with what was going on in the ether. Any apparent regularity was noted and special cases and exceptions to the rule studied. And as a result of many years spent analysing such things it became perfectly possible to say: 'If RB-7665-I went on the air it means that in four days' time there will take place a mass take-off at Ramstein.' It is an inviolable law. And if a station which we call C-1000 springs suddenly into action even a child would realise that the battle readiness of the American troops in Europe was raised to a higher level. And if, for example . . . .

'Listen, Vitya, we understand very well that you can't talk about it . . . . But you just . . . what shall I say . . . anyway, look after that guy.'

They were checking up on me. All my life they would be checking up on me. It was part of the job. They checked up on my self-control, my stamina, my mental reactions and my loyalty. But I was not alone in this. Everybody was being screened all the time. Who you smiled at and who you didn't smile at, who you drank with and who you slept with. And if you didn't drink or sleep with anybody there was a further question: why not?

'Come in.'

'Comrade colonel, senior lieutenant . . . . '

'Sit down,' he ordered.

He was Colonel Marchuk, Kravtsov's new deputy. Soviet military intelligence doesn't have any special uniform. Everybody wears the uniform of the troops from which he came into intelligence. For example, I wore the uniform of the tank troop while Kravtsov wore an artillery officer's uniform. In the Intelligence Directorate we had infantry men and airmen and sappers and chemical warfare men. Colonel Marchuk was a medical officer. On his crimson lapels he wore the medic's badge: a serpent entwined around a golden cup. It is an attractive badge. Not as attractive, of course, as ours, but still attractive. Soldiers say the medical badge means: cunning as a serpent and not bad at drinking.

Marchuk stared at me earnestly, overpoweringly. Was he trying to hypnotise me? His stare made me feel uncomfortable. But I withstood it. I had had a sound training in that. Everyone in *Spetsnaz* trains on the dogs. If you look straight into a dog's eyes you find it cannot withstand a man's stare. A man can stop a howling dog with a look, but only if the dog is alone and not in a pack. Facing a pack you have to use a knife to help your eyes. Look it in the eyes but get the knife into its flanks. Then start looking at another one.

'So, Suvorov, we have been studying you carefully. You work well and we like you. Your brain seems to work like an electronic machine. An untuned one . . . but you can be tuned. I'm sure of that. Otherwise we wouldn't keep you here. You have an exceptional memory. Your capacity for analysing matters is sufficiently developed. You have good taste. That's a nice girl you've picked from the control group, a very nice girl. We know her. She has never let anyone near her before. So there you are. There doesn't really seem to be anything about you to comment on.'

I didn't blush. I wasn't a college boy. I was a fighting officer. And I don't have that kind of skin. My skin is Asian and so is my blood. For that reason I don't blush. Different physiology. But how the devil did they find out about my girlfriend?

'It's very regrettable, Suvorov, but we are obliged to know such things. We have to know everything about you. That's our job. After studying you we have come to certain conclusions, most of them favourable. What pleases us most of all is the progress you have made in ridding yourself of your faults. You have practically rid yourself of your fear of heights and closed premises. You are no longer afraid of the sight of blood, and that's exceptionally important in our work. The inevitability of death does not scare you. You have good relations with the dogs. You'll need some more training in that, of course. But you've really got a problem with frogs and snakes, and that's bad. Are you scared of them?'

72

'Yes, I'm scared,' I confessed. 'How did you find out?'

'That's none of your business. Your business is to learn not to be afraid of snakes. What is there to be afraid of? You can see I've got a little serpent sitting on my lapels. And there are some people who actually eat frogs.'

'The Chinese?'

'Not only the Chinese. The French do too.'

'In a famine, comrade colonel, I would sooner eat people . . . .'

'But it's not because of famine. Frogs are a delicacy. Don't you believe me?'

Of course I didn't believe him. Propaganda. Life wasn't as bad as that in France. If he insisted, I would of course agree that the proletariat in France didn't live very well. But only out loud. To myself I would remain of the same opinion. Life was good in France, and the proletariat didn't eat frogs. But there was no deceiving Marchuk. He had no difficulty in detecting the doubt in my eyes.

'Come in here.' He summoned me into the cinema where they put on secret films about the enemy. Marchuk pressed a button and we could see on the screen a kitchen, a chef, frogs, saucepans, a red dining room, waiters, and customers in a restaurant. The customers didn't look like conjurers, but they ate frogs' legs.

'Well, what about it?'

What could I say? There seemed to be no way out. Yet they had recently shown a film called *Liberation* with Hitler in it. It wasn't really Hitler, but an actor from Eastern Germany. Dietz was his name. Now if the colonel himself were to eat a frog I would believe him, but you can put on anything in a film, even Hitler, let along frogs.

'What about it?' he repeated. What could I say? If I said I accepted it he would immediately get at me, asking how an intelligence officer could fall for such rubbish. I show you some nonsense and you take it all in? How on earth can you, an officer responsible for gathering information, distinguish really valuable documents from material slipped to us by the enemy to confuse us?

'No,' I said. 'I can't believe what I saw in that film. It's a fake. A pretty poor one. If people have nothing to eat they can at the worst eat cats or dogs. Why should they eat frogs?'

It was quite clear to me that it was an instructional film. They were testing my reactions. The woman had a rather fluffy poodle with her. Now they would check to see whether I noticed the poodle or not. Of course I saw it. And I had come to the conclusion I was obviously expected to draw: no normal person was going to eat frogs if there was a poodle going begging. It wouldn't be logical. But Marchuk was getting cross.

'Frogs cost money, and quite a lot.'

I remained silent. I wasn't going to get involved in polemics. Everybody knew that frogs couldn't be expensive. But I accepted what the colonel said diplomatically, a little uncertainly, leaving myself a loophole to retreat through: 'They are getting too fussy. Bourgeois decadence.'

'There you are. At last you believe. I showed you that film for this reason:

73

people eat them, yet you are scared even to take them in your hands. To tell you the truth I myself cannot pick up a frog or a snake in my hands, but then I don't have to. But you do, Viktor, as a young officer with good prospects in intelligence.

My innards simply froze: surely they weren't going to make me eat them. Marchuk was a psychologist. He could read my thoughts like a book. Never fear – we're not going to make you eat frogs. Snakes perhaps, but not frogs.

He was just a private, very short and with a child's face and long eyelashes, like a girl's. But he was in *Spetsnaz*. Four battalions of the *Spetsnaz* brigade were made up of really huge soldiers who strode around the town like a herd of bears. But one company in the brigade consisted of soldiers of various sizes, some of them very small indeed. This was a special professional company, and it was more dangerous than all the other four battalions put together.

The soldier had a very thin neck. His name – Kipa – was not Russian. But he was certainly in the special company for some good reason. It meant he was an expert in some special way of killing people. I once watched him beat off an attack by four men dressed in protective armour and armed with long staves. He defended himself against the staves with an ordinary sapper's spade. He did it without passion but with skill. Such fighting always attracts attention. However much of a hurry he might be in, if a man in *Spetsnaz* sees a fight going on in the main square he will inevitably stop to have a look. And what a fine fight it had been! Now the little soldier was in front of me. He was going to teach me something. He took out of a bucket a little green frog and explained that it was best to get used to it by playing with it. You could do amazing things with a frog. You could, for example, put a straw into it and blow it up. It would then float on the surface but would not be able to dive, and that was very funny. You could 'undress' the frog – do a sort of strip-tease. The soldier took a small knife and showed me how it was done. He made little slits in the corners of the mouth and in one movement removed its skin. The skin appeared to come off as easily as a glove from your hand. Kipa then put the skinned frog down on the floor. You could see all its muscles, bones and bloodvessels. The frog jumped about the floor croaking, and it seemed as though it felt no pain. The soldier reached into the bucket, took out another frog, skinned it like skinning a banana and put it down on the floor. Now there were two of them to jump about, so they shouldn't be lonely.

'Comrade senior lieutenant, Colonel Marchuk ordered me to show you the whole of my set-up here and to get you used to dealing with these little beasts.'

'Are you just as good at handling snakes?'

'I handle them too. I keep the frogs only to feed the snakes with.

'Will you give these to the snakes?'

'The undressed ones? Sure. No sense in letting good stuff go to waste.'

He took the two naked frogs and led me to where the snakes were kept. It was very humid and airless. He opened the cover and dropped the two frogs into a large glass box where a repulsive grey reptile lay curled up in a corner.

'What sort of snakes do you keep?'

'Adders and rattlesnakes. We've asked intelligence in the Turkestan district to send us a cobra, but it hasn't arrived yet. Not a big thing, but very expensive to transport. It has to be kept warm and given food and drink on the way. It's a very delicate thing, and if you upset its régime it will certainly die on you.'

'Who taught you this trade?'

'I am self-taught. Just an amateur. Been at it since I was a kid.'

'Are you fond of them?'

'Yes, I am.' He said it without emotion or any intention to create an effect. I realised the scoundrel was not lying . . . . Jesus Christ! I had never thought of a man loving snakes.

At that moment the two naked frogs let out piercing screeches. The fat lazy reptile had at last deigned to pay them some attention.

'Sit down, comrade senior lieutenant.' I glanced first at the chair, to make sure there wasn't a cold slippery reptile curled up on it. Then I sat down . . . . I was scared stiff. Kipa smiled: 'After ten lessons you will be asking to come here yourself.'

His prophecy did not come true. I still found snakes just as repulsive. Nevertheless I could hold one in my hand. I knew how to grab hold of one. I knew how to clean it out and grill it on a long stick or a piece of wire. And if I were ever to be faced with the choice – to eat human flesh or snake, I would eat the snake first.

The helicopter had dropped us on a marshy island. It would soon pick up Kravtsov and take him off, leaving me alone at the control post.

'If a group opens up communications without having first set up an observation post and proper defences, give it an extra hour's punishment.'

'Very good.'

'For any violation of the regulations in the preparation of coded messages, exclude the whole group from the competition altogether.'

'Very good.'

'Make sure they drink water properly. It mustn't be gulped down. You have to take a little into the mouth and keep it there for a few seconds to moisten the tongue and throat. A person who gulps water down will never slake his thirst, will start sweating, will never have enough water, and will soon be out of action. If you see anyone drinking water in the wrong way you can given him an extra five minutes, or even ten minutes, of punishment.'

'I understand very well, comrade colonel. This isn't my first time as an umpire. You'd better get a bit of sleep. The helicopter will be back in an hour. Just right for you. How long is it since you had a sleep . . . .'

'Never mind about that, Viktor. It's all in a day's work. It's worse when the

Party leaders start bothering you. We're lucky. In Lvov we have good relations between the Party leaders and the district command. But in Rostov the Commander of the North Caucasus military district, Lieutenant-general of Tanks Litovtsev doesn't have it so good. The local Party bosses have ganged up with the KGB against him and don't give him a moment's peace. They have been sending complaints to the Central Committee. They've already written more complaints and denunciations than Dumas wrote novels.'

'And nobody can do anything to help General Litovtsev?'

'What shall I say . . . . He's got a lot of friends. But what can one do to help? We are not masters of the situation. We stick to the regulations, our manual and military law, we don't break them . . . . But how can one help him and stay within the law?'

'Comrade colonel, maybe I can help in some way?'

'How could you, Viktor, a senior lieutenant, help a lieutenant-general?'

'I've got a long night ahead of me, I'll do some thinking . . . . '

'Actually there's no need to do a lot of thinking . . . . Everything has been thought through. It's action we need . . . . I can hear the helicopter. That's for me, no doubt. Look here, Viktor, there's a personal friend of mine, the Head of Intelligence from the North Caucasus military district, Major-general Zabaluyev – one of Litovtsev's colleagues – attending these exercises. He wants personally to watch the competition of the *Spetsnaz* forces, but he doesn't want to embarrass the troops with his rank. Tomorrow he will take up position with you at this control post. He will be wearing our usual uniform: a grey overcoat without any distinguishing badges. He won't interfere in the work of the groups. He just wants to observe what goes on and to have a chat with you. If you really want to help, why don't you ask him?'

I thought for a moment. 'Do you feel, comrade colonel, that when the exercises are over I might have to go sick?'

'I have given you no such order. If you feel it necessary, then of course. But just remember that it's not so easy to go sick in our Army. You have to get a chit from a doctor.'

'I'll get one all right.'

'Only watch out – there are times when a man feels ill but when the doctor doesn't share his feelings. That's very awkward. You have to go sick in such a way that the doctor has no doubt about it. You've really got to have a high temperature. You know what can happen: you feel ill yourself, but you've no temperature.'

'I'll have a temperature.'

'All right, Viktor. I wish you well. Have you got something to give General Zabeluyev to eat?'

'Yes, I have.'

'Only don't hit the vodka . . . unless he asks for it.'

Nine days later I reported to Colonel Kravtsov's office and informed him that I had gone sick following the exercise but that I was now feeling fine. He smiled at me and took me down a little. A well-trained intelligence officer never went sick, he said. You had to keep control of yourself. You had to drive the illness out of your body. Our bodies were subject to our will, and by sheer willpower you could drive any illness out of yourself, even cancer. Strong people didn't get ill. Only the faint-hearted went sick.

He was giving me a good talking-to, but was himself quite radiant. He just couldn't suppress a smile. He smiled happily and openly. It was the way soldiers smile after a bayonet fight: just don't touch our people! Touch them and we'll have your guts out!

A *Spetsnaz* soldier has many enemies. An early dawn and a late sunset are against you. The buzz of a mosquito and the roar of a helicopter are also enemies. It's bad for you, my boy, when the sun's in your eyes. It's bad for you when you find yourself in a searchlight beam. It's bad when your heart is galloping. It's bad when thousands of electronic installations are scouring the ether, trying to catch the sound of your hoarse whisper and your bursting lungs. It's always bad for you, brother. Really bad is when your principal enemy appears. They will think up many more different devices to catch you, anti-personnel mines and electronic sensors of every kind. They will set you against other soldiers, highly trained men. But your principal enemy always remains the same. Your principal enemy, my friend has its ears standing up, yellow fangs with drops of evil saliva, a grey fur and a long tail. Its eyes are brown with yellow spots and its coat is red-brown beneath the collar. It is your principal enemy because it is quicker than you. It detects your scent with its nose. And it has a tremendous leap when it hurls itself at your throat.

That's it, the enemy. The most important. The most important of all. See how it bares its fangs. Its hackles up, its tail too, and its ears flat just before it leaps. Now the brute jumps. It doesn't growl; it just wheezes. Sticky saliva round its jaws, as though mad. The KGB provides a special entry in its records, headed 'Viciousness'. And the experts write terrible words under the heading: 'good viciousness', 'excellent viciousness.'

This particular dog probably had only exclamation marks under the viciousness heading. It was called Mars and was the property of the KGB frontier troops. I wouldn't say it was a huge dog. I have seen even bigger ones. But Mars was very experienced. And everybody knew it.

On this occasion I had not been put against Mars. Today it was Zhenya Bychenko's job. We shouted words of encouragement to him: hang on, Zhenya, give it to him, show him how they taught you to fight in *Spetsnaz*. It was not allowed and not the custom to shout advice on such occasions. Even the most excellent advice might at the last moment distract the fighter's attention and allow the fierce animal to get his teeth into his throat.

77

Zhenya was holding a knife in his left hand and a tunic in his right. But he hadn't wrapped his hand in the tunic. He was simply holding it out with his hand stretched forward. The dog didn't like that: it wasn't what he was used to. Nor did he like the knife in the left hand. Why in the left hand? The dog was in no hurry. He shifted his animal eyes from the knife to the throat and from the throat to the knife. But he also eyed the tunic. Why had the man not wrapped it round his hand? With his canine reasoning the grey animal knew that the man had only one key hand and that the other one was only supporting and diverting. And the dog must not make a mistake. He must attack the hand which was the decisive one, the most dangerous. But maybe he should go for the throat? The dog shifted his eyes, trying to choose. Once he had made his decision his eyes would hold still and he would attack. The man in the arena and we who were watching were waiting for that very moment. Before it leapt the man would have a split second to strike a counter-blow. But Mars was experienced. He attacked suddenly without a snarl or a growl. He did not attack as other dogs do, he pounced without concentrating his eyes and without straining back before the leap. His long body was suddenly suspended in the air. His mouth and his wild eyes flew at Zhenya without a noise of any kind. Nobody actually caught the moment when he sprang. We expected the jump a second later. And so in that silence the dog flew at Zhenya's throat. But Zhenya's tunic whipped across the dog's eyes. We caught sight only of the sole of his black boot. The dog howled as it landed in the corner. We roared with delight. We howled like wild boars. We screamed with pleasure.

'Cut him up, Zhenya! Cut the grey one! Give him the knife! Zhenya! The knife! Finish him off before he gets up!'

But Zhenya did not attack the snarling animal. He did not try to kill the panting dog. He hopped over the barrier straight into the arms of the delighted company of *Spetsnaz* spectators.

'Oh, Zhenya! The way you got him with your boot! You got him breathing out, and in mid-air! What a man!'

Meanwhile in the arena a little soldier with bright green epaulettes was weeping beside the panting dog, and for some reason stuffing a lump of sugar covered with saliva into the dog's bloody mouth.

'Comrade senior lieutenant, you are wanted by the head of the admin. section.'

'I am on my way.'

Of all the departments at HQ the administration department is the smallest. At the headquarters of military districts departments are usually commanded by colonels and directorates by major-generals, and it is only in the admin. department that the chief is a major. But when an officer is summoned to the department he pulls himself quickly together. What on earth have they got for me? The administration department is in a small room occupied by an elderly grey-haired major, a real paper-pusher, with three lance-corporal clerks. But everybody is scared to be called to the admin. department, regardless of whether he is a lieutenant or a major-general. The admin. department is the place where the wishes of the district commander are turned into a written order. And what is written in black and white . . . . The admin. department is the channel by which the Supreme Commander, the Minister of Defence and the Chief of the General Staff convey their orders to their subordinates. The admin. department transmits those orders to the people to whom they are addressed.

'Comrade major, Senior Lieutenant Suvorov reporting on your instructions.'

'Put your identity card on the table.'

I took a deep breath and placed the little green booklet with its golden star on the table in front of the major. He calmly took the 'Certificate of Officer's Identity', studied it attentively and for some reason spent some time over page 11, on which my personal weapon was recorded, and page 14 where my blood group was noted. Not a muscle on his flabby face moved. He did his job just like a machine, as impassively as a hangman. The major then handed the booklet to the lance-corporal, who had everything ready on his desk. He dipped his long gold pen into a pot of black ink and wrote something carefully into the book. I remained standing at attention but with my shoulder dropped so that I could glimpse the lance-corporal. Patience. In a minute the major would announce some decision. The corporal dried what he had written and handed the book back to the major. The major glanced at me enquiringly, took a very complicated-looking key from a little secret pocket, opened the huge door of the safe, took out a big seal, slowly took aim and then suddenly and sharply brought it down on the page of my booklet just written on.

'Listen to the order!'

I drew myself up.

'Order concerning the personnel of the Carpathian military district No. 0257. Secret. Clause 17. Senior Lieutenant Suvorov, V.A., officer of the 2nd Directorate of the District HQ to be promoted prematurely to the military rank of captain in accordance with representations made by the chief of the 2nd Directorate Colonel Kravtsov and the Chief of Staff of the District Lieutenant-General Volodin. Signed: Lieutenant-General of Tank Troops Obaturov.'

'I serve the Soviet Union!'

'I congratulate you, captain.'

'Thank you, comrade major. Please accept an invitation to the wake.'

'Thank you, Viktor, for the invitation. But I can't accept it. If I accepted every such proposal I should have drunk myself to death long ago. Don't be offended. Today alone there are 116 men on the list, eighteen of them premature. So don't take offence, Viktor.'

The major handed me back my identity book.

'Once again, thank you, comrade major.'

I flew back down the stairs and along the corridors as if on wings.

'How come you're so cheerful?'

'How come you were summoned to the badger in his lair?'

I answered no one. I mustn't satisfy their curiosity – it would bring bad luck. The first to know about my promotion had to be my commanding officer and no one else.

'Why are you looking so pleased, Viktor? Been promoted?'

'No, no. I've eighteen months to wait yet for captain.'

I wanted to get back to the department as soon as possible. The blessed metal doors and permits held me up.

'Comrade colonel, may I come in?'

'Come in.' But Kravtsov did not look up from the map.

'Comrade colonel, Senior Lieutenant Suvorov. I am reporting to you on being promoted ahead of time to the rank of captain.'

Kravtsov looked me over, but for some reason he kept looking down.

'Congratulations, captain.'

'I serve the Soviet Union!'

'In the Soviet Army a captain has more stars on his shoulder than anybody: four of them. You Viktor have the maximum. Consequently I do not wish you many stars; I wish you only a few stars, but big ones. You have a great future ahead of you.'

'Thank you, comrade colonel. Permit me to invite you to the wake.'

'When?'

'Today – when else?'

'What do you say to our postponing it until tomorrow? Tonight we've got to go and prepare an exercise. If the lads drink too much this evening we'll never get them together. Let's get the job done and then celebrate tomorrow.'

'Fine.'

'Today you're free. But remember: we set off at three in the morning.'

'I shan't forget.'

'Then off you go.'

'Very good.'

Exercises are usually carried out year after year on the same training grounds and firing ranges, and the staff officers are well acquainted with the area where the training battles take place. All the same, before largescale exercises take place the officers who are to act as intermediaries and umpires have to visit the area again to make sure that everything is ready for the event: the whole area cordoned off, models representing the enemy in place, dangerous zones indicated by special signs. Every umpire in his section has to have a good idea of the forthcoming battle and must prepare for the forces he is observing and training the sort of questions, suggestions and situations appropriate for just that area and not somewhere else.

Because the umpires knew the territory where the exercises were to take place pretty well (many of them had served there as lieutenants and had themselves been tested there at some time), the trip to the exercise area before the exercises became a sort of little picnic, a little group excursion, a chance to unwind in the course of the helter-skelter of staff work.

'Has everyone got it clear?'

'All clear,' roared the staff officers as one man.

'Then it's time to have some supper. Let's go to table. Today Viktor Survorov is host.'

There is actually no table, just a dozen grey soldiers' blankets spread out on a clear spot in a fir wood near a stream. All we had was on the table: tins of preserved fish and meat, slices of pink bacon fat, onions, cucumbers, radishes. The army drivers had baked some potatoes over the camp-fire and boiled up some soup.

I offered Colonel Kravtsov the seat of honour. Such is the tradition. He refused and offered me the place instead. Also a tradition. I had to refuse. Twice. But the third time I had to accept the invitation and invite Kravtsov to take the seat on my right. The rest took their seats according to seniority: Kravtsov's deputies, heads of departments, their deputies, then the senior men from the groups, then all the others.

It was the duty of the youngest of those present to set out the bottles on the table. He was Tolya Buturlin, a lieutenant from the 'Inquisition', from the translators, that is. A good lad, who took his duties seriously. Tradition forbade him to smile or to say anything. The others also kept straight faces. It was not done to smile or to talk. Nor was it permitted to ask why there was a senior lieutenant sitting at the head of the table. It was obvious to everybody why the chilled bottles were being put out, but it was not considered proper to speak of them or about the reason for their being there. You were expected to sit still and keep a respectful silence.

Tolya brought the bottles from the stream. They had been stored there in a carefully arranged pile in icy water. The water swirled around the clear glass, bubbling and frothing.

'Where's your glass?' The enquiry was traditional.

'Here.' I handed Kravtsov a large cut glass tumbler. Kravtsov filled it right up to the very rim with the transparent liquid and placed it before me, very carefully. Not a single drop should be lost.

But the glass had to be full. The fuller the better. Everybody kept silent, as though they were not concerned with what was going on. Then Kravtsov took out of his officer's case a small silver star and dropped it carefully into my glass. There was a faint tinkle as the star bobbed around in the glass and glittered.

I took my glass, being careful not to spill anything, and put it to my lips. You are not suposed to reach out with your lips to meet the glass, although nature prompts you to sip off just a drop, so as not to spill any. Higher and higher I raised my glass. The sunlight shone through the liquid and threw out multi-coloured rays. Then I had to move the glass away from the sun and lower it to my lips. Then my lips touched it. It was very cold. I began to drink the fiery liquid, raising the bottom of the glass even higher. The little star at the bottom shifted and slid slowly towards my lips, until it touched them. Thus it is as if an officer were welcoming his new star with a kiss. I held the star lightly in my lips until all the fiery liquid had run down my throat. And that was it. I took the star carefully with my left hand and looked around me: I had to break my glass. With this in mind someone had thoughtfully placed a large stone on the soft grass. I hurled the glass against the stone and the ringing splinters scattered around. Then I handed Kravtsov my wet star. With his little officers' ruler he measured out the right place on my right epaulet. The fourth star had to be exactly on the red stripe and its centre 25 millimetres above the previous one. So it was put in its place. Now it was my chance to take a little food and counter the effect of the vodka with salted cucumbers.

'Where is your glass?' I was asked again.

Two shoulders. Two epaulettes. Consequently, two stars, which meant two glasses . . . at the start of the ceremony.

I proffered a second glass. Once again the fiery-icy liquid swirled around in it. Again to the very brim.

I stood up. It's easier to drink standing up, and it is permitted. Nobody would object. I could have drunk the first glass standing. Tradition does not prevent it. So long as the glasses are full. So long as the officer does not spill of the precious sparkling drops.

A second star glittered in the stream of vodka. Down went the vodka, and crash went the glass, and the star appeared on my other epaulette. Then Kravtsov poured himself a drink, right to the brim. And everyone else quietly poured himself what he felt like. If you admired Viktor you would pour a full glass. If not, you poured as much as you wanted. But you had to drink it all at one gulp.

'Let us drink,' the colonel proposed quietly.

It was not done at that point to say what we were drinking to. We drank and that was that. They drank slowly and solemnly, but always in a single gulp. I alone did not drink. It was then my right to look at each one to see how much each had poured himself: who had a full glass and whose glass was only two-thirds full. But they were all full; and then they were all empty.

According to tradition I was still a senior lieutenant, although the order had been posted the previous day and although I already had the new stars on my epaulettes. Kravtsov drank up, and took a sip of water. That was followed by the words of the ritual: 'There is a new force in our regiment!'

It was from that moment that I was considered to have been promoted. Only then was I a captain. Then at last I could smile.

Then there was shouting and much noise, everybody smiling. There were good wishes and congratulations. Everybody was talking and laughing. The ceremony was over: no more tradition. The officers' drinking bout was beginning. And if there is truth in wine, then that day it would be wholly on our side. Tolya rushed off to the stream. Young Tolya would have his day and a chance to celebrate. One day.

Blistering heat. Dust. Sand between your teeth. And the flat, dreary steppe whichever way you looked. The sun, bright, cruel and impersonal, shining mercilessly into your eyes like an interrogator's arc-lamp. Only very occasionally did an ugly piece of tree, bent low by the blizzards of the steppe, break up the appalling monotony of the landscape.

Anybody in his senses would spit, cross himself and go back home. There was nothing to do there. But we unfortunates carried on to where the arid steppe came suddenly to an end at the steep banks of the muddy river Ingul, where the stark outlines of watch-towers stood out in the shimmering heat and dozens of rows of barbed wire formed a barrier round the stunted bushes. The trees were practically bare, their scanty leaves grey from a thick layer of dust. But were those really watch-towers? Perhaps they were for geological work? Or for oil prospecting? No, they had nothing to do with oil: those towers were equipped with searchlights and machine-guns. There were a lot of watch-towers, a lot of searchlights and a lot of machine-guns. So we had not gone wrong. We were on the right road. You're doing fine, comrades! This way for us. Zheltyye Vody. The time would come when that name would have the same terrible significance as Katyn, Oswiecim, Sukhanovo, Babi Yar, Buchenwald or Kyshtym. But that time had not yet come, so that most people hearing that name did not shudder. And it wasn't only the man in the street for whom it had no special associations. It meant just as little to the prisoners who were being marched in an endless column from the station towards the watch-towers. Many of them were really pleased. It wasn't Kolyma or Novaya Zemlya: it was the Ukraine, for goodness' sake, which meant they'd survive. It would be some time before they learnt – and maybe they would never learn – that the Party bosses in Moscow had a direct line to the manager of the 'clay plant' where they were going to work. They were not to know that the top brass at the centre phoned the plant manager every day to get the production figures. Because it was a very important plant, more important than the Chelyabinsk tank factory. And the prisoners who were sent there were not in fact as lucky as they thought. They had no reason to rejoice at the plentiful rations they would receive. The ones whose teeth or hair began to fall out would be transferred elsewhere. The ones who guessed what sort of 'clay' they were handling would also be quickly moved on. And if, one day, all the camp inmates rose in revolt, the guard at Zheltyye Vody was thoroughly reliable; if need be, we would come to its aid. Because right next to the plant was the biggest *Spetsnaz* training camp. Our lads were not to be fooled with. Better carry on without complaining in the 'clay plant'.

Dust and heat and the endless steppe. We are making a lot of parachute jumps. From great heights, from low levels and from very low levels. We jumped in twos from an Antonov-12 and in fours from an Antonov-22. Can you imagine what it means to jump in fours? Four men leaving the aircraft within two and a half seconds? Of course not. Only someone who has done it can know what it's like. We jumped in the daytime and we jumped at night. Zheltyye Vody is actually in Europe, not far from Kirovograd. But summer there is always hot and dry, sultry and cloudless. The weather is always good for flying, and that is why the *Spetsnaz* companies, battalions, regiments and brigades were assembled there from all corners of the Soviet Union for parachute training from June to September. We simply longed for a storm of rain to soften up the accursed flying field. It was as hard as granite, though it was only clay. There was no point in laying cement because the sun had baked a better surface than any engineer could have done. So we longed for rain: we prayed for it; all of us, tens of thousands of us.

A thunderstorm was advancing like the world revolution – slowly and uncertainly. The steppe was completely dried out, and the wind was raising sand-storms. The horizon was lost in darkness, the sky shone bright in the distance. Thunder could be heard rumbling faintly far away. But still no rain. I longed to expose my face to big drops of summer rain. But it wouldn't come. Tomorrow there would still be nothing but the debilitating heat, the hot wind full of fine sand, and the endless, burnt-up steppe. And with our dried-out throats we would be shouting, 'Hurrah!' As we were today. The cream of the *Spetsnaz* was drawn up from one end to the other of the runway. The sea of dusty, faded blue berets swayed slightly.

'ATTENTION! EYES RIGHT! PRE – SENT ARMS!'

The band struck up the ceremonial march, and I no longer bothered about water or rain. The sound of the march lifted me out of myself. In the distance appeared a car bearing a more than life-size Marshal of the Soviet Union. As they caught sight of him the first battalion roared, 'Hurrah!' and the soldiers' welcome ran along the ranks – 'A – a – a – ah!' It was probably with a similar cry that the battalions were sent into battle. Hurrah – a – ah.

'Comrade Marshal of the Soviet Union, I hereby present the combined units of *Spetsnaz* for review and march-past. Head of the 5th directorate – Colonel-General Petrushevsky.'

The marshal looked at the endless ranks of *Spetsnaz* and smiled.

Then General Petrushevsky presented his units:

'The 27th brigade of *Spetsnaz* of the Belorussian military district!'

'Greetings!' came the roar from the marshal's throat.

'Greetings . . . marshal!' the 27th brigade roared in reply.

'The 3rd naval brigade of *Spetsnaz* of the Black Sea Fleet!'

'Greetings!'

'We serve the Soviet Union!' shouted the 3rd in reply.

'The second independent training battalion of *Spetsnaz*! . . . The 13th brigade of *Spetsnaz* of the Moscow military district! . . . The 224th independent company of *Spetsnaz* of the 4th Guards Tank Army!'

The marshal shouted his greetings and his words echoed across the parade ground into the distance.

A military parade is a very strict and serious ceremony. But it is a happy one too. And there is good purpose to these reviews of the troops. General Petrushevsky's car went to the right of and a little to the rear of the marshal's car. And one could see the general's eyes glowing with pride. He was proud of his dashing troops and wanted the marshal to admire them.

'The 32nd brigade of *Spetsnaz* of the Carpathian military district!' ...

'Greetings!'

There seemed to be no end to the aerodrome. The *Spetsnaz* formed an endless wall.

It had become traditional after every major exercise to parade the troops for a general inspection. The tradition went back hundreds of years. So it was in much earlier days that the warrior chief would gather together those who had survived, count the casualties and congratulate the victors. With the exercises, which had been on a tremendous scale, now over, it was possible to get some idea on this seemingly endless parade ground of the incredible power of the 5th Directorate of the GRU. Even so, not everybody was present.

'703rd independent *Spetsnaz* company of the 17th Army!'

As the marshal drove past the rows of men a thought must have passed through his mind. Against whom was this great host to be unleashed? Against Europe? Against Asia? Or perhaps against the comrades in the Politburo?

Come on, marshal – what are you waiting for? All of us here are with you. We're all fighting to go. Come on, let us off the leash. We'll make the whole of Russia run with blood. Just give us the order. We won't kill them all, of course, not all of them. Anyone with a big country house and a big car we'll leave alone. There's no harm in having big cars and houses. And those who talk about social justice we'll also leave alone. That's a fault, but not a very big one. People go astray, and what can you take from them, from the crazy ones? We shall kill, marshal, only the men who link these two things together into one: the men who talk a lot about social justice *and* go around in big cars. They are the ones for the lamp posts and the telegraph posts. They are the cause of all our country's misfortunes. So let us off the leash, marshal! Of course you can't do it, though, can you? Hurrah – a – ah!

The roar of voices rolls across the field, and it echoes in the dried up waterways in the distance.

'Are we going to work, men?' asks the marshal.

'A – a – ah,' roared the troops, full of enthusiasm in reply. We'll do our job, don't worry.

We worked all right. We worked day and night. We scarcely could distinguish between day and night. Just one thing after another. Parachute jumps in the daytime and parachute jumps at night. Jumps from very low levels and from medium heights. Jumps with the aid of catapults. Thank goodness this is not for everyone. Jumps from the stratosphere. Luckily, too, only for the chosen few. Competition after competition. Then more jumps. Bitter-tasting dust on your lips. Bloodshot eyes. Our feelings wanted to find release. Sometimes we were in a state of complete apathy. We were already packing our parachutes without much concern. We just wanted to get them packed and then to grab half an hour's sleep. Perhaps we should check them again? To hell with it . . . . Training battles. Napalm. Dogs. MVD. KGB. More shooting and more jumping.

And death walked alongside us all the time. It didn't take anyone under its black wings. But it was there, watching us. In the 112th independent battalion they were testing a new parachute, the D-I-8. It was a bad parachute, and the *Spetsnaz* were scared of it. They didn't want to jump with it: there was something wrong with it. At least once in every hundred jumps the lines fouled the fabric. The designer of the parachute and the examiners were there too. They told us we hadn't packed them properly and hadn't stored them carefully. To hell with them: it was we who ran the risks. A sergeant-major in the 112th battalion jumped with one of these, the lines got caught up in the canopy and he cut them free with a knife. He landed safely and gently. But once he was down they told him in fun that he shouldn't have been in such a hurry to cut the lines, that he should have found where they were sewn with a silk thread and have carefully undone the thread. After a jump like that the sergeant was in no mood for jokes. He gave them all a good lashing with his tongue, the designer too.

Death was very close to us. Just on the other side of the fence. Zheltyye Vody was close by. A concentration camp. Uranium, 'cold clay'. Which meant death. Was it not there that every commander got hold of his 'puppets' and 'gladiators'? Forbidden zones. Guard towers. Parachute towers. All close by. We and the concentration camp. But why? To frighten us? Or maybe there was some other reason for having the main Spetsnaz training centre next to uranium mines. Next to the concentration camps. Next to death.

More jumping. 'Captain Suvorov. I folded this parachute myself.' The first operation. The top of the canopy had been strengthened. 'I folded this parachute myself.' Ready? Jump. On and on it went. 'Major-General Kravtsov. I folded this parachute myself.' For a long time I looked blankly at the signature of my neighbour, who had completed his packing. There was something about it I couldn't understand. Something wasn't right. But my brain wasn't working. Lack of sleep. I made a painful effort to concentrate my mind and suddenly I realised:

'Comrade general!'

'Sshh, not so loud. Yes, Viktor. Yes.' And he laughed. 'Only don't let on. I've been a general for the last thirty-two hours. You were the first to realise it.'

'Congratulations.'

'Thanks. But don't make a fuss about it. We'll have a drink later. This is not the time. Oh, damn, I'm tired out. Have you packed your parachute?'

'Yes, both of them, comrade general.'

'Give them back.'

'Very well.' And, sensing something contrary to the regulations, I put another question:

'Am I not jumping today?'

'You're never going to be jumping again.'

'I see' – although I understood nothing.

'You are to report to Kiev. And from there you will probably be sent to Moscow.'

'Very well.'

'Don't tell anyone about your movements. When they make out your documents in the admin. department you will say that you have been ordered to report to the Tenth Chief Directorate of the General Staff.'

'Very well,' I almost shouted.

'Then goodbye, captain. I wish you well.'

'Captain, there is a provisional decision of the General Staff that you are to be dropped in the enemy's rear to carry out a special task'. The unfamiliar general measured me up with a serious gaze. 'How long do you need to prepare yourself?'

'Three minutes, comrade general.'

'Why not five?' For the first time he smiled.

'I only have to pop into the toilet – three minutes will do.' And, realising that he might not appreciate my joke, I added: 'I have been travelling in a bus all night and had no opportunity.'

'Nikolai Gerasimovich,' the general said to someone, 'escort the captain to the toilet.'

Two and a half minutes later I was again standing in front of the general.

'Are you ready now?'

'Yes, comrade general.'

'To go anywhere?'

'Through fire and water, comrade general.'

'And you are not interested in where you are going?'

'I am interested, comrade general.'

'Supposing we decided to take a long time preparing you for carrying out a task? Five years, for example. What would you think about that?'

'I would welcome it.'

'Why?'

'Because it would mean that the task was a really serious one. And that suits me.'

'What do you know, captain, about the Tenth Chief Directorate of the General Staff?'

'It deals with the provision of weapons for all those who are fighting for freedom, trains commanders for national liberation movements, and sends military advisers to Asia, Africa, Cuba . . . .'

'What would you feel about becoming an officer in the Tenth Chief Directorate?'

'It would be the highest honour for me.'

'The Tenth Chief Directorate sends advisers to countries with a hot humid climate and with a hot dry climate. Which would you prefer?'

'The hot and humid climate.'

'Why?'

'Because that would mean Vietnam, Cambodia, Laos. There's fighting going on there. The fighting has come to an end in the hot and dry countries.'

'You are mistaken, captain. There is always fighting everywhere. There's never any peace anywhere and never will be. There's war going on all the time. Open warfare stops sometimes, but never the secret warfare. We are considering the question of sending you to the war. To the secret war.'

'To the KGB?'

'No.

'Can there really be secret warfare without the participation of the KGB?'

'There can.'

'And it is directed by the Tenth Chief Directorate?'

'No – it is directed by the Second Chief Directorate of the General Staff. To conceal its existence the GRU makes use of various organisations including the Tenth Chief Directorate. We shall send you, captain, for examinations at the GRU's secret academy, but everything will be so organised as to give the impression that you are to become a military adviser. The Tenth Chief Directorate will be your cover. All your documents will be made out only in the Tenth Chief Directorate. It is they who will summon you to Moscow, where we will take you over to do your examinations.'

'What if I don't pass the examinations?'

He gave a snort of disgust. 'Then we really would hand you over to the Tenth Chief Directorate and you really would become a military adviser. They would take you on – you would suit them well. But you suit us too, and we are sure you'll pass our examinations, otherwise we wouldn't be talking to you here.'

'I understand, comrade general.'

'In that case it is necessary for you to complete certain formalities.'

He extracted from the safe a sheet of paper, crisp as a new banknote, clearly marked 'Top Secret'.

'Read it and sign it.'

There were twelve short points on the sheet of paper. Each began with the phrase 'It is forbidden' and ended with the ominous warning 'is punishable by death'. The final point read: 'Any attempt to reveal the contents of this document or any part of it is punishable by death.'

'Are you finished?'

Instead of replying I nodded my head. He moved a pen towards me. I signed, and the sheet of paper disappeared into the depths of the safe.

'Till we meet in Moscow, captain.'

After handing my papers to a quite young senior lieutenant I presented myself to the officer who was now my former commander:

'Comrade general, this is Captain Suvorov reporting on being transferred to the Tenth Chief Directorate of the General Staff.'

'Sit down,' said Kravtsov.

I sat. He looked me straight in the eyes for a long time, and I withstood his stare. He was smartly turned out and looked very stern, without a suspicion of a smile.

'You, Viktor, are entering into a very serious business. You are joining the Tenth, but I believe that's only a cover. It seems to me that you will go somewhere higher up. Maybe even into the GRU. Into the Aquarium. They are simply not allowed to talk about it. But mark my words. You will arrive at the Tenth Chief, but you will be taken over by another outfit. That's the way it will probably be. If my assessment of what is going on is correct, then you will have to go through very serious examinations. If you wish to pass them you must always be yourself. There is something crooked, something faulty about you. Don't try to conceal it.'

'I am not going to conceal it.'

'And be good and kind.' Always be good. All your life. Promise me?'

'I promise.'

'If you have to kill a man, be kind! Smile at him before you kill him.'

'I'll try.'

'But if you are going to be killed don't whine or weep. That will never be forgiven. Smile when they are trying to kill you. Smile at the executioner. By so doing you will make yourself immortal. Every one of us has to die some time. Die like a man, Viktor. Die with pride. Promise?'

Next day a green coach delivered a group of officers to a deserted railway station where a military train was being put together. They had all been summoned to Moscow by the Tenth Chief Directorate of the General Staff. They were all going to become military advisers in Vietnam, Algeria, Yemen, Syria, Egypt. I was in the group. For all my friends, colleagues, commanders and subordinates from that moment I ceased to exist. The first point in the document that I had signed forbade me to have any contact with any of the people I had known in the past.

Chapter 6

As the train sped along the rails towards Moscow the boundless expanse of the country was spread out before me. A child waved at the train from a railway embankment. Poplars, birch trees, fir trees, ruined and looted churches, girls haymaking, factory chimneys. More children on an embankment, waving and smiling at me. One bridge after another. Then the train rumbled across the steel girders above the Desna river. Konotop, Bryansk, Kaluga. The regular beat of the wheels on the rail joints. The carriage was very noisy, and there was a lot of drinking going on. It was a military train, with no outsiders. There were only military advisers in my carriage. Potential advisers, anyway. They were all drinking to their future. To the Tenth Chief Directorate. To Colonel-General Okunev. Another bottle was going the rounds. Drink, captain! Bags of promotion for you! Thanks, major, for you too! Everybody's eyes were bright. We were all little boys who were crazy about war. Had we gone away for training in order to come back capable of inspecting a battalion's kit? No, we had been carried away by the glamour of war. And these were the lucky ones to whom the Tenth Chief Directorate had given their chance. So drink to the Tenth, lads!

There were a lot of us in the carriage. Gunners, airmen, infantry, tank men. Yesterday they had not known one another. Now we were all friends. Another bottle was handed round. To you, my friends, to your success. To promotion. But where on earth was I going? In my documents it said Cuba, but that was only because there was nobody else in the group going to Cuba. Many were going to Egypt and Syria. Some were heading for Vietnam. If there had really been somebody marked out for Cuba, they would have thought up something else for me. Kravtsov was of course right in supposing that Cuba was just a cover. But he didn't know much more. Kravtsov – now a general. I had seen him after his promotion, but then he had been in dust-covered overalls and a faded blue beret, like everybody else, with nothing to distinguish him from the *Spetsnaz* soldiery. I tried to imagine what he would look like in a real general's uniform with gold epaulettes and wide stripes down his trousers. But I couldn't do it. I see him always as he was at the time of our first meeting: in a clean tunic with a lieutenant-colonel's epaulettes and the features of a young captain. Good luck to you, Kravtsov.

Krasnaya Presnya is the biggest military rail junction in the world. Train after train. Thousands of people. All behind barbed wire and high fences. And all under the blinding glare of searchlights. Trainloads of tanks for Germany. Trainloads of recruits for Czechoslovakia. The clanging and rumbling of wagons on the move. Shunting engines putting the trains together. A train loaded with guns for the Far East. Then some big container trucks, with a guard as big as Brezhnev's. Stores everywhere. Loading and unloading. A trainload of demobilised soldiers from Poland. Then there were prison trucks with long narrow windows covered with white paint. Grilles over the windows. Krasnaya Presnya is not just a military centre; it is also a transit prison. Soldiers with guard dogs. Red shoulder straps. A trainload of prisoners moved slowly into the special zone. Huge steel gates. Barbed wire. A blinding blue light. Trainloads of prisoners. For Bodaibo. For Cherepovets. For Severodvinsk. For Zheltyye Vody. The huge grey building of the military transit camp. The group of advisers for South Yemen – to block B, room 217. Adviser for Cuba! That's me. Captain Suvorov? Yes. Follow me. A smart young major led me past a long fence and stacks of green boxes. This way, captain. In a small courtyard there was an ambulance with red crosses on it waiting for us. After you, captain. The door was slammed shut behind me and the vehicle moved off. It stopped a couple of times, probably to be checked as it left the forbidden area. Then I was being driven through Moscow. I could tell that we weren't going along a straight road but round the streets of a big city. The vehicle made frequent turns and stops, probably at traffic lights. But that was only my guessing. I could see nothing: the windows were opaque, as in a prison truck.

What is 262 multiplied by 16? Quickly, in your head. It was not a very difficult sum. You had first to multiply by 10, add half the product plus another 262. But the piercing eyes of the examiner made it difficult to think quickly. Wiping my forehead with the palm of my hand I raised my eyes to the ceiling and then lowered them again to look at the sheet of green paper covering the table. Right in front of me on the green paper covering the table one of my predecessors had solved this very sum in very faint pencil. It was written very clearly and accurately, but would be quite invisible to the examiner. I was going to make use of the ready-made answer when it occurred to me to wonder how my predecessor could have got hold of a pencil and how he could have used it under the searching gaze of the examiner. It was put there simply to tempt me. I raised my eyes, then thought again for a second and gave my own answer – 4192. The examiner then started his stopwatch and set me another question. I glanced quickly at the answer written on the table and saw that it was wrong. It was certainly a trick, an attempt to thrust ready-made but wrong answers on me. But the questions kept coming thick and fast, as if tumbling from a conveyor belt. 'What is the specific weight on the ground of an American M60 tank? Why do spiral staircases in old castles go from left to right and not the other way round? How many weeks in a year? How much does a bucket of mercury weigh? What is the price of gold on the international market? Which firm produces the Phantom fighter? What is the output of steel in the Soviet Union? Which are the better anti-tank shells – American or French? What design faults are there in the rotary engine? When was the first Sputnik launched?' There was no time to think up answers; at the slightest hesitation another question was set and then more and more. 'What do you know about Chekhov?' 'He was a well-known sniper in the 138th rifle division of the 62nd Army.' 'Do you know Dostoyevsky?' What an odd question. Who doesn't know Dostoyevsky? 'Nikolai Gerasimovich Dostoyevsky is a major-general, chief of staff of the 3rd Shock Army.' For some reason the examiners gave a long laugh. But they accepted my answer: 'Never mind, captain, your answers are not quite what we wanted, but they are correct and they give us quite a good idea of your character. If we laugh occasionally, pay no attention, don't be embarrassed.' Was I really ever embarrassed?

It seemed to me as if I had been asked a million questions. Then I worked out that there had been only 5000 – fifty questions an hour, seventeen hours a day, for six days. Some questions needed five or ten minutes to answer, others took only a few seconds. You were not allowed to refer to anything or write anything down or consult with anybody. You had to reveal exactly what you knew and thought. What you had to avoid was trying to be too clever, to lie or to embellish things for the examiners. If you tried to skate round some tricky questions they would catch you out later contradicting yourself. The examiners changed round; sometimes there was only one, at other times the room was full of them. The examinee was alone from seven o'clock in the morning till midnight.

There were no breaks. To go to the toilet you had to ask permission each time. The request might be approved immediately, but sometimes one had to ask two or three times. The food was brought directly into the classroom. Sometimes it was a magnificent repast which made you sleepy; sometimes for a whole day they would 'forget' to bring food and water, yet questioning went on the whole time. 'What would you have done in the place of the gangsters who robbed the mail train in Great Britain?' 'Imagine that all the buried money has been divided out and you have received your portion.' 'What do you know about Johann Straus?' 'If you had to modernise the American B58 strategic bomber, to what would you attach special attention and why?' 'How many columns are there on the façade of the Bolshoi Theatre?' 'What type of woman attracts you specially?' 'What is 4416 divided by 8?' 'How many vodkas can you drink at a sitting?' 'Here are photographs of some people whom you have seen in the last few days—you have three minutes to sort them out into ones that you have not seen at all, ones you have seen once and ones you have seen twice or more.' The last two days were completely taken up with answering questions which had already been set during the first four days, but this time the test was undertaken in conditions of a strong radio interference. 'You have one minute to cross out on this page all letters 'B', underline all the letters 'T' and put a red ring around the letters 'R'. At the same time a tape recorder was switched on which bellowed in your ear something completely different, like '"R" cross out, "A" underline, "U" encircle with a red ring.' 'You have three minutes to add up all the 3's on this sheet of paper on which are simply written hundreds of different numbers. Don't pay any attention to what my colleague is doing. Begin.' Then the colleague began to shake the table, make faces, shout obscenities in your ear, catch hold of you by the hand, strike your legs and shake the chair. But you were advised not to pay any attention to all this.

At the end of one of these days you are in a state of complete collapse. That was the moment the examiners were waiting for, when you had sunk into a black abyss of exhaustion. They would rush into the room together, switch on the bright lights and shake you awake. '262 by 16.' And they shout: 'It's so simple – don't you remember? You've already done it; you did it this morning; it's so simple.' '4192,' I mumble sleepily, and the light goes out.

In the space of a week they got to know practically everthing there was to know about me. They established the extent of my knowledge in every field which interested them. Apart from that they assessed my capacity for work, my memory, my resourcefulness, my ability to orientate myself, my honesty, the presence or absence of a sense of humour, my stamina, my reactions to various situations, my ability to remember faces, names, numbers and titles, my ability to take independent decisions, and a lot more besides.

'You suit us very well, young man,' a grey-haired man in civilian clothes told me, after I had endured a week of examinations and tests. 'But there is only one way out of our organisation. That is through the chimney of the crematorium. So think again. And so that you shall have something to think about, we'll show you a film. . . .'

I thought that his face would pursue me in nightmares throughout my life. But that was not the case. I never dreamt of him. But I often thought about him, and there was something about the affair that I couldn't understand. The official version said that a GRU colonel sold himself to the British and American intelligence services because he was fond of the opposite sex and that that was why he needed a lot of money. Let us suppose that was true. But if it was just a question of women why on earth did he not simply defect to the West? In America or Britain he would have had enough money and enough women to last him all his life. A man with the information he had would have been welcomed and treated at his true worth. He had plenty of opportunities to defect. But he didn't do it. He went on working in Moscow, where he had no opportunity to spend that sort of money. Which meant that it wasn't a matter of money or of women. So what was it then?

If he had been nothing more than a womaniser he would have escaped and settled for women and money. But he didn't. He finished up in the crematorium, the man I had seen silently screaming. But why, for goodness sake? I twisted and turned on the hot pillow and just couldn't get to sleep. It was my first night without examinations. But was I being observed at night by closed-circuit television? Oh, to hell with it! I got out of bed and made a rude gesture to each corner of the room. If I was still being watached they wouldn't be taking me to the Central Committee of the Party tomorrow. Then I decided that it wasn't enough simply to make rude gestures, so I exposed to the camera, if there was one there, everything I had to show. We would see next day whether they would throw me out or not. Having displayed what I could I got back contented into bed and went straight to sleep, firmly convinced that I would be shipped off to Siberia the next day to command a tank company.

I slept in that bed like a babe. A really deep sleep. I knew that, if I were accepted into the Aquarium, it would be a big mistake on the part of the Soviet Intelligence. I knew that, if there remained only one exit and that through the chimney, my departure would not be an honourable one. I knew that I would not die in my bed. No, people like me do not die in their beds. It would really have been better for Soviet Intelligence if it had despatched me through the chimney right away!

Once again I was being taken somewhere in a closed van with opaque windows. I couldn't see where I was going, and no one could see me. Where was I off to? To the Central Committee or to Siberia?

Outside I could hear the sounds of a big city, the scuffling of millions of feet, so I must be in the middle of the city. Maybe at the Lubyanka? There was always a stream of pedestrians like the Niagara Falls walking past the Lubyanka on Dzerzhinsky Square. For some reason it seemed to me that that must be where we were. But there was nothing strange in that, because the Central Committee was close by. Our van remained stationary for some time and then drove carefully in to a yard of some kind. There was the clang of metal doors behind us, the door of the van opened and I got out.

We were in a little narrow, dark courtyard, with ancient high walls on all four sides. Behind us were the gates, with KGB sergeants on duty. There were a few doors opening on to the courtyard with a KGB guard at some of them. There was no guard to be seen at the other doors. Up above there were pigeons cooing on the cornice. This way, please. Another grey-haired man produced some papers. The KBG sergeant saluted. This way. Grey-hair knew the way and led me along endless corridors. Red carpets. Vaulted ceilings. Leather padded doors. Our documents were checked again. This way, please. A lift took us silently to the third floor. Another corridor. A big ante-room with an elderly woman at a desk. Wait a moment, please. We waited. come in, please. Grey-hair gave me a gentle push from behind, closed the door after me and remained in the ante-room.

The office had a high ceiling and windows well above eye-level. There was no view at all from the window, only a blank wall and the pigeons on the cornice. There was an oak desk, at which sat a very thin man wearing gold-rimmed spectacles. He was wearing a brown suit without any distinguishing marks – no medals or orders. It was so easy in the Army. You looked at a man's epaulettes and you could say at once: comrade major or comrade colonel. But how could I break the ice here? I simply introduced myself:

'Captain Suvorov.'

'Hello, captain, how are you?'

'I wish you health!'

'We have studied you attentively and have decided to take you into the Aquarium, after suitable preparation, of course.'

'Thank you.'

'Today is the 23rd of August. Keep that date in mind, captain, throughout your life. That is the day on which you are being received into the *nomenklatura**, and not just into the *nomenklatura*, but straight into a higher level – the *nomenklatura* of the Central Committee. Apart from all the other exceptional privileges you will receive yet another one. From today you are no longer subject to control by the KGB. From today the KGB has no right to put questions to you, to demand answers to them or to undertake any action against you. If you make any mistake, report it to the person in charge of you and he will report to us. If you fail to report it we shall know about your mistake all the same. But in any case any enquiry into your behaviour will be carried out only by top officials of the GRU or by the Administrative Department of the Central Committee. You are obliged to report any contact with the KGB to your chief. The well-being of the Central Committee depends on the way organisations and people who belong to the *nomenklatura* of the Central Committee are able to preserve their independence of all other organisations, The well-being of the Central Committee is also your own personal well-being, captain. Take pride in the confidence which the Central Committee has in our military intelligence and in you personally. I wish you well.'

I saluted smartly and left the room.

A lake in the middle of a forest. Reeds around the shore. A birch wood above the banks. And behind a tall fence was our house in the country, our *dacha*. There was a tiny beach with some boats turned upside down, and on the other

* Nomenklatura – list of most important posts in Soviet Union which can be occupied only by Party members with special experience and which carry numerous special privileges; the elite of Soviet society (See: *Nomenklatura* by Prof. M. Voslensky, London 1984.)

shore there were some more cottages made of logs. They were also enclosed in green fences. And they were also under guard. It was a very special area. They were country cottages, but cottages only for top comrades. And it was not at all easy to get into this area. Oak woods, lakes, dense forests. Here and there red roofs, and more green fences. There was only one road leading to our lake. Wherever you turned you kept coming up against green fences. Beyond our fence there were other people's cottages. Somebody was playing about with a volleyball. But we were not allowed to know who it was. And he had no right to snoop on us. On one side our fence is higher than on the other and we hear music coming from that direction in the evenings. Very pleasant music. Tangos.

Ours was a very big *dacha*. There were twenty-three of us living there. But there was room for thirty. Each one had a little room to himself. The walls were made of pine logs. There was a smell of tar. A small landscape painting on the wall. A huge soft bed. A bookshelf. Downstairs was a hall with a large Asian carpet. We rose when we wished and did as we pleased. There was a good breakfast, a modest lunch and a luxurious dinner. In the evenings we used to sit round the fireplace. We drank. We went hunting. There were twenty-three of us and we had all in the past been officers at the middle level of Soviet military intelligence. The group included one lieutenant-colonel, two majors and one senior lieutenant. The rest were captains. One of us had been a fighter pilot. Two had been in the missile forces. There was a man from the parachute troops, a commander of a missile ship, a military doctor, a military lawyer. Altogether a pretty mixed bunch. We had been handed over by various commanders. Each one of us had for some reason or another landed up in the wake of some military intelligence officer at the divisional, Army or even higher level. Each one of us had been picked out by someone to join his personal group. It was out of those groups that the Aquarium selected its own candidates. Of course, when it took people away from the men directing military intelligence at the middle level, the Aquarium was careful not to take all of them or even the best. If today the Aquarium were to take all his best men away from Kravtsov, tomorrow people like him would not be so painstaking in the selection of their personal staff. Consequently the Aquarium is very careful about the way it takes people away from officers at the middle level, so as not to destroy their willingness to devote so much attention to the selection of staff in the future.

I slept a great deal. It was a long time since I had slept so soundly and so peacefully. I would get up late in the morning and go down to the lake. The weather was dull but the water was warm. I would swim for a long time, knowing that the sleep I was getting and the freedom I was enjoying were not for long. We were just being given the possibility to relax after the examinations before the beginning of the academic year. So I relaxed.

A quick friendship ends in a long quarrel. I knew that and so did my comrades in the group. So we were not in a hurry to make friends. We tried each other out very carefully, chatting about trivialities and telling not very witty stories. We were sniffing around in a word. Meantime we could drink. There was a rich choice in the huge bar. You could drink as much as you wanted. But we drank only in moderation. At some point we would become friends and would be able to trust each other. At some point we would be ready to support each other. Then we would really get drinking, like real officers. But not yet.

We had been carefully measured, and here we all were in our new civilian clothes. Some of us were fated to wear uniform when we became generals. But some would remain in civilian clothes even when we reached the rank of general. That was the sort of service it was.

'I am Colonel Peter Fyodorovich Razumov.' With these words a rather plump man in a sports jacket with a volleyball in his hand introduced himself. 'I am fifty-one and I have served for twenty-three years in the Aquarium. I've worked in three countries and spent sixteen years abroad. I have seven recruitments of agents to my credit. I have been awarded four orders for active service and numerous medals. I am going to be in charge of your group. You will of course think up a nickname for me. To save you trouble I will mention a few of my unofficial nicknames. One of them is Elephant. All the teachers and professors at the Military-Diplomatic Academy are called Elephants. The Academy itself is known as the Conservatory when we are talking about you, the younger generation, or as the Elephants' Graveyard when we are talking about the staff. It is possible that one day one of your number will also become an Elephant and will come here to train some young elephants. Now I would like to talk to each of you separately. Captain Suvorov.'

'Yes, comrade colonel.'

'Call me simply Peter Fyodorovich.'

'Very well.'

'Drop the "very well". You remain an officer of the Soviet Army. Moreover you are moving on to the highest level – the General Staff. But you can forget the "very well" for the time being. Can you not click your heels when you speak with your superior?'

'No, I can't, comrade. . . . Peter Fyodorovich.'

'Your first job, Viktor, is to learn how to sit in an armchair in a slightly relaxed position. . . . You sit with a stiff back as if on parade. Civilian diplomats don't sit like that. Understand?'

'Yes.'

I had wondered for a long time how it was possible to organise a secret school for intelligence officers and train them there for many years without anybody around being able to guess what was going on and without anybody being able to get a picture of us. In fact it's very simple. The main building of the Military-Diplomatic Academy is situated in the centre of Moscow on Narodnogo Opelcheniya Street. But that houses only the administration, the central co-ordinating part of the academy. The students are scattered in small groups all over Moscow. They know only the place where they study, and then only the inside of it. But they don't know where it is situated.

Every morning at 8.30 I would turn up for work at the research institute for electromagnetic radiation of the Soviet Ministry of Communications. It is next to the Timiryazev Park. What the institute really does and to whom it actually belongs is known to very few. At the end of the 1950s there was only a four-storey building with columns on this spot – a typical piece of Stalinist architecture, in yellow stucco. In those days there were probably no more than a couple of hundred people working there. But the institute expanded at a great speed. Now there are large numbers of huge grey six-storey blocks. They are built from grey brick without any facing, in the Khrushchev style, to save money. Further on there are gigantic glass-faced blocks reaching for the sky. White concrete and aluminium. That's the grand style of the Brezhnev period.

The research institute is now a colossal complex of many workshops, with various coloured pipes steaming in the frost as they weave their way in and out, and with snow-white buildings rising up above the chaos of railway lines leading off into the depths of huge hangars. The whole complex is divided into hundreds of zones and sections by means of barbed wire, grey concrete and wire netting mounted on brick walls. The brakes on a diesel locomotive screech. Five thirty-ton trucks are swallowed up in a secret workshop. No entry! The scientists are in a hurry. So are the workpeople. We work in three shifts, without a break. Thousands of people pour into the wide corridors. The morning shift. This is big-time science. Have your pass open for inspection! Zone 12-B. At the main entrance the crowd is split up into dozens of separate streams and hundreds of rivulets. What are their jobs? What problems are they working on? Better not ask, for your own sake. Yet another passageway. Barbed wire high up above. Show your pass! Carry on. Again the human stream splits into smaller streams. It's quite right what they say in our text-books: the best place to hide is in a crowd, or a skyscraper.

I am rushing to work, lost in a crowd of scientists working on a specially protected site. The scientists are shut off from each other by walls of fear and distrust, enormous pay packets and secret privileges. They have been caught out too often by dirty tricks played on the institute by security officers. The more you keep silent, the longer you live. Nobody asks any questions. Each one lives his own life within the walls of this cathedral of science. Hurry up now! It's the beginning of the shift.

My pass is checked once again and then I find myself in a heated corridor. This is the waiting room. All my friends are already there, the other twenty-two. The eighth group of the first course in the First Faculty of the Military-

Diplomatic Academy of the GRU. For us the research institute is only an assembly point. Time to move into the departure hall next door. There's no one inside it; only a big truck without a driver with an orange-coloured container loaded on it. The leader of our group unlocks the door of the container and we all go into it. Inside there are thick carpets and upholstered seats, as in a first-class aircraft cabin. But there are no windows. So we have no way of knowing where we are taken every day. And we never see the driver. He turns up only when he gets the signal and the doors of the container are shut from within. He probably hasn't the slightest knowledge of our existence. Every day at 8.40 a.m. he comes into the hangar, gets into the driver's cab and drives a 'specially dangerous' load from one secret site to another. There he backs his container into another hangar, gets out and goes into another room while the container is unloaded. Every evening he does the trip back. For the rest of the time he is driving other orange-coloured containers around Moscow. The containers may contain detonators for atomic bombs. Or it may be a deadly virus capable of destroying the whole of mankind. Or he may be transporting apparatus intended for genetic or meteorological warfare. How is he to know what's in the containers? They are all identical, all orange-coloured. But he takes home a big pay packet. In such 'scientific institutes' as this one everybody, from the cleaners and night-staff, is very well paid. For the sake of secrecy – to keep them quiet.

One after the other we jump down from the container onto the concrete. High up under the roof of the hangar a sparrow is chirping away. He alone sees all the secrets: who drives us, who cleans up the classrooms at night, who brings in our meals and cleans up the dining room after us. But we see no one. Everything is organised so as to prevent us from being seen. If there are people laying the tables in the dining room the doors leading to the classrooms cannot be opened. As soon as all the cooks and waitresses have left the dining room and shut the doors behind them we get a signal – like Pavlov's dogs – that all is ready. If our door into the dining room is open nobody besides us can go in. It's all automatic. And the food is good. I never ate better, even in Czechoslovakia.

All the same, you never forget you're in a restricted zone. We are shepherded around like prisoners, only in greater comfort. We call the container the 'orange Maria'.

From the hangar an iron door leads into the building where the classrooms are. Our container is taken away and in its place arrives another one bringing the teaching staff.

We have five minutes to recover before the lessons start. It's a neat little courtyard. The grey concrete walls which surround it are almost totally concealed by feathery fir-trees, giving an impression of cosiness. Above the fir-trees there is barbed wire, but what is beyond the wire can't be seen. It's clear that even on the other side of the wall there are the same rounded roofs as over our swimming pool and tennis court. Perhaps on the other side of the wall there is another study centre like ours. Maybe our Polish or Hungarian colleagues are studying there. But they may be Cubans, Italians, Libyans or people of some other nationality. How can we tell? Perhaps it's not a study centre at all but a missile laboratory, a store house, or maybe a prison for especially dangerous prisoners. One thing is clear, however: that our walls do not face the outside world. If you were to break through the wall you would not find yourself in a forest or a town but on the territory of another equally well protected establishment.

I used to try to guess where we were being taken by following the movement of our 'orange Maria'. It was not very far. It seemed to me as if our study centre was right next to the Krasnopresnaya prison. But there was no way of knowing for sure.

'Are you ready now? Let's get going.'

We are all in the lecture hall. Everyone goes to the safes. Each notebook has ninety-six pages. Top secret. Take out your notebook. Lock the safe. Use your personal seal. Everyone in the hall.

The lecturer is separated from the students by a thin semi-transparent curtain. He cannot see us clearly and we cannot see him properly. Just the outline. But he can talk to us without any interference. Sometimes he has to come out from behind the curtain to write something on the blackboard or point to something on a map, but on those occasions he is not allowed to turn his face towards us.

We are taught by men who distinguished themselves as military intelligence officers. Some of them worked at the very highest level of the GRU as illegals; the others worked more openly in the guise of military attachés, military and civilian advisers, journalists, diplomats, trade representaties, or members of the staff of consulates, Aeroflot, Morflot, Intourist and international organisations. But every one of them has suffered a major failure. Otherwise they would not have been sent to the 'elephants' graveyard' but would have continued their work of intelligence-gathering or analysing until they retired.

Our 'elephant' switches on the security system, which makes the walls vibrate slightly, and starts his lecture:

'This is what a spy looks like.'

A picture came up on the screen of a tall, rather round-shouldered man in a raincoat and a hat, wearing dark glasses, with the collar of his coat turned up and his hands in his coat pockets.

'That is the idea that people who write books and make films, and consequently their public, have of what a spy looks like. But you are not spies! You are intrepid Soviet intelligence officers. And it doesn't become you to look like spies. For that reason you are categorically forbidden:

a) to wear dark glasses even in the brightest sunlight;

b) to wear your hat pulled down over your eyes;

c) to go about with your hands in your pockets;

d) to turn up the collar of your raincoat or overcoat.

'The way you walk, the way you look about you, the way you breathe, will all be put through a long training process, but you must remember from the very first day that there must be no tension in your behaviour. The furtive look and the glance over the shoulder are our enemy, and we shall punish you as severely for that as for major errors of principle in your work. You must not look like spies. Your open, honest-looking faces were one of the most important factors noted by the selection board. We study thousands of officers who are potential candidates for the GRU for a long time. Sometimes we keep candidates under observation for several years, during which each of them makes several flights in civil aircraft and in civilian clothes. The one who is stopped by the police as he is boarding a plane is no good for us. We need the sort of people to whom the police pay no attention. Now take a look at yourselves: the pleasant, rather simple-looking faces of working-class or peasant lads. Not a single intellectual in glasses and nobody looking like James Bond. That's excellent. It means that the selection board is doing its job properly.

'Least of all should you resemble spies by the methods you employ. The authors of detective stories always depict the intelligence officer as a brilliant shot and an expert at breaking his opponents' arms. The majority of you have come here from the middle ranks of military intelligence in *Spetsnaz* units in the Army or the Navy. There, of course, it was certainly necessary. But here in the intelligence service of the General Staff we are not going to teach you to shoot, to use your fists or to split bricks with the edge of your hand. You have reached the highest level of intelligence work, where all you need is your head. You will engage in very serious operations and if your stupid head lets you down some time, no amount of skill with a gun or your fists will help you. An officer who has exposed himself through his own mistake is no longer capable of obtaining secret information, and in that situation a gun won't help him.

'Japanese tricks for self-defence and attack and guns and knives are a sort of safety belt for someone working at a dizzy height above the ground. We simply don't provide you with such a belt! The fact is that it is only those steel-erectors who make use of a safety-belt who fall from high places. One day they forget to do up their belt and down they go. But those who never wear a safety belt never fall. Because they are always conscious of the fact that they are not strapped on. So they are always very careful. The safety belt reduces that constant caution.

'If your head lets you down, you will have hundreds of professional policemen on your tail with cars, helicopters, dogs, gas, weapons and the last word in equipment. No gun is going to help you in such a situation. So we don't give you one. We deprive you of every kind of illusion. Every one of you can rely only on his own head, his own intelligence. You may as well know now that there is no safety belt. One mental error, and you're down the chute. This is the essence of the way we differ from the popular idea of a spy in dark glasses. And the achievements which our service has to its credit without recourse to dark

101

glasses, sharp shooting or mighty blows with the hand are tremendous. The subject for today's six-hour seminar is: methods of penetration by agents.'

We started to study our notebooks. The training of officers in the GRU is radically different from what is written in novels. In the course of the next three years at the Military-Diplomatic Academy we were to hear quite a few surprising things.

Man is capable of performing miracles. A man can swim the English Channel three times, drink a hundred mugs of beer, walk barefoot on burning coals; he can learn thirty languages, become an Olympic champion at boxing, invent the television or the bicycle, become a general in the GRU or make himself a millionaire. It's all in our own hands. If you want it you can get it. Most important is to want something: the rest depends only on training. But if you simply train your memory, your muscles or your mind regularly, then nothing will come of your efforts. Regular training is important, but training alone decides nothing. There was the case of the odd character who trained regularly. Every single day he lifted a smoothing iron and continued this for ten years. But his muscles got no bigger. Success comes only when the training, of whatever kind (memory, muscles, mind, willpower, stamina), takes a man to the limit of his capacity. When the end of the training becomes torture. When a man cries out from pain and exhaustion. Training is effective only when it takes a man to the very limit of his capacity and he knows exactly where the limit is: I can do two metres in the high jump; I can do 153 press-ups; I can memorise at one go two pages of a foreign text. And each new training session is effective only when it becomes a battle to exceed your own achievement on the previous day. I'll do 154 press-ups or die in the attempt.

We were taken to watch future Olympic champions in training. There were fifteen-year-old boxers, five-year-old gymnasts and three-year-old swimmers. Look at the expression on their faces. Wait until the final moments of the day's training, when you can see on a child's face the grim determination to beat his own record of the day before. Just study them! One day they will bring home an Olympic gold to offer to our red flag with the hammer and sickle on it. Just look at that face: so much tension, so much pain! That's the road to glory. That's the path to success. To work only at the very limit of your capacity. To work at the brink of collapse. You can become a champion only if you are the sort of person who, knowing that the bar is about to fall and crush him, nevertheless heaves it upwards. The only ones who have conquered themselves, who have defeated their own fear, their own laziness and their own lack of confidence.

Our 'elephant' had taken us to see young sportsmen in training for the Olympics.

'That's the way our country trains the people who are to defend its reputation in the world of sport. Do you really think that our country would take the training of our intelligence officers less seriously?'

102

Chapter Seven

What happened in February 1971 was something never to be forgotten. The head of the GRU, Colonel-general Peter Ivanovich Ivashutin was promoted to the rank of Army General. There was great rejoicing in the Aquarium. The whole General Staff was delighted. It meant that military intelligence was on top. The Chairman of the KGB Yuri Andropov remained just a Colonel-general. A real slap in the face.

We knew that the Central Committee of the Party was heaping coal on the fires of conflict and that there was no way of avoiding a scrap between the KGB and the GRU. The balance between the KGB and the Army had been upset, and now the Central Committee was correcting the mistake. Very quickly there was a purge in the middle levels of the KGB and sweeping changes took place among the KGB major-generals and colonels. At the same time officers and generals of the GRU, of the whole General Staff and Soviet Army, were being promoted. For example, the commander of the North Caucasus military district, Lieutenant-general of Tanks Litovtsev became a Colonel-general. I wondered if he remembered the difficulties he had had at the beginning of his career? Someone then gave him a helping hand, at the risk of his own future. For that I had been made captain before my time. But no doubt the general himself had secretly helped and was still helping somebody or other, otherwise there would have been nobody to back him up. And today he wouldn't have been a three-star general. Good luck to him.

In February 1971 the KGB and the GRU were at each other's throats. But how could an outsider know what was going on? Everybody knew Colonel-general Andropov. But who had ever heard of Army General Ivashutin? Actually, he had no desire for publicity. Unlike Andropov, Ivashutin was in charge of a secret organisation which operated quite unseen and had no need of advertisement.

War planning is the business of the General Staff. The General Staff is the brain of the Army. Any interference by the KGB in military planning would inevitably bring the whole state to the brink of catastrophe. Therefore, in order to survive, the state is obliged to limit the influence which the KGB can exert on the General Staff. To be victorious in war the General Staff has to see the world through its own eyes. It must collect information about the enemy through the efforts of its own officers, who understand the problems of operational planning and who are capable of deciding for themselves what is important for the General Staff and what isn't. The General Staff has no time to request information from others; it *orders* its own intelligence service about what has to be given first priority. If it is to do its job properly the General Staff must have the right to encourage its best intelligence officers and to hand out severe punishment to the slackers. And it has the right. And it has its own intelligence service. It sees the world, not through the prism of the KGB, but through its own eyes.

We were to become officers of the intelligence service and of the General Staff simultaneously. And we were given a very short period to complete our training – five years. Because of that our training programme was more concentrated than anyone thought possible. We were officers of the General Staff, and if we were not capable of carrying the workload we would be dropped off at lower levels.

We did our best. We carried our workload. But not all of us.

At night I dreamt only of vast attacking operations. Deep penetration by tanks. Parachute descents. *Spetsnaz* brigades in the enemy's rear. I dreamt of gunfire and the sounds of battle. I would open my eyes and hear only the revolting ringing of an alarm clock and feel the rays of a winter dawn shinging painfully straight into my eyes. I would sit for a long time on my bed rubbing my temples with the palms of my hands. I felt I couldn't stick it out.

The time passed quickly. The winter term – eight examinations. Summer term – another eight. Fifteen days' leave in the winter; thirty days in the summer. But I didn't go on leave. I passed the tests, but then I had a lot more to do. Practically no one in our group did. There was so much work to be done, more and more of it. If you wanted to keep on top of it you simply had to work. Till green rings and black spots danced before your eyes. Nobody stopped us working. We could sit up all night. We could sleep only three hours a night if we wanted to.

Our group was slowly shrinking. The lieutenant-colonel was expelled on grounds of immorality – sexual excesses. He was exiled to the space centre at Plesetsk. It was also a GRU posting, but in fact a banishment for offenders. The major from artillery reconnaissance was expelled for drunkenness. He was sent back to *Spetsnaz* in the Baikal district. The group was shrinking. There had been twenty-three of us. Now there were only seventeen. They expelled those who began to have fainting fits from the strain of work. They expelled those who could not tell when they were being followed and those who made mistakes or lost their tempers when taking decisions. They expelled those who couldn't learn two foreign languages, learn the history of diplomacy and of intelligence work, the whole structure, tactics, strategy, armament and forward planning of our Army and the armies of our opponents.

They would disappear without warning. They would never again get promoted to the top. They would be found places where there would be no one whom they could tell about where they had been. They would be found places where there were only similar drop-outs from the GRU, where mutual suspicion and provocation flourished. Where, in fact, do they *not* flourish?

A wolf takes care of itself. We feel like wolves. Every free moment we have is given over to looking for dead drop sites. We poke about in corners. A spy needs hundreds of these sites, the sort of places where he can be absolutely sure of being alone and know that he has nobody on his heels, where he can hide secret papers and objects and be quite certain that no children from the street or chance passers-by will find them, that there's not going to be any building work going on and that there will be no rats or squirrels, no snow or water to damage what has been hidden. A spy has to have many such dead drops in reserve and must never use the same place more than once. The sites we need have to be away from prisons, railway stations, important military factories, and not in government or diplomatic districts, because in all those places there is heightened activity by the police and it is easy to be trapped. But where, in Moscow, can you find a place where there are no prisons or important government or military institutions?

We searched for these dead drops in all our spare time. We hunted for them in the woods on the outskirts of Moscow, in the parks, on patches of wasteland and in abandoned buildings. We searched in the snow and mud. We needed a lot of usable sites. And anyone who learns to find such places in Moscow can also do it in Khartoum, Melbourne or Helsinki.

We are taught how to remember people's faces. This form of mental activity has to be reflexive rather than analytical. Thousands of faces are flashed at me on a screen, as well as thousands of silhouettes. My finger is poised over a button as if on a trigger. Whenever I see the same face come up on the screen I have to press the button immediately. If I am mistaken I shall feel a slight but quite unpleasant electric shock go through me. If I fail to press the button when I should I also get a shock. We have regular sessions of this and the speed with which the faces are shown keeps increasing. Every time they flash more and more faces, then they show the same people in wigs, in make-up, in different clothes and in different attitudes. And mistakes are always punished with the nasty little shock.

A spy has to pay attention to car registration numbers. If the same number turns up twice it could mean that you are being followed. And that means that you must abandon the operation you are on. I am shown thousands of registration numbers, flashed on the screen as fast as a French express train.

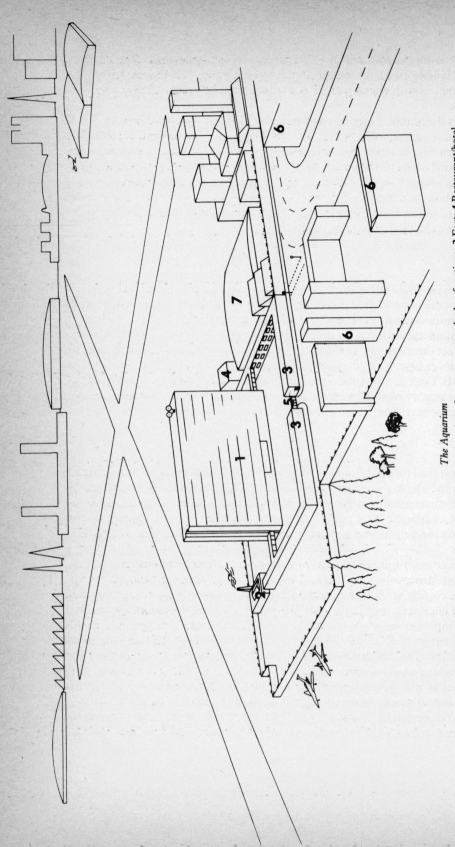

The Aquarium

1 The glass tower of the central building; 2 Crematorium, for the burning of secret papers and other functions; 3 Fort; 4 Restaurant/hotel, containing the security entrance from the Khodinka airfield; 5 Central entrance, which remains permanently closed; 6 'The colony', containing the living quarters of resident GRU officers and retired GRU officers; 7 Space research centre.

There is no need to memorise them, only to recognise them. An analytical mind is of no use in this: you need an automatic reflex. And they are developing it in me, as with dogs, by the Pavlovian method. Mistake – shock; mistake – shock.

But the numbers on cars can be quickly changed, so you need to be able to recognise cars not only by their numbers but simply by their appearance. In a modern city, however, there are millions of cars and our brains are not capable of memorising even hundreds, especially when so many of them are identical. This is where the spy's reflexes come into play. Our brains are capable of taking in millions of details, but we are simply not able to make use of that colossal store of information. Never mind: the Aquarium will teach us. In five years' time we shall have the right reflexes!

We are General Staff officers. So we are taken to Gogol Boulevard to learn how to take decisions in the course of large-scale operations. On huge maps and on the limitless expanses of the Shirokolanov training ground, at first with much hesitation and little confidence and only on paper, but later in practice, we try to direct the movments of huge masses of troops in modern warfare. Maybe we will never have to do it in reality but, once having moved the 5th and 7th Guards Tank Armies on the map from Belorussia into Poland, you suddenly realise exactly what information and what a quantity of information is needed by the General Staff to make such a move in a real war.

We searched for dead drop sites all over the city. We learnt how to detect with certainty whether we were being followed. Before any operation, an intelligence officer must be absolutely certain in himself whether he is being followed or not. A straight yes or no. In today's secret war for which he is being trained nobody can help him and nobody will share the responsibility for any mistakes made.

Yes or no. I followed a previously worked-out route, twisting and turning around Moscow for four hours. I switched taxis, buses and trams. I left the dense crowds at the centre and reached the deserted parts of the city, then dived once again into the crowds. The KGB also had something to learn. It is very important for it to learn about its own mistakes in following people. In this the interests of KGB and GRU coincide, and these two hostile organisations cooperate. The 'Elephant' knew that I was training in the city that day and that my training would begin at 1500 hours at the Metropole hotel, which was being treated as if it were a Soviet embassy in a hostile country. Once I left the 'embassy' it was up to the 'Elephant' to decide whether to phone the KGB or not. Yes or no. Once a week the 'Elephant' would send each of us out on different routes which we prepared ourselves. Last time there had been no doubt at all that I was being followed. I had been quite sure. But now? Yes or no? I wasn't sure. I didn't want to have to return to the 'embassy' and report to the 'Elephant' that I wasn't sure. If I did, he would send me out again to walk around Moscow and I would have to give a definite answer by the next morning. Yes or no. A spy's eyes are one of his most important tools.

His tongue is another. The Aquarium does everything possible to persuade its officers to acquire foreign languages. For knowing one Western language they raise your salary by 10 per cent. For every Oriental language they pay you an extra 20 per cent. So if you learn five Oriental languages you can double your salary. But not to learn two languages would mean being sent off to the Plesetsk space centre, and I had no desire at all to go there. So I studied hard. It was a big problem for me to learn a foreign language: I just don't have a musical ear. My hearing was damaged through working with tanks and their guns. I did my best, but in language studies I was the worst in the group. There had been others worse than I was, but they had already been dropped. I was next in line. Even if my pronunciation was awful, I would catch up in other respects or die in the attempt.

'I had the same problem,' said Elephant by way of encouragement. 'Learn off whole pages by heart. That's the way to acquire fluency. Then you will always have in hand a supply of everyday phrases and whole sentences for use in speaking and writing.'

So I learnt whole pages by heart. Then I would write them down. Then I'd re-write them. I would do it from memory thirty times over so that I could do it without mistakes.

My eyes served me even worse than my tongue. I had had experience in the *Spetsnaz* of staring dogs in the eye. But this was no longer sufficient. They trained us to use a mirror, to look yourself in the eyes without blinking, or shifting your gaze. If you are trying to recruit someone you have first of all to withstand his stare. Friendship begins with a smile; recruitment with a stare. If you can't withstand the first earnest stare of your interlocutor there's no use trying to recruit him later, because he is mentally your superior. He won't fall for you.

I left the underground at the Krasnaya Presnya station and headed for the zoological gardens. If you ever have the same problem, go along there towards closing time: there will be nobody to bother you. I stared the tigers and leopards in the eyes. I strained my will and clenched my teeth. The motionless yellow eyes of those awe-inspiring beasts held my gaze. I clenched my fists tigher, digging my nails into my palms. You have carefully to narrow your eyes and then open them wide very slowly, so that you don't blink. It makes the eyes burn and tears come welling into them. Another moment and I blinked. The huge, lazy brown cat-like creature smiled at me contemptuously and turned its head away in disappointment, as if to say, 'You're too weak to try those games with me, Suvorov.'

Never mind, big cat. I am not easily put off. I'll come here again next Sunday. And the next, and the next. I'm pretty tough too.

Once again the days and nights began to fly by, scarcely distinguishable from one another. Our course could well have been spread over ten years, but it had been compressed into five and for that reason not everybody could see it through. Perhaps this was in itself also a sort of examination? Perhaps this was the main point of our training – to get rid of the weaker ones now while they were in the Soviet Union, so as not to have to do it later?

In spy work there is one quite simple rule: breakaway forbidden! If you have discovered that there are people following you, first of all don't give any indication that you've noticed them, don't behave nervously and don't start rushing about – you are, after all, a diplomat. Better to go on wandering round the city. You must not, of course, carry on with the operation you were engaged on. They may pretend they have stopped following you, while in reality they are close by you, only with more people and different ones. Whenever you discover you are being followed, you must without exception suspend your operation, however urgent it may be. Every operation is planned in many different versions. You're being followed today, so we will repeat the operation tomorrow, or in a week's time, or in a month. But don't dream of trying to break away from your tail. Even if you break away for the very best of reasons you will be telling them that you are a spy and not just a diplomat, that you know how to detect that you are being followed secretly, and that you have some reason or other for evading them. If you let them see that, they will never let you out of their sight. They will follow you every day and never give you a chance to do your work. You may, of course, get away from them once, but they will then class you as a dangerous man, and you will never get away from them again. Instead you will have thirty of them on your heels every single day. That is why breaking away is forbidden. But not on that day . . . .

That day we are given permission to break away. 'To hell with your diplomatic careers,' said Elephant. 'There are situations in which the Aquarium orders you to carry through an operation at any price. So break away!'

There were two of us. Genka and I. Break away, he said. Just try and do it in Moscow, where it was already dark and cold and empty. In three days Moscow would be drinking and having fun. There would be celebrations, parades and bands on the streets. But on that day, just before it exploded in a bout of drunken joy, Moscow had fallen silent. There were the two of us, Genka and I, and some dark shadows behind us. Our own shadows, and someone else's.

They were running all over the place, not trying to conceal themselves. If each of us had been on his own we would have got away from them long ago. Breaking away was forbidden, but we had been taught how to do it.

The first time we made a dash for it was when we were in the Petrovsky Arcade. It was a good place. Lots of people there. We dived into the crowd, pushing people aside, rushing up narrow stairs, into the crowd again, out of the back door and into the underground. But the shadows were still on our tails and wouldn't be shaken off. When the train reached the Lenin Hills station we had another try. Just before the doors closed as the train moved off we hopped off on to the platform. But our shadows were too smart for us.

Moscow was empty. Cold and dark. But Genka knew of some other place on Marina Raskova Square. Let's go, then!

The bastards! How many could there be of them? A great many, curse it. It was a pity we were not allowed to separate. It was a two-man operation. Should we separate anyway, Genka? No, that would be to exceed our rights. But what if the operation was a failure – would that be better? Genka led me around some empty side streets where he had a place he had prepared long ago. Then we were running down the lanes. But it was no good: there were three big youths right behind us making no attempt to conceal themselves. The tail was deliberately conspicuous, intended to play on our nerves. There were many more following us without being seen. More side streets, and now there were three of them behind us, laughing openly at us. 'What if they try to get away?' a loud voice behind us asked. 'We would catch 'em up,' another voice replied reassuringly. More laughter in our backs. Then Genka gave me a dig in the ribs, meaning 'get ready'. I was ready: only snow was falling lightly on us. The very first snow. It would have been nicer to be strolling down the street and savouring the crystal air. But that was not for us. It was time to break away.

Genka grabs me by the hand and we fly into a door and down and then up some filthy stairs and along dark corridors, trying not to break our legs. Down another stairway. Some buckets and an awful smell. Another door and more stairs and corridors. Genka is out of breath, though he is a good runner. He is big and heavy. But he has cat's eyes in the dark. More doorways, rags, rubble and broken glass. Then we come out on to the street, goodness knows where. I have walked the whole of Moscow but have never come across such places before. There are three side streets ahead of us. Genka pulls me into the first one. It seems we have got away. It is a good place Genka has found. How many months has he been traipsing round Moscow to find it? A place like that ought to be framed in gold, to be shown to young spies: see what a magnificent place it is! A model. If you are going to work in London, New York or Tokyo – everyone ought to have such a place for himself. So as to be able at any time to get away from the police. But it won't do us any good today. Snow is falling lightly over Moscow. The first. It stuck to the soles of our shoes so that Genka's and my tracks are as clear as those of the first astronauts on the Moon. It's known as Murphy's law. According to that unbreakable law, a slice of bread and butter always hits the ground butter downwards. We'll never get away,

Genka! Yes we will. And Genka drags me by the hand. Empty Moscow. Honest citizens have all shut themselves away in their little homes. There is only Genka and I in the whole of Moscow . . . and the big boys from the KGB. Genka is out of breath again. Are you scared to jump off a train, Vitya? he asks. No, Genka, I am not scared. I have a chance. You go on the operation and I'll cover you from behind. We'll run down the sidestreets and courtyards, and if we come out on the main road we'll leave no tracks, but there will be their cars and you can't get away from them.

We hop over a fence and there is a train platform and the screech of a train's brakes. Genka is puffing. And behind us are three big boys, also puffing. They have also jumped over the fence like mad horses. Genka pulls me into the train. We scramble into the last door and run down the centre of the carriage. If only the door will slam behind us! But it doesn't slam. There is a noise like galloping horses behind us and our three followers are also in the carriage and running after us. We rush through one carriage and then another. Genka pushes me ahead but holds back himself. He goes like a fighter plane into a head-on attack. He is a tough lad, Genka. But they are tough too. They are fighting it out in the carriage, while I get to the door. If only it will stay open now! I throw the whole weight of my body against one half of the door, while the other half clicks shut behind my back and the train moves off.

You should always jump off a moving train backwards and to the rear. But I remember that only much later. I shoot out of the door forwards and towards the front. You ought to keep your teeth clenched together, but I forget that too, so they they come together like a trap and nearly bite off the end of my tonge. The train hasn't got up much speed when I shoot out of it and I'm not far off the ground: the platform is a lone one. Only I twist my ankle as I fall and cut my hand. To hell with that: I jump up and the end carriage bumps past me, the brakes screeching. The KGB men have pulled the emergency brake. They have been trained too. I am acting as I would in a real situation, and so are they. They have examinations to pass; they are constantly being assessed. They need to catch me now at any price. But they bloody well won't! I rush towards the fence and over the top. Let's put on some speed! Thanks, Genka!

It is already after midnight. The trains are now quite empty. I rush through the subways and dark sidestreets and then dive into the underground. There I am sure that no car can follow, so the KGB people will have to keep close to me. But the carriage is empty. It's late, and I have got clean away. The most important thing now is to keep out of sight of the television cameras. There are more than you can count in every underground station. If the KGB have lost track of me they will already have sent a description of me to the central control point. All the cameras will long have been scanning underground Moscow.

But I have already had experience of this. I'll get out at the Izmailovo Park station, where I've discovered only four TV cameras and know precisely where

111

they are situated. If I travel in the last carriage I can slip quickly past the camera there into the underground passage where there is a concrete barrier with a narrow gap for pedestrians and a dozen footpaths leading into a dense wood. Try and find me there!

The first snow squeaks beneath my feet. But it has already been trodden down on the footpaths. In the evening crowds of elderly pensioners stroll there, and further on among the fir trees there are always a lot of young people, more or less drunk. Now, later on, there is nobody about. I follow a roundabout route in the wood and stop and listen for long periods. There is no sound of footsteps on the snow behind me. Reassured, I look round in all directions, feeling, as they say in novels, like a thief. But there is nobody to cause me any concern. I have got clean away. And I am the only one who knows where the secret hiding place is. It is right there, in a dark corner where a couple of dozen garages have been built against a concrete wall. Between them and the wall is a narrow and evil-smelling gap, reeking with urine. That's a good thing: it means that people are not likely to want to poke about in the gap. They do their business there and hurry away. But I have different work to do. I look round once again to be quite sure and then squeeze into the gap. It is very narrow, and I have to work my way three metres down it to where the first two garages meet. Once there I can push my fingers in and feel whether somebody has left a packet. But it is easy for me to cover the last metre. Genka would never have been able to squeeze through such a space. I breathe out and press forward another few centimetres. I take a quick breath, breathe out and move forward again. What a fool I am! I should have taken off my overcoat before getting into the gap. It's a long time since I discovered this place. I squeezed into it then without much difficulty, but that was in the summer. I breathe out again and move a little further. Then I stretch out my right hand. A little more, and it's round the corner. Then I spread out my fingers and feel up and down.

Ouch! Somebody grips my hand as if in a vice and a blinding light shines into my eyes. I can hear a dozen voices talking quietly around me, and my hand feels as if it is in a trap. It is very painful. Somebody with powerful hands grabs me by the legs and pulls. They drag me right out, my nose in today's snow and yesterday's urine. Then a car appears from somewhere with a screech of brakes, although they are not allowed in the Izmailovo Park. My arms are twisted behind my back and somebody slips a pair of handcuffs on my wrist.

'Call my consul!' This is what I am supposed to shout in such circumstances.

The rear door of the car is thrown open. There I have to protest again: I refuse to enter the car! But someone gives me a sharp kick to knock my legs from under me. They are a tough bunch of boys! I grit my teeth and there I am sitting in the car between a couple of Hercules.

'Call my consul!'

'And what are you up to here, you scoundrel?'

'Call my counsul!'

'Every move of yours has been photographed!'

'It's just a crude act of provocation. I can produce a film of you screwing Bridget Bardot! Call my consul!'

'You had secret documents in your hands!'

'You forced them into my hands. They were not mine!'

'You were feeling for a secret hiding place!'

'That's pure fabrication: you seized me in the centre of the city and forced me into this stinking hole! Call my consul!'

Tyres screeching on the turns, the car rushes me off somewhere in the dark.

'Call my consul!' I shout.

They get tired of my shouts.

'Listen, young man. That's enough training: stop shouting.'

But I am up to their tricks. If they let me go there and then it means that the training session is over. And if they don't let me go it means that the training is continuing. So I take a really deep breath and shout at the top of my voice:

'The consul, you bastards, call my consul. I am an innocent diplomat! The consul!'

'Call my consul!'

There is no shortage of light. Two arc-lamps shine straight into my face, bringing tears to my eyes. Call the consul! They sit me down on a chair, and a big scowling character takes up position behind me. Call the consul! I stand up. But the big fellow presses his huge hands on my shoulders and sits me in the chair again. As soon as the pressure on my shoulders eases I again try to stand up. The big fellow again presses me down into the chair and brings his heavy boot into play as well. He skilfully knocks my feet from under me, like a wrestler, so that I fall into the chair again. I get a sharp kick on the shin that hurts. From somewhere beyond the lights I can hear a voice saying:

'You're a spy!'

'Call my consul. I am a diplomat of the Union of Soviet Socialist Republics!'

'Everything you've done has been recorded on film!'

'It's been faked! It's a crude provocation! Call the consul!'

I try again to stand up. But the big fellow knocks my left leg from under me with a quick movement of his big boot, the way an executioner kicks the stool from beneath his victim. Then I lost my balance. Again I feel pain. He has given me a very light kick, but on the bone, just above the heel. I would never have thought it could be so painful.

'What were you doing at night in the park?'

'Call the consul!'

Again I stand up. And again he kicks me gently but in the right place. This treatment leaves no bruises and nothing to prove that I have been maltreated. I stand up again and again he sits me down with a quick blow.

The big fellow doesn't seem to realise we are only training. Why is he being so rough? I stand up again and he sits me down as before. I glance over my shoulder to see what sort of a face he has. But I can make out nothing. I have rings dancing before my eyes from the lights and cannot see. The room is in darkness except for the two arc-lamps. I can't even tell whether it is a big room or a small one. It is probably pretty big, because there is an unbearable heat coming from the lights, but occasionally there is a cool draught blowing through. It is never like that in a small room.

'You have broken the law . . . . '

'Tell it to my consul.'

I am in pain and have no desire to get another blow on the leg, so I decide to repeat my attempt at standing up only three more times. Then I will simply remain seated. I don't really want to get out of the wooden chair at all. But I try. I dig my feet into the brick floor, carefully transfer the weight of my body on to the muscles of my legs, take a deep breath and force myself upwards. He strikes me just as I am pushing myself up. My left foot shoots up and I fall into the chair again with a little groan. Pity it isn't a soft chair: it would have been less painful.

'Who were you getting material from through the drop?'

'Call my consul!'

I know that the one who is kicking me in the leg is under training. That is the sort of work he will have in the future: standing behind a chair and making sure the person under interrogation does not get out of it. It is a difficult business. But he is a diligent student. Persistent, an enthusiast. Each of his kicks is harder than the previous one, or at least so it seems to me, because he keeps hitting me in the same place. When all is said and done, why do I try to stand up? I can simply sit still and demand to see the consul, and so long as they carry on not calling the consul I shan't let them involve me in conversation. So I'll stop trying to stand up. Twice more, and finish.

The next kick is performed with skill and great devotion to the job. Consequently I don't understand the next question. I know there has been a question but don't know what it was. For a few moments I wonder what to reply and then suddenly find the answer:

'Call my consul!'

I begin to tire of this sort of questioning, and so do they. Then the big hands again force me down into the seat and someone pushes pencils between my fingers. I know their little game. You can try it on a friend. A mild handshake produces a shudden and horrible pain. A little harder, and unconsciousness follows immediately. It is very simple and very effective and moreover leaves no traces. I quickly recall how to resist this treatment. First, you don't cry out; second, you take pleasure in your own pain and wish for more of it. That's the only salvation. Somebody's sweaty hand feels the palm of my own, straightens up the pencils between my fingers and suddenly squeezes my hand hard. The two lights wobble, shake and swing

114

around madly. I float away somewhere out of the big dark room with its brick floor. I just want more pain, and I am jeering at someone.

It is a cold, grey November morning in Moscow. Everyone is still sleeping. A mail van drives past. A street-cleaner, half-asleep, is sweeping the pavement. I am lying back on the soft seat of a car, with the houses of Moscow speeding past me. The side window is slightly open and an icy draught is blowing away the remains of my nightmares. I can feel that my face is unshaven and that my hair is stuck to my head. For some reason my face is wet. But I am all right. Somebody is driving me somewhere in a big black car. I turn to the driver. It is Elephant. He is my driver.

'Comrade colonel, I didn't tell them anything.'

'I know, Viktor.'

'Where are we going?'

'Home.'

'Did they let me go?'

'Yes.'

I remain silent for a long time. Then suddenly I feel scared. It seems to me that I told them everything when I laughed.

'Comrade colonel, did I give anything away?'

'No.'

'Are you sure?'

'Quite sure. I was right by you all the time, even as you were arrested.'

'Where did I make a mistake?'

'There was no mistake. You broke away from them and made for the hiding place with no one on your tail. But it was too good a place: the Moscow KGB knows it. You used a place which is used by real foreign spies. It's a very good place, and that's why it's under constant observation. They took you for a real spy, not knowing who you were. But we intervened at once. It was a genuine arrest, but the interrogation was just training.'

'How's Genka?'

'Genka's all right. They held him for a while, but he also gave nothing away. In this business you have to relax. It's no good being sorry for yourself or dreaming about revenge. If you get over that, then you can put up with anything. Get some sleep. I shall recommend you for real work.'

'What about Genka?'

'Genka too.'

'Have you ever been to Mytishchi?'

'No.'

'So much the better.' Elephant suddenly became very serious. 'Listen: this

115

is a serious training project. The target is the Mytishchi missile factory. The task is to find a suitable person and to recruit him. The first aim is to gain experience of a real recruitment. The second aim is to discover possible ways which an enemy intelligence service might use to recruit our people working in especially important plants. The limitations imposed on the exercise are as follows. The first concerns your time. For carrying out the recruitment you may use only your own time, your days off and holidays. You will not be given any free time for doing the job. And the second concerns finance – you will use only your own money, as much of it as you like, even all of it, but not a kopek of government money will be allotted. Any questions?'

'What does the KGB know about this?'

'The KGB knows that, with the permission of the administrative department of the Central Committee we are continually carrying out such operations all over Moscow. If the KGB arrest you we will rescue you, but then we shan't send you abroad.'

'What can I tell the person I recruit about myself and my organisation?'

'Anything you like, except the truth. You are not recruiting him on behalf of the Soviet State (any fool can do that) but on your own behalf and at your own expense.'

'That means that if I recruit him he will be regarded as a real spy?'

'Precisely. With the one difference that the information he hands over will not go abroad.'

'But that doesn't make his guilt any less.'

'Certainly not.'

'So what will he get?'

'Article 64* of the Criminal Code. Surely you know that?.

'I know, comrade colonel.'

'Then I wish you success. And bear in mind that you are doing an important job for the Soviet state. You are not only training: you are helping our state to get rid of potential traitors. Your whole group will be given similar tasks, but with other targets. The whole academy does the same. Every year. I wish you success. And finally – sign this paper to say you have been given the task. It's a very serious job.'

According to the theory, the first think you have to do in recruiting is to identify the set target. This wasn't difficult. Mytishchi is a small town with a huge factory in it, surrounded by barbed wire. At night the factory is bathed in a sea of blinding light. Guard dogs can be heard yapping inside the fences. There can be no mistake about it. But a factory has to have a name. If it says at the gates that it is a tractor factory that may mean that, apart from armaments, the factory produces something for tractors. But if the name at the gate tells

* Article 64: Betrayal of the homeland.

116

you nothing, if it is something like 'Uralmash' or 'Lenin Forge' or 'Hammer and Sickle', then you can cast all doubt aside: it is an armaments factory pure and simple.

The second rule of recruiting says that there is no need to clamber over the factory fence. People come out of a factory of their own accord. They go to libraries, to sports centres, to restaurants, to bars. Around a major factory there is bound to be an area where lots of workers live and where there are schools and nurseries for their children. There will be a medical centre, a tourist office, a park and so forth. You just have to find it all.

The rules say that there's no need to recruit the factory manager or the chief engineer. It's easier to recruit their secretaries, who are by no means less well informed than their bosses. But unfortunately it is one of the conditions of our training in recruiting that we are forbidden to recruit women. Recruiting women, they say, is no training because it is too easy. It's all right when you are working abroad, but not when we are being trained. It's not really so bad. You can find a draughtsman or computer programmer, or someone in charge of secret documents or a copying machine.

Every one of us was given a similar task and every one of us drew up his own plan, as if he were preparing for a major battle. Recruiting as part of training was no easier for us than the real thing. If you are arrested for such activity in any Western country there is only one consequence – you are sent back to the Soviet Union. But if you make a mistake under training and are arrested by the KGB the consequences are much more serious – you will never be allowed to travel abroad. When you are working abroad all your time is your own and there is no limit to what you can spend, whereas under training you have examinations to worry about – in strategy, in tactics, in the armed forces of the United States, in two foreign languages. You have to make the best of it. If you want to get on you have to pass your exams *and* do your recruiting.

My first move was to draw in my mind a circle, about a kilometre across, round the vast factory site. Within that area I decided not to show myself under any pretext. I knew that every centimetre in that area was under observation by the KGB and that there was no point in my going there.

One evening I was outside the zone waiting for the end of the day shift. A stream of people came rushing along the pavements. There was much noise, clatter and laughter. A maelstrom of people.

There was a great crowd at the bus stop, snow underfoot and freezing fog around the street lamps. People crowded noisily into the bars. But that did not interest me for the time being: that was the easy way and I would resort to chance meetings only if other ways did not turn up. What I needed now was a library, and I had no difficulty in finding the usual factory library nearby. Anybody could go in and I soon found myself among the bookshelves. As I moved along them I tried to see who was interested in what subjects. I needed a

117

contact. I noticed a ginger-haired fellow in glasses studying books of science fiction. I decided to speak to him.

'Excuse me,' I said quietly in his ear. 'Where can I find science fiction here?'

'Right over there.'

'Where exactly?'

'Come here – I'll show you.'

I came across a contact on my third evening.

'I'm looking for something about astronauts and about Tsiolkovsky.'

'You'll find it here.'

'Where?'

'Come along—I'll show you.'

Spy films always depict intelligence officers as brilliantly eloquent and witty. The spy's arguments are always irrefutable and his victim always agrees with his proposals. This is nonsense. In real life the reverse is true. The fourth law of recruitment says that every man has his head full of bright ideas and that everyone suffers, mainly because no one will listen to him. The biggest problem for everyone is to find a good listener. That's impossible because everybody else is after the same thing, seeking their own listeners, so that they've no time to listen to other people's silly ideas.

Most important in the art of recruiting is the ability to listen patiently to one's interlocutor. Learning to listen without interrupting is the guarantee of success. It's a difficult art to acquire. But you can make a good friend if you are prepared to listen to him. I had found a friend. He had read all the books on Tsander, Tsiolkovsky and Korolev. And he talked also about others about whom it was not yet permitted to write books – about Yangel, Chelamei, Babakin, Stechkin. I just listened.

We couldn't talk properly in the library. In fact we were not supposed to talk at all. So I listened to him among the snowdrifts in a clearing in the woods where we went skiing. And in the cinema and in a little café where we drank beer.

My friend was fascinated by the various systems for delivering fuel from the tanks to the rocket engines. The fuel can be delivered by means of either turbo-pumps or a displacement system. I listened and agreed with him. The first German rockets used turbo-pumps. Why then had that simple, cheap system been forgotten? Why, indeed? Although this method involved the use of very reliable and accurate pumps it would guarantee against a major accident – a burst tank full of fuel due to an increase in pressure in the displacement mixture. I agreed with this entirely.

At our next meeting I had in my pocket a tape recorder in the form of a cigarette case. A wire from the recorder went down the sleeve of my jacket to my wristwatch, which contained a microphone. We sat in a restaurant chatting about the possibility of using nitrogen tetroxide as an oxidising agent and liquid oxygen along with kerosene as the main fuel. It seemed to him that, although this mixture was old-fashioned, it had been thoroughly tested and could be depended on for the next couple of decades.

Next morning I played the tape over to Elephant. I had committed a fairly serious technical error: a microphone could not be put in a watch to record a conversation in a restaurant. The constant rattle of knives and forks next to the microphone is deafening, and our voices sounded too far off. This greatly amused Elephant and only when he had stopped laughing did he ask:

'What does he know about you?'

'That my name is Viktor.'

'What about your surname?'

'He didn't ask.'

'When's your next meeting?'

'On Thursday.'

'Before then I will lay on a meeting for you in the ninth directorate of GRU Information. You will talk to an officer who analyses American rocket engines. Of course he knows a great deal about *our* motors too. He will provide you with the real questions, about the things which would interest him if you had got to know an American missile engineer. If you succeed in extracting from your bespectacled friend a sufficiently intelligible answer you can reckon yourself lucky . . . but not him.'

The Information department of the GRU wanted to know what my friend could say about hydrogen fuel.

We sat in a dirty bar and I told my friend that I didn't think hydrogen fuel would ever be used. I don't know why, but he thought I worked in the fourth shop in the factory. I had never told him that: I could hardly do so, since I didn't know what the fourth shop was.

He stared at me enquiringly for some time and then said: 'That's the way you people in the fourth think. I know how you always want to play doubly safe. You fear toxicity and the danger of explosions. That's all very well. But think of the huge output of energy! The toxicity can be reduced and we are dealing with that in the second shop. Believe me: we shall be successful, and then limitless possibilities will open up before us. . . .'

At the next table I thought I recognised a familiar back. Surely not Elephant? But it was. And along with him were some other rather impressive characters.

Next morning Elephant congratulated me on having carried out my first successful recruitment.

'It was just a training exercise. But never mind. If a kitten wants to become a real cat it has to start with fledglings and not with full-grown sparrows. Meanwhile you can forget all about hydrogen fuel. That's none of your business.'

'I'll forget.'

'You can forget about your bespectacled friend as well. We'll pass his file with your reports and tape recordings over to the right people. The Central Committee needs concrete evidence of the KGB's poor work to keep the security people on a tight rein. But where can they find such material? Well, there it is!' Elephant opened the safe to show me the pile of reports by my comrades on their first attempts at recruiting.

But I was to come across displacement systems and hydrogen fuel once again. Just before passing out from the academy we were given an opportunity of talking with weapons designers so as to get a general idea of the problems facing the Soviet armaments industry. They showed us tanks and guns in Solnechnogorsk, the latest aircraft in Monino and rockets in Mytishchi. We spent several whole days with leading engineers and designers, without of course being told their names. They also had no idea who we were, and probably thought we were some young lads from the Central Committee.

In Mytishchi I was led through three control points and a whole army of security men, and in a high, well-lit hangar we were shown a green fuselage. After hearing long explanations I asked why we did not revert to the use of turbo-pumps instead of the displacement systems.

'Are you a rocket specialist?' the engineer enquired.

'Sort of,' I replied.

Chapter Eight

On the third day following my arrival in Vienna Major-general Golitsyn, the 'resident', or head, of the GRU's diplomatic *residentura*★ in Vienna summoned me to his office.

'Have you unpacked your suitcases?'

'Not yet, comrade general.'

'Don't be in any hurry to do so.'

I looked at him enquiringly. His huge fist crashed down on his oak desk and a delicate coffee cup rattled plaintively.

'Because we have a plane leaving for Moscow on Friday. I'll send you back there, you lazy devil. How many agents have you recruited?'

I left the general's office and burst, blushing with shame, into the main office of the *residentura*, where not a soul paid the slightest attention to my entry. They were all too busy. Three of them were bent over a huge map of the city. One was hastily typing something out on a typewriter. Another two were trying unsuccessfully to fit a huge grey electronic unit with French markings into a diplomatic bag. Only one elderly experienced intelligence officer looked up. He, apparently realising how I was feeling, said sympathetically:

'The resident has of course threatened to throw you out on the next plane.'

'Yes,' I said, in the hope of gaining some support.

'And he will. That's the sort of chap he is.'

'What am I to do?

'Just get on with your work.'

It was good advice, and I could hope for no better. If someone knew where and how to get his hands on some secret document he would go and try to get it himself. Why should he want to share his success with me?

And so I went to work. In the course of the next four days I did not, of course, recruit anybody. But I took the first steps in the right direction. Consequently my return to Moscow was delayed for another week, and then for another. Like that I continued working for General Golitsyn for four years. It did not take long to understand that every member of Golitsyn's staff, including his First Deputy, was in exactly the same situation.

★ Contained within a legitimate diplomatic establishment (a Soviet embassy, a consulate), the *residentura* or residency is the major base for GRU activity abroad. (See V. Suvorov, *Soviet Military Intelligence*, London 1984.)

I am a spy.

I graduated from the Military-Diplomatic Academy and worked for six months in the 9th Directorate of the Information Service of the GRU. Then I was transferred from analysing information to the business of gathering it. Intelligence-gathering is not only carried on abroad.

The Soviet Union is visited by millions of foreigners, some of whom know things which are of interest to us. These have to be sorted out from the rest and recruited, and their secrets have to be extracted from them by force, cunning or cash.

The business of intelligence-gathering is a furious battle carried on by thousands of officers of the KGB and GRU among likely foreigners. They work just like a pack of hounds, and it is no accident they are called wolfhounds or Borzois. The man in charge of intelligence-gathering in Moscow and its surrounding territory is the soulless Major-general of GRU Boris Alexandrov, for whom any achievable standards are regarded as too low and who is ready without a moment's thoughts to ruin the career of any young officer for a moment's oversight. I worked in General Alexandrov's directorate for a year, and it was the most difficult year of my life. But it was a year in which I made my first recruitment and obtained on my own initiative my first secret document. Only someone who has been able to do that in Moscow, where there are not very many secrets we don't know about, has a chance of going abroad. Anyone who is able to work in Moscow can work anywhere. That is how I came to be sitting in a little Viennese bar holding in my hand a cold and slightly moist mug of sweet-smelling, practically black beer.

I was engaged on the gathering of intelligence. I had been very busy in Vienna from the outset. Not because I had been very successful in seeking out people with secrets. By no means. It was simply because my superior officers were having such success in their work, and every one of the operations they carried out had to be provided with proper cover. The attention of the police had to be diverted, the officer on an operation had to be followed and protected during his secret meeting, the information he obtained had to be taken over and delivered to the residency at some risk. Secret letter-drops and meeting places had to be checked, secret signs inspected – there were a thousand different jobs to do for various people, and you often could see no sense in what you did. It was all hard work and risky.

The Soviet Embassy in Vienna is very similar to the Lubyanka. The same style, the same colour. Typical Chekist tastelessness. Artificial grandure. Lubyansky classicism. There was a time when my country was filled with this fake Chekist grandeur – columns, façades, cornices, spires, turrets and mock balconies. Inside the embassy, just like the Lubyanka, it is dismal and boring.

Artificial marble, moulded cornices and columns, leather doors, red carpets and the undying smell of cheap Bulgarian cigarettes.

However, not all of the embassy looks like a branch of the Lubyanka. There is an independent island there, a sovereign and independent branch of Khodinka: the GRU *residentura*. We have our own style, our own traditions and rules. We pour scorn on the Lubyanka style. Our style is simple, yet strict, no embellishments, nothing superfluous. But our style is concealed under the ground. We are the only ones to see it. It is all the same in Moscow, with the huge KGB buildings in the very centre of the city, no view to all. The GRU building however is utterly hidden from the eyes of outsiders. The GRU distinguishes itself from the KGB by the fact that the GRU is a secret organisation. Here in Vienna too, the style of the Lubyanka is on view to all. The style of the GRU is hidden from everybody.

But in the Soviet Embassy there is also a third style. In the dense garden there towers the strict and solemn Orthodox Church. There are five cupolas with golden crosses, and above them one more cupola with its own golden cross. Why they did not remove this church immediately after the revolution, I do not know. It stands proud and detached, its golden crosses higher than the red flag. In the early morning mist, the first rays of the sun fall on the highest of the golden crosses and fragment into thousands of flashing sparks. I know full well that there is no God. I have never been in a church in my life. I have never even stood for any length of time outside a church, not even a ruined one, except that here in Vienna, I pass by the church every day. I don't know why, but it disturbs me. There is something mystical and magical about it. It has stood here now for more than a hundred years. It goes without saying that for the last fifty years, no services have taken place in it. Its bell rings not the slightest sound, not even the faint tinkle of a music-box. But even without this, the ringing of bells, it is beautiful. The builders in no way strove to emphasise its greatness, but it is majestic. In its severe appearance, there isn't the slightest trace of falsity. There are so many colours and patterns brought together, but each pattern and each nuance blends in with the next, and together they embody a kind of great harmony. I fear these patterns. I walk past, and look down at my feet. If I don't look down, I feel I could end up on my knees before this mysterious, beckoning beauty, and stay there for ever.

I was reporting on my first moves. The resident (we called him 'the Navigator') listened to me without interrupting, staring down at his desk. That seemed strange to me, because one of the first things they teach a spy is to look your interlocutor straight in the eyes, to withstand long stares and to control your gaze like a fighting weapon. So why did that hard-baked officer not obey those elementary rules? There was something wrong. I remained tense without dropping my eyes, preparing myself mentally for the worst.

'All right,' he said at last, without raising his eyes from his papers. 'In future you will work under the personal control of my First Deputy, but twice every month I shall hear your report myself personally. You have done quite a lot in these first few weeks, so I am going to give you a really serious task. You will have a meeting with a real person, a person recruited by the First Deputy. I cannot take the risk of sending him on the operation. So you will go. The man who has been recruited is of exceptional importance to us. Comrade Kosygin* himself is being kept informed about our work in this field. We cannot afford to lose such a contact. He works in Western Germany and provide us with parts of the American 'Tow' anti-tank missiles. We shall get you secretly into Western Germany where you will have the meeting. You will be given parts of a missile. You will pay the man for his services. You will cover a lot of kilometres to cover up your tracks. You will be met by an assistant to the Soviet military attaché from Bonn. You will hand the goods over to him, well packed up. He is not to know what he is receiving. From there the goods will go by diplomatic bag to the Aquarium. Any questions?'

'Why shouldn't our officers in Western Germany be instructed to carry out the meeting?'

'Because, in the first place, if Western Germany expels all our diplomats tomorrow we don't want the flow of information about Western Germany to be reduced in any way. In the same way we receive secret information through Austria, through New Zealand, through Japan. If all our spies were to be expelled from Great Britain, it would be a catastrophe for the KGB. But not for us. We would continue to receive secrets about Britain through Austria and Switzerland, Nigeria, Cyprus, Honduras and all the other countries where there are officers of the Aquariuim.

'And because, in the second place, after receiving the missile parts we have obtained, the head of the GRU will summon all the diplomatic and illegal residents of the GRU in Western Germany and ask each of those eight generals the question: how is it that Golitsyn in Austria can get hold of such things in West Germany while you in West Germany can't? You are only fit for pick-up or support work, he will tell them – and the appropriate conclusions will be drawn. That's the only way, Suvorov, that competition is encouraged. And it is through bitter competition that we have successes. Follow me?'

'Absolutely, comrade general.'

'Want to ask anything?'

'No.'

'Yes you do, and I know what your question is! What's worrying you now is the fact that the First Deputy will receive a medal for obtaining the missile parts, but it's the young captain who is running the risk and won't get a damned thing for it. Is that what you're thinking?'

Suddenly he raised his eyes. That was his trick. He kept his eyes away until the very last moment. He had cruel eyes without a single spark in them. His

---

* Kosygin, Aleksei Nikolayevich (1904–1980): Soviet prime minister 1964–80.

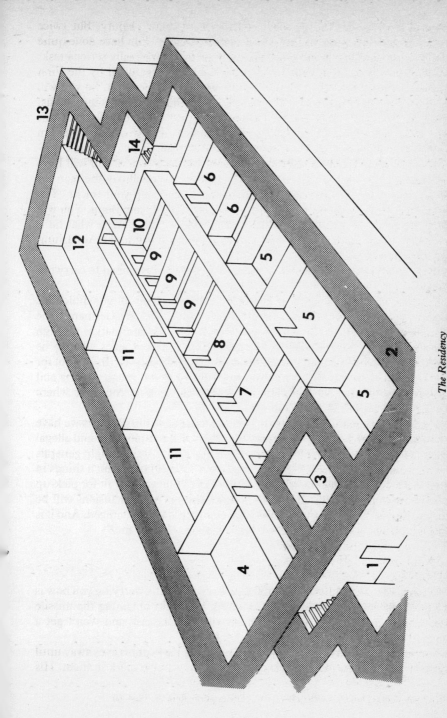

The Residency

1 Central door to underground rooms with access from interior of embassy; **2** Reinforced concrete wall; **3** Pass-check room; **4** Guard room for *Spetsnaz* officers; **5** TS service rooms for central government and military communications; **6** Interception service rooms for local surveillance; **7** Navigator's office; **8** Briefing room ('the cabin'); **9** First Deputy's and deputies' offices; **10** Darkroom; **11** Common rooms for officers; **12**? (use not known); **13** Supplementary access to residency, normally locked; **14** Access to bunker.

look was like a whiplash. He made use of it suddenly and swiftly. I wasn't ready for it. I withstood it, but realised that I would not be able to lie to him.

'That's what you were thinking?'

'Yes, comrade general, that is exactly what I was thinking.'

'Get on with your work. Try and find an agent to recruit. Then we shall be providing support for you. Then you will be working with your head alone. Someone else will be risking his skin for you.'

His cheeks twitched a little, but his look remained leaden.

'Agree the details with the First Deputy. Off you go.'

I clicked my heels, turned smartly about and marched out of the Navigator's room. There was nobody in the corridor and nobody in the big room. Nothing but the gentle hiss of the air-conditioner, sending an icy stream of air into the semi-darkness of the room. I turned up the blue-tinted light a little and strode across the room to the safes at the far end of the room, my footsteps muffled by the thick carpet. For a few seconds I stared dumbly at the bronze disc, then sighed and dialled the numbers of the combination. The heavy fire-proof door swung open smoothly and silently, revealing twelve small but massive doors. I unlocked my own door clearly marked with the number 41. Inside was my briefcase. I closed the safe, put the briefcase on my desk and pulled carefully at the two silky tapes, thus destroying the imprint of the two seals, first the one with the coat of arms, then my own personal seal. From the briefcase I took a smooth sheet of thick white paper bearing a neat column of signatures. With another deep sigh I wrote on it: 'Briefcase No. 41 opened July 13, 1243 hours local time.' Then I leaned back a little and signed my name.

After returning the piece of paper to the briefcase, I next took out a shiny green folder bearing the number 173-V-41. The first sheet of paper in the file was covered with writing, but the rest had nothing on them at all. I held one of them between two fingers and placed it in front of me. I put my personal stamp on the top left-hand corner and then inserted the sheet in the typewriter. In the top right-hand corner I quickly typed the words 'Top Secret' and then, a few lines lower down and right in the centre of the page, the single word: 'PLAN.'

Having done that I clutched my head in my hands and stared gloomily at the wall. Inwardly I was seething with rage. I hated the whole world, I hated myself, I hated the desk, the blue light, the brown carpets and the green folders.

Then, from out of the crowd of people and objects attracting my hatred, there emerged slowly one single face which I now hated even more than I hated the typewriter. It was the face of the Navigator, curse him.

It was easy to give orders. But this wasn't a matter of commanding a division. Go there, do this. I had never been in West Germany. Fancy sending me on such a job after only three weeks of practical work. And what if I wrecked the operation? To hell with it: I would fetch up in prison, but he would lose his officer and his agent.

If at that moment there had been someone around whose face I could have punched I would not have hesitated. But there was no one handy. I looked around the polished surface of the desk in search of something on which I could vent my wrath. My eyes fell upon a cutglass tumbler full of pens and pencils. I took it in the palm of my hand and after studying it closely suddenly hurled it with all my force at the wall. It broke into a thousand pieces.

'Going off your rocker?'

I turned round to find my First Deputy standing by the safes. Lost in my thoughts I had not noticed his arrival.

'I'm sorry,' I said without raising my head, still staring down at the floor.

'What's the matter?'

'The Navigator has ordered me to carry out the meeting with your agent. . . .'

'Well – go and do it. What's the problem?'

'Frankly speaking, I don't know where to begin or what to do.'

'Draw up a plan!' he burst out suddenly. 'Write down your plan, I'll sign it and off you go.'

'But what if events don't work out in accordance with my plan?'

'W-h-a-t?' He looked at me with wide-open eyes full of incomprehension and fear. He looked at his watch and at me, signed and then said with reproach in his voice:

'Pick up your papers. Let's go.'

The briefing room always reminded me of a cabin on a luxury liner. When the security systems were switched on the floor, ceiling and walls throbbed with a very slight, scarcely noticeable vibration, just like the deck of a cruiser surging through the waves at full speed. Apart from that, somewhere inside the thick walls behind dozens of layers of insulating material there were powerful jammers. The deafening noise they made was reduced to a thousandth of its volume by the sound insulation so that inside the room you could hear only a muffled roar like the sound of surf on a distant shore.

The inside of the briefing room is brilliant white, which was why some call it the 'operating theatre'. But I preferred to call it 'the cabin'. It had only one table and two chairs, all completely transparent, giving an impression of luxury and distinction.

The First Deputy pointed to an armchair and sat down opposite me.

'At the "elephants' graveyard" they didn't teach you anything that's much use. If you want to be successful, you must first forget everything the "elephants" taught you at the academy. Only those who can't work independently in practice land up as "elephants". Now listen to me. First of all you must draw up a plan. Put into your plan various alternative plans and what you would do in those circumstances. The more you write the better. Your plan is your insurance in case of failure. If the Aquarium enquires into the affair you will have something to defend yourself with: you can show that you made serious preparations for the operation. Remember: the more paper there is, the cleaner your backside. When you've written your plan start making preparations. The most important element is to prepare yourself psychologically. Relax as much as possible; have a good sauna. Get rid of all negative emotions and all your worries and doubts. You must set out on the job utterly convinced of success. If you don't have that self-confidence, better turn the job down now. Most important is to get yourself into the mood of an aggressive victor. Once you've relaxed sufficiently listen to something by Vysotsky* – his "Wolf Hunt", for example. You should have that running through your mind throughout the operation. Especially on your way back. It is after a successful meeting, on the way back from it, that we make the biggest mistakes. We are too pleased with ourselves and forget the feeling of the aggressive victor. Don't lose that feeling until you get inside our steel doors. I repeat: the most imporant thing is not the plan but the psychological adjustment. You will be a victor only so long as you feel yourself victorious. When you have written out your plan I will go through all the possible variations with you. That's very important, but remember that there are more important things. Remember that! Be a victor! Feel yourself victorious! Always. It's very difficult. But do it. I wish you success.'

I was standing in a clearing in a forest. I was in an old, clapped-our hired car. My papers said I was a Yugoslav citizen. Not a tourist. Unemployed. My goodness! It was only then that I realised how many of my brother Borzois had been involved in the operation so that I could be standing there in that forest. Somebody had got hold of the car from somewhere. And he had done it in such a way that no one would know that he was a Soviet citizen who was for some reason hiring an old worn-out car. Somebody else had helped me to cross the frontier. Not that that had been a very complicated affair. Somebody else had obtained for me the sort of papers that would not arouse suspicions if they were examined.

So there I was in the clearing. I was completely alone and ready to have my head or even other parts cut off if anyone had succeeded in following me. I had hidden a small box containing gold coins among some young fir trees nearby. If I were to be arrested during the meeting, gold coins would tell against me. I was supposed to be a poor tramp: where would I get hold of gold coins? The reason for the gold coins was that our 'friend' was a crafty one. He didn't want to be paid in dollars or in marks but in gold. If something went wrong he would be able to explain that they had been left him by his great-grandmother.

There was a long time to wait before the meeting. Huge pine trees rustled above my head. I asked myself who this 'friend' could be who was ready to hand over parts of the latest anti-tank missiles. A weapons designer? A general? The manager or owner of a missile plant? Who, apart from a general,

* Vladimir Vysotsky: Russian poet and singer, who died young in 1983.

128

an engineer or a factory owner, was in a position to get hold of parts of a missile? An ordinary worker might steal a single part, but each part was numbered. A guard might steal a whole missile, but they were all registered. How I wanted to be a big-time intelligence officer and recruit generals and engineers and obtain examples of the most up-to-date missiles.

What a hope! In my worn-out suit and ragged sweater it would be rather awkward to meet an American general. What sort of an idea would he get of the GRU? Not to mention my battered car. Shameful.

It was coming up to midday. Time for a meeting. I was holding a Japanese transistor in my hand. Some music was coming quietly over. I held the receiver with the aerial pointing to my left hand – that was the recognition sign. A watch with a dark green face was an additional means of recognition. Our friend would recognise me by those signs. He would have none. He would simply come up to me and ask the time and he would have to stop a little to my right. That would be sufficient for recognition purposes. It was already time. He was actually a minute late. Some general. Not much sense of discipline. At that moment a mud-bespattered tractor trundled out of the gate, driven by an old farmer smelling of manure. That was all I needed, for a tiresome old peasant like that to appear. I had arranged a secret meeting. For the last hour and a half there hadn't been a single living soul to be seen, and now this old boy had to turn up just at the wrong moment. In a drawling voice he asked me the time. The time? I shoved the watch under his nose. Go on, get on your way. But he didn't move. He stayed there, standing a little to my right. What do you want, old man? He pointed at his dirty old trailer. What on earth? Push off. I've a mind to. . . . He also lost his temper. And it was only his anger that suggested to me that he was the 'especially important' agent whom they knew about in the Politburo and in whose work Kosygin himself took an interest.

I had another look at him. Then at my watch. What doubt could there be? The general never existed. Whatever put it into my head that I would be meeting a general?

Then I looked at the trailer. There, in amongst a pile of wood and covered by a dirty tarpaulin, were the broken parts of an anti-tank missile. Stabilisers, broken and twisted, a tangled mass of wires and printed circuits stuck together into a ball. I quickly took it all and hid it in the wooden boxes. I shook his hand, and ran to the car. But the German was banging on the car with his crutch.

What did he want now, the old fool?

He then indicated by a sign recognised all over the world that what he wanted was money. I had quite forgotten. I ran to the little fir tree, took the box from beneath the moss and gave it to him. He opened it and looked in with obvious pleasure. He examined the coins. He smiled. Go on, try them with your teeth, you old devil. What the hell do you need so much for? You're soon for the grave. You can't take it with you, you know. He simply smiled at me. Then I remembered my training. You have to smile at secret agents. To smile in a friendly way, with warmth and humanity. So I did as I had been taught. I smiled. *Danke schön.* He bowed to me, and pressed the money to his heart. I set

129

off in my battered old car in one direction. He went off on his muddy tractor in another. A meeting had taken place.

I dodged around the side roads, getting as far as possible away from the meeting. And quite unexpectedly I hit upon the relatively simple mechanics of this particular contact. There in Bavaria, not far from Ravensburg, was the base of the First American armoured division. The division was already equipped with the 'Tow' anti-tank missile, and the anti-tank units of the division were already firing the missiles, using dummy warheads. When the missile hit the target it didn't explode but simply broke up. It was a genuine missile but without the warhead. That didn't matter. Our warheads were no worse than the Americans'. It was not the warheads we were after at the moment, but the guidance system, the control mechanism and the chemical composition of all the components. And that is what I now had with me in the car. The mud would be removed and the wires disentangled. Whatever pieces were missing we would get our hands on next time. Whether they weighed a hundred kilograms or two hundred. Whatever could be got into the car.

In the Soviet Army, when we fire '*Shmel*' or '*Falanga*' missiles, miles and miles of tarpaulin sheets are spread out and whole regiments are sent to gather up the smallest fragments that fall. But with the Americans it's the other way round. They don't pick up the twisted bodies of the missiles, the crumpled circuits or the bent stabilisers. Consequently there is no need to recruit generals or designers. It is sufficient to make contact with a shepherd who tends his sheep on the vast lands near the military base. A forester, a road-mender or a lumberman can be an 'agent of special importance' and for thirty pieces of silver will deliver to you just what comrade Kosygin needs.

I drove my battered car as fast as it would go along the wide German autobahns. Built by Hitler. Well built. I kept my foot down and wore a faint smile on my face. When I got back I would apologise to the Navigator and the First Deputy. I was not sure exactly why, but I would simply go up to them and say quietly: 'Comrade general, forgive me, please.' 'Comrade colonel, forgive me if you can.'

They are top-class intelligence officers. And that was exactly how to operate. Quietly and without attracting attention. I was ready to risk my career and my life for the success of our simple but brilliant operations. For the sake of our common aims. Forgive me.

It is generally reckoned that a young spy, operating under cover of being a diplomat, a journalist or a businessman, should not be active in the first months of his appointment abroad. He has to get used to his role, to learn his way round the city and country in which he is working and get to know the laws, the customs and the way of life. Young officers in many intelligence services do just that in their first months – they are simply preparing themselves for carrying out important operations. At such a time the local police devote little attention to them: they have enough problems with experienced spies.

But the GRU is a special kind of intelligence service. It is not like many other intelligence services. Since you are not being followed in the first months, you should take advantage of that fact, if nothing else.

In my first months in Vienna I placed a packet in a dead drop, for a whole week kept under observation a place where a signal from someone was expected, took over some boxes one night in a wood and delivered them to the embassy, and withdrew some officers from an operation when our radio monitoring group detected increased activity on the part of police radios in the area of our operations. Everything I did was back-up for someone else's operations, helping somebody, participation in operations the purpose of which I did not know. Out of forty intelligence-gathering officers in our residency, more than half were doing the same kind of work. It was known as 'covering the tail'. Those who did this work were spoken of with scorn as 'Borzois'. The Borzoi is a hunting dog which doesn't need a lot to eat but which can be coursed through fields and woods after foxes and hares. You can let it go after bigger animals but not on its own, only in packs. the Borzoi is made up of long legs and a small head.

Everything in the world is relative. I was an officer of the General Staff. By comparison with hundreds of thousands of other officers in the Soviet Army I was a member of the top élite. Within the General Staff I was an officer in the GRU, that is in the highest grade compared with thousands of other officers in the General Staff. In the GRU I was a foreign service officer, which meant that I could be sent to work abroad. Foreign service officers belonged to a much higher class than those GRU officers who were not allowed to travel abroad. Even among the foreign service officers I also belonged to a superior caste, because I was engaged in intelligence gathering, which was far more important than the work of maintaining security, dealing with technical questions or managing radio communications and monitoring. But within that upper élite I belonged only to the rank and file. Intelligence-gathering officers are divided into two classes: 'Borzois' and 'Vikings'. The 'Borzois' are the oppressed, under-privileged majority in the upper class of intelligence officers. Each one of us worked under the total control of one of the Navigator's deputies and practically never came face to face with the Navigator himself. We went hunting for secrets, or rather for people in possession of secrets. That was our main work. But apart from that we were used mercilessly to provide protection and support for secret operations at the true significance of which we could only guess.

Above the Borzois are the 'Vikings', who in folk-myth tradition were ferocious, perfidious, quarrelsome, cheerful and daring men. The Vikings work under the personal control of the Navigator, with due respect for his deputies but operating mostly on their own. The most successful Vikings become deputies to the Resident. They no longer work without support but with a group of Borzois at their complete disposal.

131

The Resident's First Deputy kept an eye on everybody. He was himself a very active and successful intelligence-gathering officer, but in addition to his work of intelligence-gathering and managing his own group of Borzois he was in charge of the radio monitoring group, he was responsible for the security and safety of the residency and for the work of all the officers, including the purely technical men. The only people not answerable to him were the cipher clerks. They were handled by the Navigator personally. The Navigator was the resident, the commanding officer, everybody's father; he was responsible for everything. He had practically unlimited authority. He could, for example, on his own authority execute any of his subordinate officers, including his own First Deputy, in the event of a threat to the security of the residency in which it was impossible to arrange for the evacuation of the guilty officer. Apart from residents, only the Supreme Court has the right to order the execution of GRU officers, and then only if it is the wish of the Central Committee. So that in certain matters our Navigator had more powers than the Supreme Court because he did not need to seek anyone's advice and he did not depend on votes or support from the press. He took his decisions independently and had sufficient power to put them into effect regardless of the consequences. Our Navigator was answerable to the head of the 5th department of the 1st Directorate of the GRU. For a number of matters he was answerable only to the head of the GRU himself. He even had the right, in the event of a disagreement between him and the top brass of the GRU in very exceptional circumstances, to appeal to the Central Committee.

The vast powers of the GRU resident are counterbalanced only by the existence of an equally powerful, independent and hostile residency of the KGB. Neither resident is subordinate to the ambassador. The ambassador's function is simply to camouflage the existence of two groups of shock troops within the Soviet colony. In public, of course, both residents treat the ambassador with a certain deference because both residents are high-ranking diplomats and a failure to treat the ambassador with respect would make them stand out from the others. But that public respect is the beginning and end of their dependence on the ambassador. Every residency has its own area inside the embassy, protected against others like an impenetrable fortress.

The door into our residency was green. It was a very low door, and you had to stoop to get through it. Many years previously some joker had brought from Russia a metal sign taken from an electric power pylon. It had a skull and crossbones on it and written underneath: 'Keep out! Mortal Danger!' The sign had been welded to our door and became our common talisman, protected as strictly as the secrets inside.

'Do you realise that in the last war there were two categories of pilots in our air force? Some, the minority, had dozens of enemy planes to their credit, while the others, the majority, had practically none. The first lot had their chests covered in medals, while the others had just a couple. The majority of the first lot survived the war, while the others perished by the thousands and tens of thousands. The statistics of war make very painful reading. The majority spent no more than nine hours in the air before they met their end. Fighter pilots were shot down on average on their fifth sortie. With the first category the opposite happened: they carried out hundreds of sorties and each of them spent thousands of hours in the air. . . .'

The speaker was Major-general of the Air Force Kuchumov, a Hero of the Soviet Union, a wartime ace, and one of the most determined officers in Soviet military intelligence after the war. On orders from the head of the GRU, he was carrying out an inspection of the GRU's posts abroad operating under legal cover. He visited some countries as a member of a delegation dealing with arms control or something similar; in others he turned up as a member of a group of war veterans. But he certainly didn't regard himself as a veteran; he was an active soldier on the secret front. Even while he was inspecting us I swear he carried out dazzlingly brilliant secret operations with lightning speed. We were alone together in the 'cabin'. He summoned us to him one by one. As he talked with us he was, of course, checking up on our chief, but at the same time he was helping him.

'In between those two categories of wartime pilots there was absolutely nothing, an abyss. There was no link between them, no middle class. Either an ace, a hero, a general, or a lieutenant shot down on his first sortie. Nothing in between. And I'll tell you how this came about. All the pilots received the same training and passed through the fighting units at practically the same level. In the first battle the commanding officer would divide them into those who were 'active' and those who were 'passive'. A pilot who was keen to get into a fight, who didn't fly off into the clouds away from the enemy and who wasn't scared to go into a head-on attack – pilots like that were immediately made leaders and the rest were ordered to cover the active ones. Sometimes the separation of the more active ones took place in the very first air battle. All the commanders of flights, squadrons, regiments, divisions, corps and armies threw all they had into helping the active ones in battle, to protect them and take care of them in the most furious dogfights. And the more successful a pilot was the more they did to protect him in battle and to help him. I saw Pokryshkin* in battle when he had more than fifty German aircraft to his credit. Stalin personally issued an order that he was to be backed up in battle by two squadrons. When he went hunting for enemy planes he would have his no. 2 on his tail and two squadrons behind him, one a little higher and the other a little lower. Today he's got three gold stars on his chest and a diamond star hanging from his neck and he's an air marshal. But don't imagine that it all happened automatically. By no means. It was simply that in his first battle he showed himself to be an active fighter and they began to protect him. The more daring and ability he displayed, the more they helped him and valued him. If that hadn't happened he would have been

* Pokryshkin, Aleksandr (b.1913): Russian flying 'ace' of the Second World War.

put among the passive pilots from the very beginning and given the thankless task of protecting somebody else's tail in battle. As a junior lieutenant. And according to the statistics he would have been shot down on his fifth sortie, if not sooner. Statistics smile at some and pull faces at others.

'I am telling you this because our intelligence work scarcely differs in any way from air battles. Soviet military intelligence trains thousands of officers and throws them into battle. In real life they are quickly divided into active and passive officers. Some attain glorious heights, while others fade out on their first foreign assignment. I have been going through your papers and I like the look of you. But you are now working as a back-up for other people. That support work is difficult, dangerous and thankless. Someone else gets a medal while you are risking your whole career carrying out the dirtiest and most difficult jobs. Remember: nobody will take you off that work. Any commander of our organisation abroad who receives a fresh group of young officers uses them on back-up operations and they quickly fade out. They get arrested and are thrown out of the country and they spend the rest of their lives in the GRU's information service or working in one of our 'fraternal' countries. But if you show yourself to be really keen and start looking for people to recruit, the commander will soon take you off back-up work and, on the contrary, someone else will be covering your tail and taking risks to promote your success. That's the way to look at it. A few years ago the GRU chief in Paris ordered an assistant military attaché to be sacrificed to ensure the success of some other officers. You can be sure that the commander sacrificed a passive officer. He would never give such a thankless task to an active and successful one, and in that we would support him. The men in charge of the GRU strive to produce active, daring and successful aces. Never fear – there will always be lots of passive, gutless and inert men to protect such people. Don't imagine that I'm telling you all this because I think you are better than the others. Not at all. I tell this to all the young people. That's my job – to raise your fighting spirit and your effectiveness in battle. The trouble is that it doesn't sink in to many. We have a lot of good lads who will yet never become leaders, who will cover other people's tails and come to an inglorious end. I wish you success and a following wind. Everything is in your hands: make an effort and you will have two squadrons covering your tail.'

'In the name of the Union of Soviet Socialist Republics the Minister of Foreign Affairs of the USSR requests the governments of friendly states and their military and civil services to allow the diplomatic mail of the USSR to pass freely without it being subjected to any interference or customs examination, in accordance with the Vienna Convention of 1815. Minister of Foreign Affairs of the USSR, A. Gromyko.'

The policeman read this text printed on crisp parchment-like paper with elaborate patterns and coats of arms. If there was anything he couldn't understand the same text was there in French and English. It was all there in print, short and clear: diplomatic mail of the USSR. The policeman ground his teeth and eyed the huge truck. It was rather unusual.

Soviet diplomatic mail passes through Vienna in a great flood, a veritable Niagara Falls. It is one of the main routes for the diplomatic bags. Once a week Soviet couriers stop off in Vienna on their way to Berne, Geneva and Rome. Later they return. On the outward journey they leave the 'bags' – actually large containers—at the Soviet embassies. And on the way back they pick up full containers and take them to Moscow. They would usually bring from Moscow between five and ten containers, each weighing about fifty kilograms. On their way back they might take as many as thirty or forty containers, sometimes even a hundred. For losing a container a courier can be sentenced to death. While it is in an embassy the ambassador is responsible for it, under the same terms. It is his duty to organise the reception and despatch of the diplomatic mail, so it fell to the other Borzois and myself to meet it and see it off. As long as the couriers are in the country with their containers, they are always accompanied by a Soviet diplomat who is ready if necessary to remind people that, in the event of anybody trying to seize the containers, the Soviet Union can resort to sanctions, including the use of military force. The use of weapons to protect the containers is provided for in the convention, so the couriers are powerful men and well armed.

The diplomatic couriers handle a lot of goods. A tremendous lot. Everything that we collect they transport in the containers: bullets and shells, optical and electronic equipment, pieces of armour and parts of missiles, and documents, documents and ever more documents. All kinds of documents: military plans, technical specifications, designs for new weapons, some that will one day be manufactured and some that will never be made. The couriers transport what the West has accepted and what the West has rejected. We examine it and we think about it. Perhaps we shall accept what the West has turned down, and perhaps we shall develop an antidote against something the West is planning to manufacture. All the information goes in green boxes. The police grind their teeth. Such a lot of boxes. Top Secret! In the name of the Union of Soviet Socialist Republics! In accordance with the Vienna Convention of 1815! Off they go, the couriers with their containers, while the police grind their teeth.

But on that day they were especially worried. It was a very unusual case. The couriers didn't have fifty-kilo containers, but one huge one weighing five tons! In the name of the Union of Soviet Socialist Republics! All the top police officers were gathered. They were cursing quietly and looking askance at our container. I was accompanying the container and I had already produced all the documents for them. And I had the formula ready: 'Detention of the diplomatic mail of the USSR or any attempt to seize or examine it may result in. . . .'

The container had been delivered to Vienna on a special wagon and seen at the customs to be empty. But now it was loaded up and sealed with huge red seals: 'Diplomatic Mail of the USSR. Despatcher – Soviet Embassy, Vienna.'

Now our couriers were in charge of the container. And they were armed. Now there was a Soviet diplomat present. He had a low diplomatic rank. That was the way it was always done. He had immunity as representative of the USSR. He was not to be touched. An attack on a diplomat was an insult to the state which he represented. An insult to a diplomat could be interpreted as an attack on the state itself. The police ground their teeth.

'May we see whether the container is correctly attached to the truck?'

'You have the right to do that,' I agreed. But they did not have the right to touch our container with their hands. Just let them try. I was in direct contact with our Consul-general in Vienna, and he had a direct line to the Foreign Ministry in Moscow. Let them have a look.

The police officers walked around the container. How they longed to know what was inside. But you are out of luck, gentlemen. It's already beyond your grasp.

When the container was transported out of the embassy all our neighbours in the KGB cursed us enviously, quite sure that this time the GRU had managed to get hold of a piece of a nuclear reactor. The local police probably thought the same. One of them was moving close to the container, probably with a radiation meter in his pocket, trying to find out if we were taking an atomic bomb. I couldn't stop the policeman doing that. He was not touching the container, just walking along it. Let him walk. It was his right. But his meter wasn't clicking. There was no atom bomb inside and no piece of reactor. Another policeman went close to the container. It was a hot day but he was in a rain coat, probably to conceal some electronic apparatus. He's probably trying to make out whether there's metal inside or not. Perhaps we've stolen the engine from a new tank? But they can't find out anything with their apparatus. They had dogs as well, apparently for our safety. But the dogs were sniffing around too. They wouldn't have any luck either.

Our couriers eyed me with respect. They could tell that I was directly concerned with the affair. But they did not have the right to know what is in the container, and they never would know. They knew that it was not the KGB which had loaded the container but the GRU. The diplomatic couriers have a special nose for that. They have been on the job for years. They know who will take over the baggage and from that they know who is despatching it, KGB or GRU. In this case they had only to see the container across the frontier, and in Bratislava a Soviet military convoy would meet it and transport it to its destination.

What a shock both the diplomatic couriers and the policeman would have had if they had learnt that, once it reached Bratislava, the container was to be transported to the nearest Soviet military airfield, and that there the whole of the contents would be burnt in a furnace. But that was what was going to happen.

For years our Navigator had been asking the ambassador to let him have the embassy attic. But the ambassador had refused. No, he said; and that was that. But our Navigator's department kept growing. Every year the number of grey boxes with little lamps and aerials increased. the Navigator needed the attic. He asked the ambassador again, he begged him. The space wasn't being used and he had nowhere to instal his electronic monitoring equipment. At last the ambassador gave in. Take it, he said. But it's the Augean stables up there. If you can clean it up it's yours. Only mind you don't get me into trouble. And you've got to clean the place out with your own people. 'Is there a lot of rubbish up there?' asked the Navigator. 'Everything there is yours,' the ambassador replied: 'I don't know how to clear it out. If I'd known I'd have done it long ago. We inherited a lot of stuff from our predecessors.' They shook hands on it. The ambassador gave the Navigator the key and asked him once again not to let other people know what was lying in the attic. The Navigator opened up the place, removing the ambassador's personal seal, switched on a torch and was struck dumb. The attic was chock full of books. Beautiful books – on rice paper and fine bindings. The books had various titles, but only one author: Nikita Sergeyevich Khrushchev.*

Our Navigator quickly realised what had happened. Many years previously the Party had wanted the whole world to hear its voice. So the speeches of the most learned man in the Party had been printed on the best paper, illustrated with good pictures and distributed round the world. Embassies had given copies away free to all comers and had sent them to all the libraries. And the Party had paid careful attention to the matter of which ambassador distributed the books well and which did not. There developed a competition between the ambassadors: who had given most books away free. Their reports came in: I have distributed a hundred thousand! But I have sent out two hundred thousand! I've done three hundred! All right, they said in Moscow, if it's so easy to distribute them, and since the peoples of the world are so interested in the works of our dear leader, here are another hundred thousand. Distribute them – but bear in mind that the ambassador in Paris is doing better than you. Interest in Stockholm is exceptional! In Canada people are queuing up to get their hands on copies! How they managed to get rid of the books in Paris and Ottawa I don't know, but in Vienna they were found many years later – in the attic. The Navigator approached the ambassador:

'We must throw them on the rubbish dump,' he said.

'For goodness' sake,' the ambassador beseeched him. 'The western press would get to know; they would say that we had tricked the former leader of our party and that we may well be deceiving our present leader. Supposing an article like that appeared?'

'So let's burn them,' the Navigator suggested. But he stopped short at once, realising that it was impossible to burn such a pile of books. Everybody knew that, if suddenly several tons of paper began to be burnt in an embassy, it was a very bad sign, traditionally a prelude to war. There would be panic in the fine city of Vienna, and who would have to answer for it? Burning them bit by bit was also impossible, because it would take more than a year to do it.

* Khrushchëv, Nikita (1894–1971): First Secretary, CPSU, 1953–1964.

137

The Navigator swore, then went to send a coded message to the Aquarium: We are getting the attic for our equipment if we can get the ambassador out of this scrape without too much fuss. The Aquarium agreed, and sent the container and the appropriate documents.

For two nights we, the Borzois, carted books down from the attic to the container. You only had to touch them to sneeze for hours. The attic was nothing but dust and heat. The stairs were steep. Just going up and down set your heart thumping, and the sweat running. How we cursed our dear Nikita Sergeyevich. . . .

We had to bring the container close up to the doors of the embassy, cover the gap with tarpaulin, and station a guard. Our neighbours in the KGB eyed the guard and the huge container and whistled with envy.

The police officers looked again at the container, checked the papers once more, shrugged their shoulders and waved us on. They could do nothing. It was clear to the police that Soviet military intelligence had got their hands on something very important, and they couldn't understand how we had managed to get the thing into the embassy. But since we had done it there was nothing they could do. And off the container went.

Chapter 9

The winds of change were blowing through the GRU and new people were coming to the top. But the names of the new men at the head of many of the most important departments and directorates meant nothing to me. There were some generals and admirals among them. But the name of the new head of the 5th directorate was only too well known to me. Kravtsov. Lieutenant-general. Five years previously, when I had entered the Academy, he had just received his first general's star. Now he had two, and would probably have three very soon. All his predecessors in that job had been colonel-generals. The 5th directorate! The whole *Spetsnaz* of the Soviet Army under the control of that wiry little fellow. He had under him the *Spetsnaz* troops and agent networks of sixteen military districts, four groups of forces, four fleets, forty-one armies and twelve flotillas. And he was still only forty-three. Much success to you, comrade general.

Meanwhile I was having no success. I knew I had to find ways of getting at secrets, but I just didn't have enough time of my own. Day and night, without any days off or holidays, I was working on agent support. Not a week went by without my adding another thousand kilometres on the speedometer. Sometimes the kilometres were added at a catastrophic rate, so that Seryozha Nestorovich, our mechanic, had to turn the kilometrometer back on the First Deputy's instructions to get rid of a few thousands. He had a special little tool for the job: a box and a long metal wire in a tube.

I was not the only one whose kilometrometer he turned back. There were a lot of us Borzois in the residency, and every one of them was rushing around Europe like Henry Kissinger.

A kilometrometer is a spy's face. And we do not have the right to show our true faces. So Seryozha just kept turning.

The Navigator rubbed his hands.

'Come along in and sit yourselves down. Are we all here?'

The First Deputy glanced round at us and counted heads. Then, with a smile at the Navigator, he said;

'All here, comrade general, with the exception of the cipher clerks, a radio communications group and a radio-monitoring group.'

The Navigator walked about the room looking at the floor. Then he raised his head and smiled happily. I had never seen him looking so cheerful.

'Thanks to the efforts of Twenty-nine our residency has succeeded in obtaining information about the security arrangements at the forthcoming "Telecom 75" exhibition in Geneva. The GRU in the diplomatic missions in Marseilles, Tokyo, Amsterdam and Delhi managed to obtain similar information. But our information was the most complete and was obtained sooner than the others. For that reason the head of the GRU' – and here he waited a moment so as to give the end of his sentence more weight – 'so the head of the GRU has entrusted us with the task of carrying out a large-scale recruitment at the exhibition.'

We howled with delight. We shook hands with Twenty-nine, whose name was Kolya Butenko. He was a captain, like me. He had arrived in Vienna after me but had already managed to recruit two new agents. He was a Viking.

'Twenty-nine.'

'Yes, comrade general.'

'We are grateful to you.'

'I serve the Soviet Union!'

'And now listen. We'll do the celebrating after the exhibition. You know how we carry out a large-scale recruiting effort – you are not children. The whole of the *residency* will go to the exhibition, and we shall all work purely on information-gathering. The GRU's residency in Geneva under Major-general Zvezdin, and its residency in Berne under Major-general Larin, will be responsible for back-up. If for any reason we have to get out to France, the GRU residencies in Marseilles and Paris will be ready to help. The general command of the operation is in my hands. During the operation I shall have under me temporarily the head of the third department of the 9th directorate of the GRU Information Service, Major-general Feklenko. He will be arriving here at the head of a powerful delegation. Nikolai Nikolayevich. . . .'

'Here, comrade general.' The deputy for information stood up.

'The reception of the delegation, its accommodation and transport are your responsibility.'

'Of course, comrade general.'

'In the course of this large-scale recruitment drive we shall be employing the usual tactics. If anyone does anything stupid I shall sacrifice him in the interests of the success of the whole operation. My First Deputy' – and the First Deputy stood up – 'will acquaint each of you with those members of the delegation with whom you will be working. I wish you all success.'

The express from Moscow arrived in Vienna at 5.58 in the evening. The green coaches slid slowly past us with a slight grinding of brakes. Greetings, comrades! Welcome to hospitable Austria! No need to shout for porters: there were plenty of them. They knew that an official Soviet delegation was not mean when it came to tipping.

It was a huge delegation. Officers of the GRU Information Service, officers from the Military-Industrial Committee of the Soviet government, experts from the armaments industry, and weapons designers. Of course, you wouldn't find any of that in their passports. To judge from their passports they were from the Academy of Science, from the Ministry for Foreign Trade and from some non-existent institutes. But who takes any notice of what is in our passports? Do you think it says in my passport that I am a GRU intelligence officer?

The most amazing things take place on our funny little planet. But for some reason they amazed only me and no one else. Nobody showed any interest in the huge Soviet delegation. Nobody asked any questions. Yet there were many things that were not clear. Why, for example, did the Soviet delegation not travel straight to Geneva; why did it spend three days in Vienna? Why did the delegation arrive in Vienna in a single monolithic formation, like a battalion, and then in Vienna suddenly break up and disintegrate? Why did the delegates set off for Geneva by various means and routes, some by train, some by bus and some by air? How very strange, to travel to Vienna slowly by train and to finish the journey by air. Why were the Soviet diplomats accompanied at the exhibition by Soviet United Nations officials from Vienna and not by Soviet UN officials in Geneva? There were lots of questions in the air. But nobody was interested. Nobody was seeking answers to those questions. Oh, well, all the better for us.

In the room used for giving confidential instructions, sitting in transparent chairs in which it is impossible to conceal any apparatus, were two strangers. The First Deputy introduced me:

'This is Viktor.'

I greeted each of them quietly.

'This, Viktor, is Nikolai Sergeyevich, an engineer colonel from scientific research institute No. 107.'

'How do you do, comrade colonel.'

'And this is Konstantin Andreyevich, an engineer colonel from the First department of the 9th directorate of the GRU Information Service.'

'How do you do, comrade colonel.'

I shook them both by the hand.

'What interests me,' said Nikolai Sergeyevich, taking the bull by the horns, 'are the arrangements for receiving the reflected laser beam which is used to light up moving targets when firing from concealed positions. . . .'

'You do realise that my knowledge of such matters is very superficial.'

'Of course we understand that. That is why we're here. Your business is to recruit; our business is to carry out the technical supervision. Nikolai Sergeyevich opened his briefcase: 'According to information obtained by the Information Service of the GRU, the greatest success in this field has been achieved by the firm of Hughes in the USA.'

141

'I cannot work against them at the exhibition.'

Both men looked at the First Deputy with incredulity. But he backed me up: 'That's our rule. At the big firms' stands at these exhibitions, the firm's security officers are always on duty. So we operate only against the smaller firms, where there's usually no more than one man on the stand. As a rule, he is the owner of the firm. These are the people we can do something with.'

'It's a pity.'

'You can't do anything about it. Our style of work has to conform to the circumstances. . . .'

'All right. Here are some prospectuses and articles about smaller firms which are dealing with this problem. Here is a plan of where they are situated at the show. Here is a picture of what we need. The Military-Industrial Committee is ready to pay 120,000 dollars for that black box, for example, because it would take us many years and cost us millions to develop a similar system. It's cheaper to copy.'

'Have you brought money with you?'

'Yes.'

'May I look at it? I need to get used to it.'

Konstantin Andreyevich placed a brand new rectangular briefcase on the transparent table and opened it. Inside it was crammed full of newspaper cuttings, business prospectuses and some other papers. At the entrance and exit to the exhibition there would be a police check, which this collection of papers was intended to deceive. The man turned a little catch and revealed a false bottom to the case.

What a wonderful sight! The sight of the green printed banknotes entranced me. I was struck dumb, like the Count of Monte Cristo looking at his treasure. How much human effort and what luxury was concentrated in those carefully sorted packets of crisp green notes. I am indifferent to money— or, rather, practically indifferent. But what I saw in that little briefcase made me almost bite my lips.

'This is a demonstration briefcase,' Konstantin Andreyevich explained. 'The money there is genuine, but there's not as much as there appears to be. We can't take a lot of money with us into the exhibition. For that reason the secret compartment is made to give the impression that there are several hundred thousand dollars there. It's not really at all deep. We don't pay anyone while we're at the exhibition. We just show them the money. For that purpose it's better to use large, new notes. We make the payment a long way from the exhibition and then use smaller and older notes. Like these. . . .'

He opened an old worn suitcase which was stuffed to the top with bundles of banknotes. I touched them and picked up a dozen bundles. I smelt them and put them back. The others all laughed at me. Why? I wondered crossly.

'Don't take offence, Viktor.' The First Deputy explained: 'There is a great deal more money in the second case than in the first one, but you weren't at all excited by it, whereas you were simply struck dumb by the first one. It was so striking that we couldn't help laughing. We're just delighted that the demonstration briefcase has such an effect, even on you.'

An exhibition – and especially a major international trade show – is a battlefield for the GRU. It is also a field from which the GRU can gather a rich harvest. In the last half-century there has not been a single exhibition on our little planet which the GRU has not attended.

An exhibition is a place where real specialists gather together. It is a club for fanatics. And a fanatic needs an audience. He needs someone who will listen to his wild talk and quietly nod his head. That's why exhibitions are organised. Anyone who is prepared to listen to a real fanatic and agree with what he says is his friend, and the fanatic will trust him. Believe me, fanatic. My work is such that I need to be trusted. I am like a friendly little spider. Trust me, and you'll never get out of my clutches.

Every exhibition attracts the GRU's interest, whether it be an exhibition of military electronics, of tanks, of cats or agricultural machinery or flowers. One of the most successful cases of recruitment by the GRU was carried out at an exhibition of Chinese goldfish. Who goes to these exhibitions? People with a lot of money, who are connected with the world of finance, of big business and big politics. Exhibitions are attended by counts and marquises, ministers and their secretaries. All sorts of people go to exhibitions. Of course you have to know how to select.

An exhibition is a place where it is very easy to make contacts, where you can speak to anyone you like without bothering about their rank or position. But the GRU never goes to work on the first day of an exhibition. The first day is the opening – speeches, toasts, crowds, officials and an over-anxious police guard. But the exhibition is ours from the second day. None the less, the opening day of an exhibition is important for each one of us, like the day before an attack. That day officers spend exhausting hours scanning the battlefield through their binoculars: a ravine to avoid, a group to be protected by a smoke-screen, a scarcely visible bog where the men might sink in, and over there space for a barrage of a dozen batteries to head off the counter-attack.

An enormous force of intelligence officers, analysts and support officers was now gathered in that pleasant city. But we spent the day strolling round the boulevards and along the lakeside, through the narrow lanes and broad avenues. Every one of us was going over his particular battlefield again and again, lest he might be overtaken on his flank or attacked from behind.

I don't know why, but the next day's recruitment drive did not excite me for the time being. My heart did not beat any faster. Not because I was a great spy, going fearlessly into a risky operation. It was probably simply because I was taken up with something else. It was not the forthcoming recruitment drive that took my attention, but the great city of Geneva. It was as though some kind magician had cast me back to the kingdom of the past where all epochs

143

came together on one street. That street – the rue de Lausanne – was the street of the GRU. At one time it had been the address of several GRU residencies at once, none of which had even suspected the existence of the others. The GRU had known devastating success on the rue de Lausanne. The failures had been devastating too.

It was a bright autumnal day, and very warm. There were already leaves rustling underfoot. Foreign workers, Spanish or Italian, clad in orange overalls, were busy clearing up the first golden carpet of autumn from the paths in the park. Why do you do it? I thought to myself. Surely it's nicer to walk on carpets of crimson and golden-brown leaves? Are you really not moved by the whispers and crackling of autumn? Is grey asphalt really better? The street cleaners obviously had no poetry in them. So the little greedy street-cleaning machine sucked up the beauties of nature. Had they been a little more poetic they would have stopped work and enjoyed themselves. So many colours, such magnificence! Such richness! Man can never do a better job than nature. Just opposite the entrance to the Mon Repos park was a school, as beautiful as a castle. With a clock on the tower. A beautiful sight. But it was so grey.

Beneath the clock on the school tower was the date: 1907. That meant that Lenin had also admired that school. But perhaps the bourgeois style did not please him? In any case he lived here, on the rue de Lausanne, where later the GRU residency was established and where now there were huge blocks of flats for diplomats. I would swear that the GRU's undercover residency was still at work there, no less productive than before. It was a good spot. Vladimir Ilich knew where to live and which parks to stroll in. He loved the workers and hated the bourgeoisie. That was why he never lived in the working-class quarters of Manchester and Liverpool. But he lived in Geneva in the enemy camp, in the bourgeois districts. He probably wanted to study more profoundly the psychology and manners of the bourgeoisie, so as to be able to destroy them and make everybody free and happy.

In those days there were terrorists strolling around the Mon Repos park and down the rue de Lausanne, dreaming of killing the Russian Tsar – Gotz, Azeff, Brilliant and Minor. When they met Lenin they probably bowed to him, removing their bowler hats and pressing their hands to their starched shirt-fronts. Or perhaps they did not acknowledge each other as a matter of principle. In any case, when Lenin took power he shot all the terrorists who fell into his hands and the Tsar as well—whom the terrorists had not managed to kill after all.

I had just one day, the last day before the battle, before my first recruitment of an agent abroad. I had to get to know the battlefield like the palm of my hand, as a battalion commander knows a battlefield full of craters over which his men will attack the next day. But I was not hurrying. I was fascinated by the old park which had seen so much. It was on a bench there in October 1941 that a conference of illegal residents of the GRU in Europe had taken place. As long as the Soviet Union was not taking part in the war in Europe, the Gestapo did not interfere with its network of agents, although they had some information about it. But on the first day of war the network began to fall apart, and large-scale arrests began. Efforts to localise the collapse proved ineffective. The number of arrests increased, by a sort of chain reaction, like the rings from a stone dropped in a pond. Communications broke down, meeting places proved unreliable. Everybody was under suspicion. Every resident suspected all his officers and agents, and each one of them suspected all the others. Every resident could feel the Gestapo breathing down his neck and the smell of warm blood in the torture chambers.

It was in those circumstances that they gathered in Geneva in 1941, in the Mon Repos park, although they were forbidden to do any such thing. No one of them had the right to know anything about what other residencies of the GRU were doing. Such a gathering was, in Moscow's eyes, a crime, the punishment for which, if Moscow got to know about it, was death. Yet they held their meeting.

They did it on their own initiative. I've no idea how they got in touch with each other: probably by instinct, as a prostitute can identify another member of her profession among thousands of women in a huge crowd. Or as one thief can recognise another. Or as a man who has served a prison sentence can recognise, by hardly visible signs, another man who has been in prison.

So they had their meeting. They sat there, probably looking rather grim, under that chestnut tree. Hard-bitten spies. The very élite of the spy network – the illegal residents. Navigators and commanders. They sat there and probably spent more time in silence than in talking. Perhaps their silence was a way of saying goodbye to life, moral preparation for the tortures ahead and mutual support for each other.

An outsider seeing that group could hardly have thought that they were the leaders of an all-powerful organisation which had more than once taken Europe by the throat in its invisible grip of iron. Looking at those men, no one could have believed that each one of them had exclusive control of a secret organisation capable of penetrating into the highest realms of political power and of shaking the very foundations of states, removing ministers and even whole governments, making European capitals reverberate with the tramp of millions of demonstrators. Who would have thought that those men sitting in the Mon Repos park were in possession of practically unlimited wealth? They sat there in worn-out overcoats, ragged jackets and down-at-heel shoes. A real spy must never attract attention to himself. He should be unnoticed, like the asphalt he walks on. Just grey, at least on the outside.

They were wolves at bay. They had no way out. For what they were doing they would pay the supreme penalty in the Soviet Union; it was known as 'vertical contact with the agent network'. And the Gestapo was hot on their heels.

They sat there for a long time, arguing about something. Then they took some decisions. They changed their tactics. They changed their communications systems, their ways of localising breakdowns, and the arrangements for security and recruitment. Each one acted on his own initiative without

145

reporting to the GRU about their secret agreement. In any case at that time they had no contact with Moscow. But they all survived the war, and they all had remarkable success. Jointly in 1956 they informed the leaders of the GRU of their illegal conference in 1941. They all became heroes. Victors are never punished.

But has anybody abroad ever weighed the contribution which those men made to the victory? Did anyone take them into account when they were planning the lightning rout of the Red Army? From the very day that Lenin's régime was established, people had been forecasting its speedy and inevitable collapse. People will always make forecasts, forgetting earlier, now vanished prophecies. Those men in the worn-out jackets sitting on the bench in the Mon Repos park should not be forgotten.

The 'Ascot', the 'Epsom', the '*Amat*', the 'Derby' are hotels in Geneva. They are also the GRU's fortresses. In fact any hotel in Geneva in the rectangle bounded by the Mon Repos park, the rue de Lausanne, the shore of the lake and the rue de Mont Blanc has for many years been the GRU's happy hunting-ground. From those hotels, early in the morning, groups of Soviet officers would stream across to the left shore. Their destination was the Palais des Expositions, a gigantic building with a huge central hall linked with smaller ones which together formed a vast expanse of concrete floor beneath a single roof. The concrete was covered with carpets, the space was divided up by screens, and there was room for everyone to display his wares.

It was upon that building that groups of GRU officers of all kinds were now descending. If every one of our Vikings and Borzois and each of our cars had been picked out by a little moving light it would have made a marvellous sight. Like swarms of rats slowly encircling a lion about to be eaten. Like innumerable Soviet divisions advancing to storm the embattled Reichstag.

So many cars with diplomatic number plates gathered in one place! And so many less noticeable grey Fords *without* diplomatic plates. So many buses and estate cars. The Consul-general from Berne and the Consul in Geneva had parked their black Mercedes at different ends of the Plaine de Plainpalais. They were not involved in the intelligence-gathering; they were part of the rear support. If one of us got arrested they were there to intervene, to protest, to threaten a worsening of good-neighbourly relations or sanctions by Moscow, and to keep the police at bay. The Soviet ambassador to Switzerland, Gerasimov, and the Soviet ambassadress to the United Nations in Geneva, Mironova, were also at their posts, ready for action. They were also part of the support force. They didn't know what was going on, but they had received coded instructions from the Central Committee to be ready at any moment to threaten, intimidate, exert pressure and keep the authorities away. The diplomatic couriers were also at the ready. There might be an urgent package for Moscow. Aeroflot was also ready for action, ready to fly home immediately anyone who had been arrested the minute he was released, so that there would be less fuss, and so as not to give the journalists anything to work on. To prevent it blowing up into a major scandal, to make sure everything stayed quiet and peaceful.

There were many entrances, with a queue at each. That was a good thing: we were less noticeable in a crowd. Seven francs to enter. Three tickets, please. Twenty-one francs. Excellent. A good number. Everyone in intelligence was as superstitious as an old maid. There was only one briefcase in our group, for demonstration purposes. Check it if you wish – just papers, nothing more. Put it through the X-ray machine or though the magnetic gate: nothing but paper.

My colleagues were in a hurry to reach their stands. To hell with them! I was my own boss now. I had got to recruit somebody and work with him, so I didn't want to rush. We talked with one old chap and drank coffee with him. We stopped in other places, sitting down, chatting with representatives, nodding our heads, admiring the wares.

The bigger firms had the more important goods to display. We stopped off at them too, looked enviously at the grey boxes and moved on. A lot of people had gathered round the big stands. The firms' experts were providing explanations, and the firms' security men were obviously in attendance. On we went, until we reached a stand on which a man of medium height was sitting alone near some grey boxes and looking very bored. He was on his own – his was obviously a small firm. He was probably the owner or the manager of the firm, and he was his own security officer.

'Good morning.'

'Good morning.'

'Your little boxes are of great interest to us. Fantastic product.'

My colleagues pretended that they did not speak anything but Russian, so that I had to act as interpreter. This was a good device, because it gave them much more time to think up their replies. Apart from that, it also pushed me slightly into the background.

They talked about all sorts of technical stuff and quoted strings of figures, which sent my head spinning. Meanwhile my colleagues kept hopping about and just could not sit still.

'How much are you asking for one box?'

'5,500 dollars.'

We all burst out laughing. I immediately opened the briefcase (there being no one behind me) and the false bottom, so that he could feast his eyes on the green notes. I shut it at once, but he continued to stare with fascination at the case.

'For that one box we are ready to hand over to you now no less than 120,000 dollars. The trouble is, however, that we are from the Soviet Union, and your governments in the West place such terrible restrictions on freedom of trade that we cannot, unfortunately, buy your box. What a pity!'

We got up and left the stand. Thirty metres away we turned a corner and got lost in the crowd.

'What about it? Is it a real box or just a model?.'

'No, it's a real one. Go and hook him!'

Our technical experts went along with me to have further conversation and also to have another look at the instrument before we bought it. I could easily be tricked, but not they. I returned to the stand, briefcase in hand. He recognised me and smiled. I walked past and also smiled. Then, suddenly, as if I had just hit on an idea, I turned to him and asked him if he would like to meet me for a drink that evening.

The smile faded from his face. He gave me a long, cold look in the eyes. Then he looked at the briefcase. Then again at me and nodded his head. I handed him a card on which was the address of the Hôtel du Lac in Montreux and on which I had already written the time – '21.00'. That was so as not to spend time explaining things to him.

As I left the stand I was walking on air. A recruitment! He had agreed. He was already my secret agent. I had to be careful not to leap for joy. If only I could wipe the smile of exultation from my face. If only my heart wouldn't beat so fast. I caught up my colleagues and told them I had carried out the recruitment.

We walked round a few more stands, chatting, admiring and nodding our heads. We had some coffee. Ought we not to display our briefcase once again? Shouldn't we try to recruit someone else?' My eyes lit up: two recruitments. . . . No, we would not recruit a second one. Greed was the priest's undoing.

The Plain de Plainpalais was packed with cars from end to end and it was difficult to find our own. The Consul-general's car was there and he was inside, which meant that he had not been needed. All was going well and dozens of invaluable recruitments had been carried out without anything going wrong. I could see also a huge coach among dozens of other similar coaches, where the Navigator was receiving the most successful of his pupils. But I had not yet reached the stage of enjoying such an honour as to report the results of my work personally to the Navigator. I was responsible to his First Deputy. Where could he be? After walking through endless rows of cars I found him in our bus.

It was already full. The front seats were all occupied by officers of the GRU Information Service and the Military-Industrial Committee. They had been helping us to recruit. The back seats were empty. The curtains had been pulled down, as though to protect us from the sun. There on the back seat was the First Deputy. He called us in one at a time and we reported to him in whispers.

We, Borzois and Vikings, were all crowding together in the aisle. Apparently without purpose. There was noise and pushing and joking. But it was a queue. We were all impatient, our eyes gleaming. And much laughter.

The First Deputy nodded to me. It was my turn.

'Recruited one. In six minutes forty seconds. First meeting with him this evening.'

'Good man. Congratulations. Next. . . .'

I had recruited a valuable agent, one who, for decades ahead would be providing us with the very latest electronic equipment for aircraft, for artillery, for military helicopters and for missile guidance systems. Neither I nor the First Deputy had the slightest doubt that he had really been recruited.

It was true that so far the GRU knew about the new secret agent only what was written on his visiting card, and no more. More was known about his apparatus: we had two small cuttings from newspapers about the apparatus RS-77. But that did not matter. More important was the fact that we needed his apparatus and that we were going to get it. We would soon get to know more about our secret agent. Most important was that he was ready to collaborate secretly with us.

In less than seven minutes with him I had got across to him a lot of important facts. I had used the most ordinary sentences, but from them it was clear that:

—we were official representatives of the Soviet Union;

—we were interested in the most up-to-date military electronics, and in his apparatus in particular;

—we were ready to pay well for them and he now knew exactly the price we'd pay;

—we worked under cover, skilfully and cautiously, without putting on pressure or making demands;

—we did not need many samples of an instrument but just one for copying;

From all of which he could himself conclude that:

—we were not competitors for his firm;

—if the production of such an instrument were organised in the USSR he would lose nothing by it, but would only gain, because the demand for his apparatus would grow and armies in the West might even order something even more expensive, something even more highly advanced;

—having sold us only one sample of the apparatus, he could easily conceal the fact from the authorities and the police: it was not like selling a hundred or a thousand;

—finally, our proposals were perfectly clear to him; he knew what we wanted and so he was not afraid of us; he realised that the sale of the apparatus could be treated as industrial espionage for which the penalties in the West were for some reason lighter.

All aspects of the deal were clear to him. In a single proposition I had informed him of our interest, conditions and what we would pay. So that, when he nodded his head agreeing to meet me, he was quite definitely saying 'yes' to Soviet military intelligence. He understood that we were engaged in a forbidden activity and had agreed to have contact with us. That meant. . . .

My brief recruiting talk with the man was roughly the same as telling a pretty young student that I was a rich debauchee ready to pay an attractive girl generously for sexual intercourse. Letting her see the money and naming a price, and then proposing to meet somewhere on our own and listen to music. If she agreed, what more was there to discuss? What else was there to talk about?

That is exactly the way the quick large-scale recruitments are carried out at exhibitions: We're interested. We're ready to pay. Where shall we meet?

On the other hand, even if the whole of my conversation with the man had been recorded on tape, there was absolutely nothing in it of a criminal nature. We had looked at his instrument, said we'd like to buy it, but that it was not permitted. Only later did I return and propose going for a drink in the evening.

I was young and inexperienced. I could be forgiven for taking seven minutes over a recruitment. A so-called 'instantaneous' recruitment ought to take only an instant. Just a dozen words. Just a proposition and a nice smile.

A recruitment should ideally be immediately and thoroughly concealed. I ought to have gone round a hundred stands saying roughly the same everywhere and smiling in the same way, though not recruiting. Then, if I were followed how could anyone know which of the hundred had said 'yes' to Soviet military intelligence? There were a lot of us at the exhibition. A lot actively recruiting and a lot backing them up. Every one of us covered up his recruiting by having hundreds of other meetings. There were thousands of people at the exhibition. A vast stream, a whirlpool, Shanghai. Just try to follow anyone there. . . .

A new agent has to be got as quickly as possible a long way from the exhibition. That same night my more experienced comrades were having meetings with freshly recruited agents in France, Italy, West Germany. I was meeting my man in Montreux. Others were having secret meetings in Basel, Zurich, Lucerne. As far as possible from Geneva, the further the better. Those were only the first meetings. Second meetings would take place in Austria, in Finland, in the United States of America. As far as possible from Switzerland! The further away the better.

I spent a long time covering up my tracks. I was being well taken care of by the others. If I had been followed I had thrown them off long ago. I had vanished into thin air. I no longer existed. I had got lost in huge department stores. I had disappeared in vast underground garages. I had squeezed out of an overcrowded lift.

I had been transported from Geneva to Lausanne in the boot of a car with a diplomatic plate. That was the first security move, the work of the Vikings from the GRU's diplomatic residency in Geneva. They had not seen me and knew nothing about me. They had left their car in an underground garage at an agreed time and had gone away, leaving the boot unlocked. Such were their instructions. They had probably guessed that their work was connected in some way with the exhibition. But how exactly? They did not have the right to look into the car's boot. They had driven at top speed down the autoroute, having spent not less than four hours making sure they were not being followed. They checked again before driving into an underground garage in Lausanne. A dark place with a lot of floors, stairways and exits. Were they being followed? They walked around the town to make sure, then back to the garage. Off they went: more stops and more garages. They didn't know whether there was anything in the boot or not. Of course there was nothing in it now. I had caught a train long ago and was on my way, an unnoticed passenger in a second-class compartment. Then I suddenly jumped out and changed trains. Then I disappeared in underground passageways, in crowds, in the basements of bars and in dark side-streets. It was a new country for me, but I knew it all by heart. Someone had carefully prepared the dark passages for me, spending months finding them and describing them to me. Someone else had done the dull job as a Borzoi, covering my recruitment operation.

There were only four possibilities which might lead to failure:
   —if I was being followed;
   —if all the people I had met that day were now under observation;
   —if my new friend was a police provocateur, or if he had taken fright, reported me to the police and thereby became a provocateur;
   —if somebody at our meeting place had recognised us quite by chance and reported what he had seen to the police.
   I dismissed three of these possibilities. First of all, I was not being followed. Secondly, I had met around a hundred people that day. It would have been impossible to keep all of them under observation. Thirdly, the Borzois of the Geneva GRU had picked a pretty good place for the meeting. The likelihood that I might run into somebody I knew was practically nil. There remained only my new friend. But it would not be difficult to check up on him. Later that night the GRU experts would check the apparatus, and if it worked it would mean that our friend was not connected with the police. The police would not be likely to pay so highly in terms of secrets to receive nothing in return.
   The meeting place chosen for me was really not bad. It had been discovered by some nameless Borzoi, who had then described it and pointed out its advantages. If I had not liked the place I could have complained to the First Deputy the next day, so that the head of the GRU would have known about it a day later and he would have torn a strip off the resident in Geneva. But I was not going to complain. I liked the place. It had to be in a big hotel, where no one paid any attention to anyone else. It had got to be a good hotel, but not the best.

151

And that was what it was. But most important was that I should have a well protected observation point to be able to keep an eye on everything that was going on for at least an hour before our meeting was due to begin. There was such a point. If my friend had reported our meeting and if the police were planning to watch us, then it was likely that there would be some suspicious things happening around the meeting place.

I waited an hour, but nothing suspicious took place. At 20.54 he appeared. He was alone in a yellow Audi 100. I memorised the number of his car, an important detail. Nobody drove up behind him. He entered the restaurant, glancing round in all directions. That was a very good sign. If he had been under police protection he wouldn't have looked around. To look around like that is very unprofessional (though I shall not tell him so). There would be other meetings and he would always be under observation by one of us. So let him look round. It set our minds at rest.

At 21.03 I left my observation point and entered the restaurant.

We smiled at each other. The most important thing then was to reassure him, to show him all my cards, or at least give the impression that all my cards were on the table. A man is scared only of the unknown. When the situation is clear he has nothing to fear. And if he is not afraid, then he doesn't do stupid things.

'I don't intend to involve you in any dubious business.' In this situation you always say 'I' and not 'We'. I spoke in my own name and not on behalf of any organisation. I don't know why, but it has a much better effect on recruited agents. Apparently the words 'we' and 'organisation' frighten a person. He wanted to believe that only he and one other person in the whole world know about his treachery. Of course this is impossible. Behind me stood an extremely powerful organisation. But I was forbidden to say 'we'. I had been punished for it at the Military-Diplomatic Academy.

'I am ready to pay you for your instrument. *I* need it. But I shan't force you.'

'What makes you think that I have come to work for you?'

'That's the way it looks to me. Why not? You have complete security. And top prices.'

'Are you really ready to pay 120,000 dollars?.'

'Yes – 60,000 immediately. So that you won't need to worry about my intentions. Another 60,000 as soon as I have been able to check that the instrument really works.'

'How soon will you be able to convince yourself?'

'In two days' time.'

'What guarantee have I that you'll return with the second half of the money?'

'You are a very valuable person for me. I reckon to get from you more than this one instrument. What would be the point of my deceiving you at our first meeting?'

He looked at me with a fleeting smile on his face. He knew I was right. And I looked at my first agent recruited abroad. He was ready to sell his beautiful country's security for thirty pieces of silver. I didn't like that at all. I was

152

working in this field because I had no choice. It was fate. If not here, then in some other place where the Soviet system would have found me some equally disagreeable work. And if I had refused, the system would simply have devoured me. I was not a free man. But this fellow was rushing, of his own free will, to help us. If he had come up against me when I was in *Spetsnaz* I would have made such a Judas suffer. Then I remembered that I was supposed to smile at agents. So I smiled.

'You are not from Europe?'

'No.'

'I think we ought not to meet in your country, nor in Switzerland. What do you say to Austria?'

'An excellent idea.'

'I'll meet you in two days in Austria. Look at this.' I handed him a card with an address and picture of an hotel. 'I'll pay all your expenses. Including the night club.'

He smiled. But I wasn't sure what the smile meant: was he pleased or not? I can interpret the meaning of dozens of different smiles. But there in the dark I wasn't sure.

'Do you have the instrument with you?'

'Yes, in the boot of the car.'

'Drive into the woods behind me and I'll take it off you there.'

'You're not going to murder me?'

'Be sensible. I need the instrument. But what use is your life to me? I need you alive. I don't intend to stop at the first piece of equipment. Why should I kill you? I'm ready to pay you a million. All you have to do is let me have the goods.'

'If you are ready to pay so much, it means that your armaments industry is saving money by buying it. Yes?'

'You're dead right.'

'You pay 120,000 for the first instrument and save yourself millions.'

'Correct.'

'In the future you will pay me a million, but you'll save yourselves a hundred millions. Two hundred. Three hundred.'

'That's right.'

'But that's exploitation! I don't want to work on that basis. I won't sell you the instrument for 120,000.'

'Then go and sell it in the West for 5,500. If anyone will buy it from you. If you can find someone who will pay you more than I will, it's your affair. I'm not forcing you to sell to me. I can buy the same instrument in Belgium or the United States.'

That was only bluff. We couldn't make an approach to a big firm. We'd get our noses broken. I had no other access to instruments for receiving reflected laser beams. But I smiled cheerfully. Don't, if you don't want to. But he had no monopoly. I could buy elsewhere.

'The bill, please!'

153

He looked me in the eyes. For a long time. Then he smiled. Light was now shining on his face and for that reason I was sure that his smile concealed nothing bad. Again I smiled back.

He lifted a package out of the boot of his car and offered it to me.

'No, no.' I waved my hands. 'Better for me not to touch it. Take it to my car. If anything went wrong you could say you accidently left the package in my car. Nothing to do with espionage. Just forgetfulness.'

He got into my car. (Of course it was not my own, but a hired car.)

The doors were locked from inside. That was the instruction. The apparatus was under the seat. I unbuttoned my waistcoat. It was a special garment for transporting money. I placed six tightly bound bundles in his hands.

'Check them.'

'Why should I check the money? I have trusted you with my life, in the belief that you won't betray me as a spy. So I'm bound to trust you over money.'

'If in two days' time you can produce the technical documentation, I will pay you the remaining 60,000, plus another 120,000 for the documents.'

He nodded his head.

I shook him by the hand.

He went to his car. I departed at speed into the darkness.

How many GRU officers were there taking care of me? I didn't know exactly. But I had two more appointments to keep that night. First of all the instrument I had obtained had to be got inside the walls of the Soviet embassy as quickly as possible. Secondly, I had to hand over the hired car and pick up my own diplomatic one.

Half an hour later, on a mountain road in the dark and fog, I met up with the second secretary from the Soviet embassy in Berne. He had a white Peugeot 504 which was hardly visible in the thick curling clouds of fog.

My goods were already packed in a tough green tarpaulin sack, closed up and doubly sealed. My contact was a diplomat and a colonel in the GRU, but he was not entitled to know who I was or what was in the sack. His orders were to meet me, take over the sack, lock the doors of his car on the inside and drive straight to the embassy. From the moment when the sack landed in the diplomatic car it was in relative safety. Once it was inside the stone walls of the embassy it would be absolutely safe.

I drew my car up close to his, side by side and dropped the window. His was already down. I handed the sack over.

He was a tall fair-haired fellow, with a serious face. By the determined folds at his mouth I felt sure that he was a successful recruiter. A Viking, without any doubt. Stubborn chaps like that didn't stay long doing back-up. But that was a mad day. Everyone in the Geneva and Berne residencies had been put on to back-up-work.

We were not allowed to speak, and certainly not in Russian. The orders were to stop, hand over the sack and disappear. In that brief moment he had time to look me over. By some faint signs he recognised in me a long-standing Borzoi, fed up with the work of covering other people's activities, who had for the first time met with success. He smiled at me, and said nothing, only slightly moving his lips. I grasped what he was saying: good luck.

Then there was nothing but the red tail-lights of his car in the white fog and the memory of his smile in the window of the car. And he had vanished.

I waited for three minutes. He had made his getaway by now. He had the goods. In two hours I would have another meeting near Interlaken, to hand over the hired car.

That night I might have been in Fribourg and in Neuchâtel. I met the dawn in Zurich. Most important now was to have as many contacts with people as possible. I could have been seen in a large library, in a shop selling guns, in a bar or at a railway station. I talked with lots of men and women. I asked the way to a firm which really existed but which I had no need of at all. I went through address books and sought out people who were really of no interest to us. They say that foxes also cover their tracks in exactly the same way.

I crossed the frontier at Bregenz late in the evening. There was no Swiss police control there, but even if there had been it was not permitted for anyone to inspect a diplomatic car. And if, in contravention of the Vienna Convention of 1815, they had used force to examine my luggage, they would have found nothing there. What might have interested them was already in Moscow in a huge building in the Khodinka, called the Aquarium. While I had been covering my tracks a special plane with armed diplomatic messengers had already delivered dozens of sealed green sacks carefully stacked in aluminium containers.

The Austrian police greeted me with a smile. With a quick glance at my documents they waved me through, showing no interest in my car or its contents. A rather plump fellow with a gun in a holster saluted.

Why should they make themselves a nuisance to a Soviet diplomat with such an open, kindly face? Did he really look like one of those long-haired terrorists whose pictures were posted up in the police office?

I drove slowly across the frontier, saluting them as I went. I was no enemy of theirs; I was almost a friend. We had carried out a large-scale recruitment drive, but there was not a single Swiss or Austrian citizen among our new agents. We recruited those in other places. My colleagues were operating against Austria inside all the other countries of the world.

But we try not to abuse hospitality. Of course Austrians are recruited from inside Austria, but you try not to.

'Well now, turn round, lad! What a sight you are!' That was how the First Deputy greeted me. 'Just take a look at yourself.'

I looked in the mirror and saw looking at me a man with an ashen grey face and a growth of dirty beard. His eyes were bloodshot and sunken. He was mighty tired.

'Go down and have a sauna. And a shave. Then come back upstairs. The Navigator's waiting for you.'

'Why?'

'Don't worry: it's not because you're in trouble.'

There were three of my friends in the same sauna: identified by the numbers 4, 20 and 32.

'Greetings, brothers.'

'Hello, Viking.'

They had obviously been in the sauna for a long time. They were red from the heat.

'Why don't you sit down, Viktor? And they all laughed. They knew that I couldn't sit after two whole days at the wheel. They were not sitting them-selves, but lying on their stomachs.

'Want some beer, Viktor?'

'Sure thing.'

Kolya was beating my back and backside with birch branches.

'Is that getting the circulation going again?'

'It certainly is.'

'But Viktor, don't go to sleep, it's dangerous. Better have some more beer.'

The table in the big hall was laid with good things as if for a party. There were no chairs. No one would be sitting down now. We smiled at each other but remained silent. Then the Navigator appeared, with the first cipher clerk behind him like a sword-bearer.

'I don't propose to discuss the details of the operation just concluded. But everybody achieved some success. Some made three recruitments. Several made two.'

The Navigator turned to the cipher clerk: 'Alexander Ivanovich, read out to the staff those parts of the message which concern them.'

Alexander Ivanovich opened a green file cover and read out in a solemn voice:

'To the commander of the diplomatic residency 173-V, Major-general Golitsyn. Eight diplomatic mail containers despatched by you from Vienna,

Berne and Paris have been received. Preliminary analysis carried out by the 9th directorate of the Information Service is positive. This enables us to make a preliminary judgment concerning the reliability of all the people drawn into collaboration with us. Head of 1st directorate of the GRU, Vice-admiral Yefremov. Head of the 5th Department of the 1st directorate of the GRU Major-general Lyashko.'

We all smiled.

'Read on.' The Navigator was also smiling.

'The operation you have carried out was one of the most successful recruitment drives of recent months. I congratulate you and the whole staff of the residency on their notable achievements. Deputy Chief of General Staff, Head of Second Main Directorate, Army General Ivashutin.'

'Champagne!'

The corks went off like guns. The golden liquid sparkled and bubbled in the glasses. The bottles were ice-cold, the buckets of ice were silver. How tired I was. How I wanted to drink – and to sleep.

One after the other we presented ourselves to the Navigator to exchange congratulations. I went up in turn.

'Comrade general, congratulations. The Japanese have got a lot and so have the Americans, but from today we have everything.'

He smiled.

'Not everything, but access to everything. Why didn't you go for a second recruitment?'

'I don't know, comrade general. I was afraid of spoiling things.'

'You did right. The two most dangerous things in our work are mutual suspicion and excessive enthusiasm. One recruitment is also a great deal. Congratulations.'

'Thank you, comrade general.'

'Alexander Ivanovich. . . . Read out the last message.'

The cipher clerk opened his file again:

'To Major-general Golitsyn. Thank you for your work. Kulikov, Army General, Chief of General Staff.'

'Hurrah!' we shouted.

The Navigator again looked serious. Solemnly he raised his glass.

The third cipher clerk woke me up four and a half hours after my head hit the pillow. There were eighteen folding beds in the rest room. Some of them were already empty. In the others my comrades were sleeping – those who were engaged on the second operation that day.

'Did I do right to wake you, Viktor Andreyevich?' The cipher clerk studied his list.

I glanced at my watch and nodded.

Breakfast was being served in the big hall where the smell of champagne still hung in the air. But I didn't feel like eating. My head was going round. I made myself drink a glass of cold juice and eat a slice of bacon. The cipher clerk announced from the doorway:

'The First Deputy is waiting for you. You may take your coffee with you.'

The First Deputy's eyes were red from lack of sleep. He had probably not been to bed all night

'Be more careful with the money waistcoat. The car door must be locked from the inside all the time. In case of trouble call for the Soviet consul. During the night your car has been washed, checked over, adjusted, filled with petrol and the kilometrometer turned back. The route and the signs for aborting the operation to be agreed with the control group. That's all. Good luck. Next one!'

I returned a couple of days later. The new agent, who was already known at 173-V-41-706, brought to our meeting the complete technical specification of the RS-77 instrument. He gave me a list of civil and military officials who dealt with his firm and who might be recruited later. Against each one of them were some brief notes, with a photograph, his address and, most important, a list of his more obvious weaknesses. I paid him 180,000 dollars. And I fixed another meeting. The information that he supplied on his own initiative would be paid for next time.

Eight days later I was promoted to the rank of major in the General Staff.

For some reason I felt very depressed. It was the first time that I did not feel happy on such an occasion. When my commander read out the message to me I duly called out: 'I serve the Soviet Union', but I thought to myself: They treat me as we treated my agent. He receives a hundred thousand, and the people at the top save millions. I am responsible for making the saving possible and all I get is a little aluminium star as a reward. And I don't even have the right to wear it, because my uniform is hanging in the cupboard in mothballs.

I was sad. I got no great pleasure from rank or decorations. There was something worrying me, but I didn't know what it was. Most important was to make sure that no one else noticed my mood. If the optimism were to fade in my eyes it would be noticed and steps would be taken. I didn't know what kind of steps, but they would be taken. And that would be no good at all.

I looked the general straight in the eyes and smiled joyfully and happily.

Chapter Ten

When I'm in bed I always cover myself up, head and all, wrapping the blanket round me like a fur coat. It is an old Army habit, an unconscious reflex. It's an attempt to preserve the warmth right through to the morning. I no longer sleep in cold tents, in wet trenches or in icy autumn forests. But the habit of sleeping beneath the covers is with me for life.

Recently the blanket had begun to frighten me. If I woke up suddenly at night in the pitch darkness I would ask myself, scared out of my wits, whether I wasn't in a coffin. I would carefully probe the blanket with my nose. Not very much like a coffin. But maybe I was wrapped in a sheet and the lid of the coffin was higher? Slowly I would feel the air above me. No, I was not yet in my coffin.

This is probably the way people start to go mad, how madness creeps up on them. But perhaps I had long been a schizophrenic, only the people around me hadn't twigged it? It could well be. Being mad was by no means as bad as it might appear. If tomorrow they wrapped me in white sheets and took me off to the lunatic asylum I wouldn't resist or even be surprised. It was the place for me. I was certainly not normal. But who of the people around me was normal, either? I seemed to be living in a madhouse. Total madness. Why on earth did the West admit us in our hundreds and thousands? We were spies. Didn't they realise that I had been sent there in order to cause them untold harm? Why didn't they arrest me and throw me out? Why did these strange incomprehensible people in the West never protest? How had they developed such slave-like docility? Perhaps they had all gone out of their minds? Perhaps we were all madmen? I was sure I was. It was no accident that I imagined myself in a coffin. It had started eighteen months ago, after my meeting with Kir.

Do you know Kir? Everybody knows Kir. Kir is a very important figure. Kir Lemzenko had been stationed in Rome, though his work was not, of course, only in Italy. Kir had had success everywhere. As the GRU's under-cover resident in Rome, Kir Gavrilovich Lemzenko had wielded enormous power. That's why he had been called the Pope of Rome. He was now a Colonel-general. He was in the Administrative department of the Central Committee of the Party, and in the name of the Party he supervised the GRU and the KGB.

A year and a half previously, when I was being screened for travel abroad, I had been summoned to Kir's presence for a five-minute talk. He always saw all the GRU and KGB officers who were due to be posted abroad. It was Kir who

159

confirmed their appointments or rejected them. He was very powerful, and everybody knew it. The fate of every officer of the GRU and the KGB was in his hands.

Staraya Square in Moscow, with the monument to the grenadiers. Uniformed police and plain-clothes men standing in groups in their grey raincoats, eyeing everybody seriously. Entrance No. 6. Show your Party card. A guard with blue epaulettes read out my name – 'Suvorov'. 'Victor Andreyevich,' another called out when he had found my name on a short list. 'Yes,' said the first guard. 'This way.' A third guard accompanied me along the corridor. 'This way please, Viktor Andreyevich.' The guard was not supposed to know who Viktor Andreyevich Suvorov was. He knew only that this Suvorov had been summoned to the Central Committee for a meeting and that it would take place on the seventh floor, in room 788. The guard was very polite. 'This way, please.'

So these were the corridors of power. Vaulted ceilings beneath which Stalin and Khrushchev had walked and beneath which Brezhnev still walked. The Central Committee headquarters is a whole town, a state in itself in the centre of Moscow, like the Vatican in Rome.

There is always building going on at the Central Committee. There are dozens of buildings, all linked together and all the free courtyards and passageways are being built over and new white glass skyscrapers are going up. It is strange, but those snow-white buildings can hardly be seen from Staraye Square. Or, rather, they can be seen, but they do not stand out. Staraye Square is overlooked by the huge windows of the grey pre-revolutionary buildings now joined together into a single unit. Inside the Central Committee's quarter it is not so stern and gloomy. All sorts of architectural styles are mixed up there.

'This way, please.' Dazzling cleanliness. Red carpets. Door-handles of polished brass. I scarcely dared to touch them for fear of leaving a mark. The lifts worked silently.

'Wait here.' I was standing in front of a huge window out of which I could see the narrow back-streets of the Zamoskvorechye district, the golden domes of the churches that had been destroyed by the Revolution and restored for the benefit of foreign tourists, and the enormous building of the Military Engineering Academy. Outside the sun shone brightly and the pigeons had settled on the ledges of the tall buildings. Kir was ready for me.

'Come this way, please.' His office was vast, with one wall entirely of glass looking out over a huddle of green roofs belonging to the Central Committee buildings. The other walls were light grey in colour and there was a soft grey woollen carpet on the floor. There was one huge desk without a single scrap of paper on it, a big safe, and nothing else.

'Good morning, Viktor Andreyevich,' a kindly voice said.

'Good morning, Kir Gavrilovich.'

He didn't like being called 'general'. Or perhaps he liked it but didn't show it. In any case the orders were to say 'Kir Gavrilovich' and not 'comrade general'. An odd name. According to his surname he is Ukrainian, but his first name recalled an Assyrian warrior. How could they keep a man with such names in the Central Committee? But perhaps it was not an anti-Soviet name but, on the contrary, a very Soviet one. Following the Revolution the orthodox Marxists invented all sorts of names for their children: 'Vladlen' came from Vladimir Lenin; 'Iskra' was the name of a Bolshevik newspaper; 'Kim' was made from the initials of the Communist Youth International. Maybe 'Kir' had the same origins – the Communist International, perhaps.

'Sit down, Viktor Andreyevich. How are you?'

'Very well, thank you, Kir Gavrilovich.'

He was quite small in stature, with only the first signs of grey hair, and nothing remarkable at all about his face. If you met him on the street you wouldn't even turn to look at him, or be struck by his appearance. He was wearing the most ordinary of suits, grey with a stripe, but beautifully tailored of course. That was all. He looked altogether like a very average man. But this was the great Kir!

I had expected to hear pompous phrases from him: 'The head of the GRU and the Central Committee have placed tremendous trust in you . . .' and so forth. But there were none of those phrases about the front-line struggle with capitalism, the duties of a Soviet intelligence office, the all-conquering ideas of Communism. He simply looked me in the face, like a doctor, silently and attentively.

'You are aware, Viktor Andreyevich, that in the GRU and the KGB we very seldom have people who flee to the West.'

I nodded.

'All those who have done so are unhappy. That is not just propaganda. Sixty-five per cent of defectors from the GRU and KGB return in the end and admit their guilt. We execute them. They know that and they still return. Those who do not return to the Soviet Union of their own free will finish up by committing suicide, drinking themselves to death or just going to the dogs. Why?'

'Because they have betrayed their socialist motherland. They have bad consciences. They have lost all their friends, family, language. . . !'

'That is not the most important, Viktor Andreyevich. There are more serious reasons. Here in the Soviet Union you are one of us, a member of the upper class. Every one of us, even the least important officer of the GRU, is a superman by comparison with all the rest. So long as you are part of our system you enjoy colossal privileges compared with the rest of the population of the country. When you have your youth and your health, your power and privileges, you forget about it all. And you recall it only when it is too late. Some of us flee to the West in the hope of having a magnificent car, a mansion with a swimming pool and a lot of money. And the West really does pay well. But once he's got his Mercedes and his own swimming pool, the traitor suddenly realises that all the people around him also have nice cars and pools. He suddenly feels like an ant in a crowd of equally rich ants. He loses the sense of superiority over those around him. He becomes an ordinary person, like the rest. Even if the enemy intelligence service gives that traitor a job he will still not recover his feeling of superiority over others, because to work in intelligence in the West is not regarded as a great honour and is not highly esteemed. You're just a civil servant, a little insect, that's all.'

'I had never thought of it that way.'

'Well, think about it, and keep thinking about it. Wealth is relative. In Moscow if you drive around in a Lada you have all the pretty girls looking at you. But if you drive round Paris in a Citroên, however big it is, nobody looks at you. It's all relative. In our Far Eastern districts a colonel is God and Tsar, master of all, a very despot. But in Moscow a colonel is just a pawn, because there are thousands of other colonels around. If you betray your country you lose everything. And you will remember that you once belonged to a powerful organisation and were a very special person, set apart from millions of others. Betray your country, and you will find yourself as insignificant and unimportant as the rest of the population. Capitalism provides money, but it does not provide power or respect. There are also among us some especially smart guys who do not defect to the West but remain among us, secretly selling our secrets. They receive money from the capitalists and still enjoy the status of a superman provided by socialism. But we quickly run them down and destroy them. . . .'

'I know. Penkovsky. . . .'

'Not only him. Penkovsky is known everywhere. But there were many who are not known. A man called Konstantinov, for example. He returned to Moscow on leave and was immediately put under investigation. The evidence against him was incontrovertible. He was sentenced to death.'

'He was put in the furnace too?'

'No. He begged not to be executed.'

'And he wasn't executed?'

'No, he was not killed. But one day he fell asleep in his cell and woke up in a coffin. Deep in the ground. He begged not to be executed, so we didn't execute him. But the coffin had to be put into the grave. Those are the instructions. Off you go, Viktor Andreyevich. Good luck. And remember that the level of betrayal in the GRU is much lower than in the KGB. Try to maintain that good tradition.'

In Munich it was snowing. There was a violet-tinted sky, and an enormous grey cloud enveloping the whole city showered snowflakes on it. The people scurried along, their noses buried in the collars of their coats. There were fir trees everywhere, and around the street lamps the snowflakes seemed denser and bigger. The falling snow deadened the noises of our cruel century and hid the dirt and dreariness of civilisation. Everything was clean, without dirty patches, even the roof of the Deutsche Bank. Everything is so quiet and warm when snow falls. If you really strained you could hear the faint noise of the snowflakes as they fell. Just listen to that snow falling! Where were the people hurrying to? When you stopped it was so clean and quiet. No driving wind, no squeal of brakes. Just peace and quiet over the white city. Why did they all rush to hide themselves away in the stuffy bars, in that poisonous air and clatter and noise?

Snowflakes were falling on my face. I liked it and did not hide my face. Snow can be sharp and painful, but not that day. It was a pleasant snow falling from the sky, so I made no attempt to turn my face away.

From the railway station I made for the Marienplatz and the centre. I was covering my tracks. I wasn't being followed, but I had to take precautions and weave about a bit. I couldn't have had better weather for it. There was nobody on the deserted streets of Munich. The people had gone to earth. I was alone in the city. Major in the GRU, 173-V-4I. I was covering up my tracks after a meeting with my friend No. 173-V-4I-706. I had had the meeting in Hamburg, where some young Borzoi from the diplomatic residency in Bonn had taken over the documents I had obtained.

In Munich I was simply covering my tracks, dodging round the side-streets in the snow and mist. Sometimes I let myself be seen where there were a lot of people – once in the endless labyrinths of the beer hall where Hitler's party was founded. It was scarcely a bar; it was a whole town with streets and squares, and endless rows of seats and thousands of people. It was one great independent beer state, like the Vatican in Rome or the Central Committee in Moscow. On I went down the rows of chairs, round one corner and then another, until I found a dark corner where I could rest for a while. Who might turn up behind me? In that dark corner, in that huge oak seat, Goering might well have sat. Now I was sitting there with a huge mug of beer. That was my work: to study the passers-by, to see who might have followed me. Was there somebody seeking me with his eyes, somebody who had lost sight of me in that whirlpool, in the gloom, in the haze of the beer-hall? There seemed to be nobody. So I went outside again, into the narrow side-streets and the blue blizzard.

Comrade Shelepin was in Vienna. In transit. He was on his way to Geneva for a meeting of the International Labour Office. Comrade Shelepin was the head of the Soviet trade union movement. He was also a member of the Politburo. Comrade Shelepin was a star of the first magnitude. Not a rising star, however, but a falling one. There had been a time when comrade Shelepin had been, unofficially, deputy chairman of the KGB and at the same time vice-president of the World Federation of Democratic Youth. Comrade Shelepin had organised demonstrations for peace and friendship between the peoples. He had been responsible for mighty demonstrations in defence of peace. Millions of stupid people had responded to comrade Shelepin's appeals. They had shouted and demanded peace, disarmament and justice. For that he had been elevated to the rank of chairman of the KGB. He ruled with a strict, firm hand. He ruled half the world, including the democratic youth who were demanding peace. But he had overdone it. Now all he ruled were the Soviet trades unions. In the Soviet Union trades unions are also KGB, but only a branch. Consequently the embassy was not showing any special respect for its high-ranking guest. Let him carry on to Geneva and not hang about in Vienna. It was quite clear to everybody that comrade Shelepin was slipping downhill. He had been chairman of the KGB, but now he was only boss of the trades unions. Once the slide downwards had begun there was no stopping it.

Everybody in the embassy knew that comrade Shelepin was in the habit of drinking himself into a state of complete madness. The leader of the Soviet proletariat would use the most frightful language. He had attacked the housemaid in his bedroom. He had thrown a heavy crystal ash-tray out of the window and damaged the Cuban ambassador's limousine. He knew himself that his end had come. The former head of the KGB was taking his leave of power.

I ran into him in a corridor. His face looked swollen and lined, not at all like the one that smiled at us from his official portraits. In fact I recognised him only by the fact that he was drunk – nobody else would have dared to go around the embassy in that state – and by the size of his bodyguard. Who else would have five men to accompany him? The bodyguards had expressionless faces, as they were expected to. They moved with self-assurance, village lads raised to the summit of power. They did not, of course, understand that once the fall had begun there was no stopping it.

It was only on the lips of the man in charge of the group of bodyguards that I caught sight of a slightly contemptuous smile. I knew exactly what that smirk meant. He was not there to protect comrade Shelepin from enemies of the people; he was there to make sure that comrade Shelepin, a leader of the most class-conscious revolutionary class in the world, did not try to escape to the West. If comrade Shelepin should try to run away the chief bodyguard would make use of his revolver. In the back of the neck, between the ears. To make sure that comrade Shelepin did not get very far. What's more, comrade Shelepin, a falling star of the first magnitude, knew that the chief bodyguard was not a bodyguard but a gaoler. Shelepin knew what orders the chief bodyguard had. And I knew too.

If only they had given me such orders.

'It is disinformation.'

The Navigator was cross. I kept quite. What could I say to such a statement? He had a coded message in his hand. Our friend No. 706 had started producing 'disinformation'. When the documents obtained from him had been studied it had been impossible to detect any attempt to deceive the GRU. But the GRU always bought several samples of every document, every apparatus and every weapon, and bought them in different parts of the world. Each piece of information was compared, every time, with every document and every other scrap of information. If anyone tried to add something of his own or to conceal something, the Information Service would discover it. That is what had happened on this occasion with my friend from the exhibition, No. 173-V-4I-706.

Everything had been going well. But then, in the last document received from him, there were three pages missing. They were important pages, and they had been removed in such a way that it was impossible to tell they had ever been there. It was only by comparing the document with another, obtained perhaps through Algeria or Ireland, that it was possible to assert that someone was trying to deceive us. The change had been very skilfully carried out, obviously by experts, and that meant that No. 706 was under somebody else's control. Whether he had gone to the police himself and confessed or whether he had been caught was of no importance. The most important fact was that he was under control.

'Do you wish me to remove No. 706?'

The Navigator shot out of his chair.

'Pull yourself together, major! Have you gone crazy? Been reading too many cheap novels? "If you betray us we shall kill you, as an example to the others." But if we were to kill a respectable middle-class owner of a firm, what would that teach anybody? Who knows that he was mixed up with us? I would put him out of the way if he were a danger to us. But he knows absolutely nothing about us. He doesn't even know whether he was working for the KGB or the GRU. We never gave him any such information. The only secret he possesses is the fact that Viktor Suvurov is a spy. But the whole world knows that. The temptation to kill is strong. That's the way many intelligence services act. They let themselves get drawn into a secret war and forget their main job, which is to obtain secret information. We need secrets, as a healthy man needs sexual intercourse. Remember, major, that only a weak, stupid man, lacking confidence in himself, ever kills or rapes a woman. That is exactly the way cheap newspapers and novelists depict us – as weak and stupid. A smart man, or a smart, strong and self-confident intelligence service does not chase after agents or after women.

'A man who has hundreds of women does not take revenge on one who is unfaithful to him, for the simple reason that he has no time to bother with her. He has lots of other girls. By the way, do you have anything in reserve?'

'You mean new friends?'

'What else do you think I mean?' He suddenly flared up.

The Navigator knew, of course, that I had no other friends apart from 706 and not even a suggestion of an interesting contact. He had put the question only to be able to rub my nose in the mud.

'No, comrade general, I have nothing in reserve.'

'Then, back to support work!'

'Very well.'

I had one more meeting with No. 706. He was under supervision, but there was not the slightest need to let him see that the GRU knew about it.

I conducted the meeting as always. I paid him and told him that for the time being we did not need any more of his material. I told him we'd meet in a year's time. Maybe we would have some request then. In a year some excuse would be found for putting him out to 'conservation'. To the sleeping network, to await a sign from us. That would be the end of our contact with him: let him wait until some very important illegal approached him. He and the police could go on waiting. They'd have to wait a long time. This was known as 'severing contact with the appearance of preserving it'. We had obtained very important apparatus from him which had saved us millions. His material, when it was first-class stuff, was also used for checking someone else's. But the time had come to say goodbye. He would be left waiting for a sign, for an especially important meeting.

I had no problems with 706. But what was I to do now? A Borzoi again. Again the dreary work of backing up others. But what did I really want to do? If I couldn't work independently I would have to work for other people.

I was again on back-up work, responsible entirely to the First Deputy and deprived of the right to approach the Navigator directly. He had no time for people like me. It is true that those who had had some success also had to do back-up work occasionally, but that happened only during a large-scale recruitment drive when the whole residency was sent out on operations whose objective had been dictated from above. They were also drawn into the work of backing up operations conducted by the GRU's illegal residencies. That was a different matter. To be ordered to back up an illegal was an honour. But we Borzois were very seldom sent to back up illegals. We were left with the difficult, thankless work which involved great risks, an enormous amount of time and no rewards. Merely supporting agents in their contacts was not considered work at all. Something like a secretary-typist working for a great writer. Neither money nor fame. But if you made a mistake you soon knew all about it.

Such was the work I was doing on this occasion. I was off for a picnic in the mountains. It was really not the right time of year for picnics: the weather was not suitable, but I had to get up into the mountains. If I was followed and we were arrested and expelled from the country, I would think up a more reasonable cover story. But we are seldom interfered with in Great Britain, practically never in the United States of America, and in other countries, well, for spies we are treated rather well. So there was no need to think up anything original. A picnic – that was good enough. I knew people did not go for picnics on their own. But does anybody really care what a Soviet diplomat does in his working day?

In the boot of my car was an anti-tank grenade launcher known as the RPG-7 and five grenades to go with it. It was all carefully packed and had to be deposited in a dead drop. The grenade launcher weighed six kilograms and each grenade over two kilograms. Then there was the packing. That made altogether more than twenty kilos in one long grey package. I had no idea for whom the weapon was intended. I had to hide it in the mountains in a place which I had spent six days searching for. Someone some time would hand over to someone else a description of the hiding place and the secret signs by which it would be quite easy to discover it. The addressee receives details of the hiding place only after the goods have been lodged in it. Consequently, even if he wanted to betray us to the police, he couldn't. He would receive the necessary directions and hurry to the spot, but I would have been long gone. So that I, my diplomatic residency, Soviet military intelligence, the whole Soviet Union – we would have no connection with it at all. A grenade launcher lay hidden in the ground – that was all. Perhaps it had always been there from the day of Creation. Unfortunately it was a Soviet grenade launcher. Perhaps the Americans had captured it in Vietnam and had hidden it in the Alps?

Who would need such a weapon? I hadn't the slightest idea. It was clearly not intended to be held in reserve in case of war. For long-term storage they use heavy containers, whereas this was very lightly packed. That meant that someone would pick it up in the next few days. It was not impossible that it was going to be used in the next few days. Otherwise it would have to be stored for a long time. That was dangerous. Damn it, perhaps I was actually making history: maybe that grenade launcher was destined to change the course of history in a quite unexpected direction. The RPG-7 was a powerful weapon, light and simple to operate. All the top people in the West protected themselves with bullet-proof glass. But supposing they were hit by a PG-7V grenade? No armour would withstand it. And it had a range of 300 metres. What a commotion there would be then. I wondered whom the GRU had got in its sights? Who were the five grenades intended for? A head of state? Some general? The Pope? But the weapon could hit more than an armoured limousine. A campaigner for the protection of the environment might hit a poison gas container or nuclear reactor as an act of protest. A peace fighter might ambush a convoy with American nuclear warheads and press the trigger. It would cause a worldwide sensation. It wouldn't cause a nuclear explosion, of course, but the newspapers would make such a fuss that the West would be in serious trouble.

I made frequent turns at crossroads, kept altering my speed, joined the autoroute for a while and then went off again down obscure country roads. It seemed that there was no one on my tail. Nobody was interested in me. I was alone, in a dense forest on a narrow road. The wind swayed the trees above my head. I parked the car on the roadside, where tourists often stopped.

I was sitting on a little hillock in a fir-wood and keeping my car under observation. I had not been followed – I could guarantee that. But it was always possible that the police had fixed a radio device to my car which was now telling where I was. Perhaps they had not been following me in the usual way but had kept at a considerable distance. If that was the case, then someone should soon turn up at my car. All around were forests and mountains, and they could approach this point only by using one road which was under my observation. They might fuss around my car for a while, trying to work out in what direction I had gone. In that case I would circle around the forest, and return to my car when there was nobody near it. I would lock the doors from the inside and weave through the forests and mountains. Then I would go back to the embassy and repeat the whole operation from the beginning the next day.

I looked at my watch again: thirty minutes had passed. No one had approached my car. The only noise came from the fir trees. I could have left the package with the weapon in the car and now, once I was sure that I was not being followed, have returned to the car, taken the package and gone off into the hills. But that was not our way of doing things.

I remained a few minutes longer sitting in the undergrowth and listening to the rustling of the forest. There was no one. Then I put rubber boots on my feet, a cap with a British lion badge on my head, and a rucksack on my back: I looked just like any tourist. I had a cigar in my hand, not because I smoke, of course – I was forbidden to do that years ago. But I always carried a strong-smelling cigar with me, so that I could break off the end, crumble the tobacco in my hands and scatter it around me. It was my greeting to the dogs. I spent a long time wandering through the bushes, reached a little river and walked up it against the current. I was not being followed, but they might turn up there in a few hours' time with dogs and helicopters.

It was a pity that the package with the grenade launcher had such an odd shape. If anyone were to see such a strange object wrapped in waterproof material sticking out of my rucksack they would be bound to assume that I was labouring for the GRU, doing a rather humdrum job as a punishment for not being able to get access to secrets on my own initiative.

I had a long way to go, and on foot. Like being in *Spetsnaz*. Along the little stream, upwards. The revolutionary units of freedom fighters needed the weapons to get rid of capitalist slavery. Perhaps the grenade launcher would be picked up by Italian or German lads and used to strike yet another blow at the decaying capitalist system.

My long walk gave me time to engage in a little mental gymnastics. What could I think up so as to get myself returned to operating on my own? I could write a report for the head of the 5th department of the 1st directorate and suggest something original. For example, that the Germans or Italians should kidnap the President or Minister of Defence. That would be good for them, for their revolutionary aims and for raising the revolutionary awareness of the masses. They could bring the kidnapped official to trial before a revolutionary tribunal and execute him. But before doing that we could have a talk with him, subject him to torture and extract some secrets from him.

I continued staggering through the water, smiling at my own fantasies. I would, of course, never propose such a thing. It was a thankless business, giving advice. The people who had good ideas were never remembered. It was not the originators but the executors who were rewarded. It was a simple idea, and they didn't need me to think of it. I needed to think of something in which I would be not only the originator but also the executor. And it needed to be not a general idea but something specific. Before putting it to the Commander I would have to prepare thousands of details and be totally involved in the plan, so that I would not be pushed to one side and that the operation would not be entrusted to more experienced men.

The clear mountain stream bubbled along beneath my feet. Sometimes I went up on the bank to get round a waterfall. On those occasions I would again break off a piece of cigar, rub the tobacco between my fingers and spread it around. And I stepped only on the rocks, so as to leave no tracks.

At last I reached the place I had chosen and which had been approved by the First Deputy and confirmed by the head of the 1st directorate of the GRU. A dead drop is never chosen in a cave or a concealed cellar. It has to be a place which can easily be found by the person who is supposed to find it and which is very difficult for anyone else to discover. It has to be a place where our goods cannot be found by chance and where they won't suffer from the weather or any natural disasters.

The dead drop I had selected complied with these requirements. It was in the mountains far from any human habitation. It was in a cleft between two cliffs and concealed by an impenetrable thicket of prickly bushes. It was a place which tourists did not frequent and where curious children did not play. There was never going to be any building there and it was not threatened by landslides or flooding. But it was easy to find if you knew how to look for it. There was a high-voltage electric power line on tall metal pylons. From pylon No. 042 you had to walk towards pylon No. 041 as far as the point where the wire was at its lowest and then turn to the left. Then thirty metres at right angles to the power cable. You had to ignore the prickly bushes and arrive at a pile of stones and the ashes of a camp-fire which had been lit many years before. Not a very pleasant place: damp, dark and prickly. The last time I was there, when I found the place, I had thrown down all sorts of rubbish that I'd found lying around – a rusty tin, a bottle and a roll of wire. That was to discourage people from picnicing there.

Once again I looked round carefully at the area. Nothing had changed since my first visit. Even the tin was in the same place. I listened carefully to the sound of the wind in the mountain tops. There was nobody. I threw off the rucksack, which was wearing me down after the long journey. I had suggested to the First Deputy that I bury the weapon in the ground, but he had instructed me simply to cover it up with stones, as heavy as possible. I had also suggested taking a stray cat from the embassy and bringing it there to sacrifice in the interests of the world proletariat. A dead cat in a state of decomposition would keep the place clear of hunters and tourists and amorous pairs seeking a secluded spot. That suggestion was also turned down. The First Deputy ordered me instead to use a liquid known as ZRG, type 4. I had a small bottle of it. It has the smell of burning rubber, and it lasts for several weeks, keeping uninvited people away and guaranteeing solitude to those due to take over my package. I could only wish them good luck, those fearless fighters for freedom and social justice. I listened once again to the wind and then squeezed in between the rocks.

I already knew Western Europe pretty well, as a hunting dog knows the neighbouring wood. I could have worked as a tourist guide in Amsterdam or Hamburg. On one occasion I was working in Basel, but not alone. I was backing up someone else. Basel is where Germany, France and Switzerland meet, and it's a very useful place, a unique place. Basel is a crossroads. You could be there and suddenly disappear. It was so easy.

I was sitting in a little restaurant directly opposite the railway station. It was in fact difficult to say whether it was a restaurant or just a bar. It was divided into two, with a restaurant on one side – quite small, with red table-cloths. On the other side was a bar with wooden tables and no table-cloths. That's where I was sitting, alone. There was some decoration and the date '1932' carved into the wooden table top. It meant that the table had been there even before Hitler came to power. It must be good to be Swiss. The frontier with Germany was right there, just across the road. But war had never reached here.

A pretty, big-bosomed woman placed a mug of beer before me on a clean beer mat. How was she to know that I was already on the warpath? That I was counting the seconds in my head, and that I was not sitting in that spot by chance but so as to be able to see the big clock on the station building? She could not know that somebody else was timing himself by that clock – someone I didn't know and would never know. Nor could she know that I had smeared the ends of my fingers with MMP cream so that they would not leave any fingerprints. Nor could she know that I had in my pocket what looked like an ordinary china handle such as hangs on the chains in lavatories. You pull it and the water flushes down. That handle, however, had been put together by the Camouflage Institute of the GRU. Inside it was a container and in it perhaps the description of a hiding place or some money or gold, goodness knows what. I did not know what was in the container. But in exactly seven minutes I would go to the toilet and in the last cabin but one remove the handle from the chain, put it in my pocket and in its place put the one that was in my pocket.

Somebody who was now also watching the station clock would then go into the cabin after me, remove the handle and put an ordinary one in its place. He had that already in his pocket and was probably also clutching it in his hand, also smeared with MMP cream. All three handles were identical. There was no way of distinguishing them. The Camouflage Institute did a good job.

The hand on the big clock trembled slightly. Another six minutes. There was building going on next to the station. Either the station was being extended or they were building an hotel. The construction behind the scaffolding looked very imposing, a sort of tower. The walls were of brown metal and the windows were also dark, practically brown. High above were workmen in orange protective hats. And pigeons on the cornices. There was one particular pigeon slowly and with concentration killing its comrade, hitting it with its beak in the back of the neck.

A pigeon is a revolting bird. Neither hawks nor wolves nor crocodiles kill for amusement. But pigeons do just that. They kill their kind simply for fun. And they kill slowly, to prolong the pleasure. If only I had had a Kalashnikov automatic in my hands. I would have pushed the safety-catch down to automatic fire and sprayed the station square of sleepy Basel with bullets. I wouldn't have bothered about my diplomatic status or feared the consequences. I would have given the murdering pigeon a long burst of fire. I would have scattered it with lead, turned it into a mess of feathers and blood. But I had no automatic with me. I wasn't in *Spetsnaz*, but on intelligence work. What a pity. Because I would happily have killed it — and not bothered about the fact that in saving the weaker pigeon from certain death I was saving another murderer. Because they are all the same by nature. It would have come round, got its strength back and sought out another, weaker pigeon to stab with its beak. It would know exactly where to strike too, just as professionally as an executioner in the NKVD. A repulsive bird, the pigeon. Yet there are people who regard this cold-blooded killer as a symbol of peace. You would hardly take a crocodile or an anaconda snake as your symbol of peace. But the anaconda is a very peaceful creature. It kills only for food, and as soon as it has eaten it goes to sleep. It finds no pleasure in torturing other beings, and nor does it kill its own kind.

The weak pigeon on the cornice had spread its wings and its head was hanging down. The strong one had drawn itself together, ready to strike and strike again. I had no time to watch the end of the affair. I was off to the toilet for a top secret operation in support of another officer.

I was not wasting any time. When I was working in Germany I thought about how to get my hands on German secrets. When I was in Italy I thought about how to get hold of Italian secrets. But in Italy you could also recruit Amercians, Chinese or Australians. I needed the sort of people who possessed state secrets. I had just returned from Basel and was reporting to the Navigator the results of

171

the operation. I usually reported to the First Deputy, but on this occasion the Navigator heard me personally. It had apparently been a very important operation. I took advantage of the occasion to offer him my suggestions about how to obtain secret documents about the 'Florida' system. 'Florida' is Switzerland's anti-aircraft defence system. It might not seem very important in itself, but it was a similar system, and thus a key, to the anti-aircraft defences of the United States. If one could get to know a Swiss sergeant it might clarify a great deal about the American system.

The Navigator gave me a very grim look. There was nothing but lead in his eyes. They were the eyes of a bull taking a long look at a young toreador before picking him up on his mighty horns. The Navigator's look put me off. I had names and addresses of people on the staff of the command centre of the Swiss anti-aircraft defence system. I knew how to get to know a sergeant there. I even knew the address of the printing works which printed secret documents for the command centre. But the Navigator was still crushing me with his look. I was put off my stride and forgot my carefully prepared list of ideas.

'I will try to do this. . . .'

He remained silent.

'I will report all developments. . . .'

He was still silent.

'Our chaps in Switzerland can recruit Swiss people if they need to. And we can do it too, from Austria.'

He drew in through his nostrils a huge quantity of air and then noisily, like a whale, expelled it.

'Get back to your present work!'

Intelligence back-up work is like sweet syrup for flies. It doesn't seem dangerous, it's quite sweet, but you can't get yourself out of it. Your wings get heavy, so you sink and perish in it. Only the man who manages to get out can become a real intelligence officer. Genka, the Consul, for example. He arrived in Vienna along with me and they gave us each three months to get to know the city, so that we would know it better than the police did. Three months later we both had to pass an examination: ten seconds to think – 'What's on the Lueger Platz? Give the names of all the shops, hotels, restaurants and the numbers of the buses that stop there. Quickly now.' Maybe there's no hotel there? Come on, come on. We had to get to know the city better than the local policeman. 'Name all the streets crossing Taborstrasse. Quickly! How many stops? How many post boxes? If you set off in the direction of . . . what's on the left of you?' And so on.

Both Genka and I passed the exam at the second try. If you didn't pass at the third go you were sent back to the Soviet Union. After the exams I was put straight on to back-up work. But not Genka. While he was learning the city he found time to get to know some crook selling and buying passports. He had passports which were partly false, some with blank pages, and some which had simply been stolen from tourists. The First Department of the GRU buys up passports and other personal documents – diplomas, driving licences, soldiers' identity cards – in huge quantities. Not for re-use but for study and as models for the production of fresh documents. None of these pieces of paper is very highly valued, and getting hold of them is by no means the higher form of intelligence work. But I was put on to back-up work, while Genka wasn't: he was getting hold of passports. And while Genka was working on passports he had plenty of time to himself, and he didn't waste it. He got to know someone else and I was put on to support Genka's operations and cover his tail. After his meetings I would be given some envelopes which I delivered to the embassy. If they were to arrest somebody going into the embassy it would be me and not Gennadi Mikhailovich. He was in the clear. But then he got involved in some more serious affairs. He would go on an operation with five or six Borzois covering him. The following year he was promoted to lieutenant-colonel prematurely. He spent only a couple of years as a major.

I am not given to being envious or jealous. I was glad Genka was doing well. Good luck to him! I would also get myself out of back-up work in the near future.

It was eight o'clock in the evening. I was hurrying home. Four hours sleep and then out again on the job.

The Navigator was smiling at me – the first time for many months.

'At last! I always knew you would eventually strike out on your own. How did you come to meet him?'

'By chance. I had a job to do in Innsbruck and on my way back I decided to look for a hiding-place to have in reserve. I stopped on the side of the road, looked at the place, found it was okay and decided to go back. But my rear wheels were on the soft earth. The earth was soggy and the wheels spun. There was a ditch behind and I just couldn't move. So I stood at the side of the road trying to stop someone to help me out. They all ignored me, until a Fiat 132 stopped with a driver alone in the car. He gave me a hand, giving my car a bit of a push. I was all right, but he was covered in mud: I had given the car too much throttle. At first I intended as a mark of gratitude to give him a bottle of whisky. But I changed my mind and invited him for a meal in the restaurant, so that he could clean himself up. The meal was on me, I said – I'm inviting you.'

'Did he accept?'

'Yes. We had supper, and he invited me for the next time.'

'Did he ask who you were?'

'No, he only asked where I lived. I told him Vienna. I do indeed live in Vienna now.'

'Did you have a diplomatic number on your car?'

'No. I was doing back-up work. In someone else's car.'

The Navigator turned the visiting card over in his hands. He was fascinated by it. An engineer. From Otto Velara. It wasn't every day that a general of the GRU held such a visiting card in his hand. 'Otto Velara'. A real goldmine! There may be some people who underestimate Italy as a country of great thinkers, but not the GRU. The GRU knows that the Italians have very good brains, the brains of great inventors. Few people realise that before the Second World War Italy's technology was at an incredibly high level. The Italians were not especially brilliant in battle, and that obscured the extent of Italian achievement in military technology. In fact those achievements, especially in the spheres of aviation, submarines and high-speed launches were really amazing. Before the war GRU colonel Lev Manevich had shipped from Italy to the Soviet Union tons of technical documentation of tremendous importance. The Italians were the unrecognised geniuses of military and naval technology. There might be some who did not believe it, but the GRU did. 'Otto Velara'! An engineer!

'You don't think he's being planted on us?' It was the last thing the Navigator wanted to believe, but he had to put the question.

'No,' I said with much assurance. 'I have checked him out. And the radio monitors detected nothing suspicious.'

'Don't get excited. You mustn't do that in this business. If he is not a plant you've been very lucky indeed.'

That much I understood myself.

'This is what we'll do,' said the Navigator. 'We have nothing to lose. Let's quickly draw up a check list. Can you do it by tomorrow?'

'I'm on back-up work tonight.'

He frowned, then picked up the telephone and, without dialling any number, said, 'Come in.'

The First Deputy came in.

'Find someone to put in Viktor Andreyevich's place tomorrow.'

'There isn't anybody, comrade general.'

'Just think.'

'There's only Gennadi Mikhailovich.'

'The consul?'

'Yes.'

'Put him on to back-up work. Let him do a bit of that; he's started to think too much of himself. Keep Viktor Andreyevich off all back-up work. He's got a very interesting scheme coming together.'

The coded reply came a couple of days later. The Navigator was not at all anxious to part with 'Otto Velara', with a firm that built amazingly fast and powerful naval ships. The Navigator didn't want to read the message out to me. He simply repeated the reply received from the GRU command point:

'No.' The message did not explain why the reply was 'No'. But in any case 'No' meant that the man from Otto Velara was a person known to the GRU's computer. If nothing had been known about him the answer would have been positive. It was a pity to lose such an interesting man. And the Navigator was probably sorry for me, perhaps for the first time. He could see that I was bursting to be a Viking, and he really didn't want to put me among the Borzois again. He said nothing. But I knew that there was a frightful shortage of manpower for back-up work.

'I have to work on back-up tomorrow, comrade general. May I leave?'

'Off you go,' he said and suddenly smiled. 'You know' – and for the first time he used the familiar form of address – 'every cloud has a silver lining.'

'I, comrade general, seem always to get clouds without silver linings.'

'Maybe not this time. You have been forbidden to meet him, and that's bad. But we have at least added one more scrap of information to our store of experience.'

I looked enquiringly at him.

'You got into trouble and as a result you made the acquaintance of an interesting person. In our work the first encounter is always very difficult. How to approach someone? How to start a conversation? How to develop the acquaintance? In future, as soon as you come across an interesting person, run into his car. Then you've got contact. Get his address from him. Apologise to him, invite him for a drink, find out what he's interested in. Coins? Stamps? You have something to exchange and there's your contact.'

'Comrade general, are you ready to pay for the crashed cars?' I was laughing.

'Certainly,' he replied seriously.

Chapter Eleven

I was being sucked ever deeper into the sticky syrup of agent back-up work. There was no way of getting out.

When a bricklayer builds a wall he gets three helpers by law – someone to mix the mortar, someone to carry the bricks and someone to cut the bricks to size when necessary. But in the work of intelligence-gathering many more helpers are needed for each operational officer. And everyone wants to be the bricklayer. No one wants to be a helper. But you can become a skilled worker only if you can prove that you can do the job as well as or even better than the other skilled men. And how can you do that if back-up work takes up all your time? Every night, every weekend and every holiday.

Nikolai Viktorovich Podgorny, the Soviet President, has disappeared. Vanished into thin air. He was around, and now he isn't. The President is of course a very small pawn, practically nothing, really just a screen. Something like a Soviet ambassador, who swaggers around the embassy, receives important people, shakes them by the hand and smiles, but doesn't take any decisions, and has no access to important secrets. Let him go on smiling and shaking hands: that's his job. But we in the GRU have a direct chain of command. The Navigator is responsible to the head of the GRU. He is responsible to the Chief of the General Staff, who in turn is directly responsible to the Central Committee of the Party. Ambassadors and presidents are just camouflage. A screen.

But, for goodness' sake, if a president, even if he is deprived of any real power, can disappear, if he is remembered for only half a day. . . . Is anybody likely to remember me if I should suddenly disappear?

I have stretched my weary legs under the table and I feel good. It is so quiet and cosy here, that one cannot help but fall asleep. I am tired. A soft melody, a grey haired pianist. . . . He is no doubt a great musician, but tired like me. He has closed his eyes, and his fingers, the long agile fingers of a virtuoso, continue to play out of habit, dancing across the keyboard of an enormous grand piano. He is good enough for the finest orchestra in Vienna, but for some reason he plays

176

in the Schwarzenberg Café. Have you ever been there? I can thoroughly recommend it. If you are burdened by arduous, exhausting work; if you are red-eyed, have aching legs and your nerves are on edge, then come to the Schwarzenberg, order a cup of coffee and settle down in a corner. Of course one can sit outside in the open, at a small white table. But that's not for me. I always go inside and over to the right, to the corner next to the large window, closed off by semi-transparent white curtains. Of course when it is hot in Vienna, everyone sits outside in the fresh air. It's very pleasant to do. But then someone might be watching me from a distance. I don't like the idea that someone might be able to see me. That's why I always go inside.

From my corner I can see everyone who enters the room. I sometimes look outside from behind the curtains, out on to the Schwarzenberg Platz. Nobody seems to be watching me now, and it's good to be alone in such comfort. Mirrors, abstract paintings, luxurious carpets. Dark brown walls of polished oak. The soft music, and the intoxicating aroma of coffee, with its stimulating and soothing effect. If I had a castle, I would certainly have walls like these, upon which I would hang these decadent mirrors and pictures, and in the corner I would place this huge grand piano with the elderly pianist. In front of me I would have a cup of coffee and sit with my legs stretched out under the table, my chin resting on my hand.

I think I have heard this tune before, a long time ago, and that I have seen these pictures on the oaken walls, and the small tables. Of course I have seen it all before, of course I remember that delicate aroma and enchanting melody. All of this I have seen before. It was long ago, years ago. There was a vast beautiful city. There was a quiet square, crossed with tramlines, and a café with large windows. There was this same unforgettable aroma and this same peaceful music. But at that time, on the square next to the café with white tables, there were parked three grimy tanks with white stripes. They stood there silently, without interfering with the wonderful music. It was a hot summer. The huge windows of the café were open and through this one flowed the melody like the sound of a woodland stream. For some reason I could picture quite clearly three grimy tanks with white stripes on the Schwarzenberg Platz.

Tanks have a quite distinctive smell about them. It cannot be confused with anything else. Do you like the smell of tanks? I do too. The smell of a tank is the smell of metal, of enormously powerful engines, of field tracks. Tanks roll into towns from the woods and fields, bringing with them the lingering smell of leaves and fresh grass. The smell of tanks is the smell of wide open spaces and of power. It is a smell that intoxicates, like the smell of wine and blood. I can sense this smell in the quiet Viennese café quite clearly, and with equal clarity I can picture the thousands of grimy tanks on the streets of Vienna. The city seethes, seized with fear and indignation, and along its streets thunder column upon column of tanks. From narrow side-streets and blind corners, more and more armoured dinosaurs appear. As the drivers change up, the engines throw out clouds of dense black smoke mixed with unburnt fuel and lumps of soot.

Grating and thundering, sparks flying from beneath the tracks. Soldiers with faces blackened by soot-laden fumes. Tanks on the wide boulevards and in the narrow streets, tanks . . . everywhere. An old man, weeping, with shaggy grey beard, shouts something and shakes his fist, but who hears him? Is it possible to silence the roaring of the tanks' engines? Too late, old man, you started to cry out too late. You ought to have done it when the leather boots crashed down on the pavements. When the air above the city is filled with the roaring and grating of countless tanks, it is too late to shout. One must either shoot, or remain silent. The city teems with people, there is smoke everywhere. Somewhere there is shooting, somewhere else people are shouting. The smell of burning rubber, the smell of coffee, the smell of blood, the smell of tanks.

I am probably going mad. There is one other possibility, that they all went mad long ago, and I alone am an exception. There is even a third possibility, that everyone went mad a long time ago. Those who appeared mounted on grimy tanks in fine tranquil cities, were without a shadow of a doubt schizophrenic. Those who still live in fine peaceful cities know that one day, sooner or later, these tanks will appear on the Schwarzenberg Platz and they will do nothing to prevent it. They too are schizophrenic.

What about me? I have already been one of the liberators, and it is not as pleasant as might appear from the wings. I no longer wish to play that role. So what do I do? Do I run away? A marvellous idea. I will go and live in the wonderful world of naïve and carefree people. I will go and sit in the café, with my legs stretched under the table, my chin resting on my hand. I will listen to this magical melody. When the grimy tanks appear with their white stripes, I will stand in the crowd, shout and shake my fist. It is bad being the citizen of a country whose streets are patrolled by the grating and clanking armoured columns of liberators. Is it better to be one of the liberators?

The Soviet military attaché in Vienna has vanished too. Disappeared. Vanished into thin air. He has been home to the Soviet Union, 'evacuated', as we say. The evacuation of GRU or KGB officers is ordered if they have committed major mistakes or if they are completely ineffective, if they are suspected of having the kind of contacts with foreigners which are not permitted or if they are suspected of preparing to defect.

Why the military attaché has been evacuated I do not know. It will never be revealed. He has vanished and that's all. He has gone on leave and will not return. The Soviet Union is large and he has got lost somewhere.

His green Mercedes has been inherited by the new military attaché, Colonel Tsvetayev. He is giving himself airs, considering himself the big boss. Our neighbours in the KGB think he is the First Deputy. But with us, as in any similar organisation, a man's official position means nothing. We have our own hierarchy which is secret and undercover. It is an unseen world.

Carry on, colonel, show off a bit. But watch out: very soon the Navigator will summon you to his office for a dressing down. He will inform you very politely that you are not responsible to the Navigator personally, nor to the First Deputy or even to one of the deputies to the Navigator, but just to one of the more successful of the GRU's operational officers, a Viking. And *he* may turn out to be anybody in the embassy, your own assistant, for example. Officially in public you will continue to smile and shake hands and the assistant military attaché with the rank of major or lieutenant-colonel will go behind you carrying your briefcase. You will go around in a Mercedes, while he's in a Ford. But that's only for the outside world, and has no real importance. In the daytime the head of the Mafia may pretend to be a waiter. But that doesn't mean that the manager of the restaurant has greater influence. In the GRU we have the same system. The rank which you have on the surface is not important. It's just for show. In fact we take care to keep our leaders and more talented officers in the background and out of the limelight, and we push on to the stage those who enjoy showing off. Behind the scenes we have our own ranks, our own relative importance and our own scale of values. And behind the scenes the Viking commands the Borzoi. The Viking – the operational officers – gets them by the throat and digs out the secrets. He has to be backed up. Your assistant has already got himself up to the level of active officer, while you, colonel, are still only a Borzoi, a little puppy-dog, a dogsbody. You will be using your Mercedes to back up your assistant. For the slightest mistake the major will ridicule you in the presence of all our spying brotherhood. And for bigger mistakes you'll go to prison. He is getting hold of secrets for the GRU and you are simply covering his tail. It is he who will write a report on you: your fate is in his hands. If you make a mistake you will be done for and you'll disappear. You will be evacuated, like your predecessor. But keep smiling, little dog, just keep smiling. And remember: in three months you will have an examination in knowledge of the city. You'd better know Vienna even better than the police do: there'll be a hundred questions and there ought to be a hundred correct answers. A wrong answer could lead to a mistake in operational work. That would mean failure, a scandal, a Central Committee commission and prison. And if you pass the examination, colonel, you will be put on to back-up work, covering other people's tails, with no days off, no holidays and no hope. Meanwhile, keep smiling.

The work of backing up operational officers may be specific or general. On this occasion the whole of our glorious residency was engaged on specific back-up. The whole team. The whole pack.

The work was being co-ordinated by the Navigator himself. The Soviet ambassador and the consul-general were on general duties and hadn't the slightest idea what was going on. They had simply received a coded message from the Central Committee instructing them to cover, protect and conceal. If we, on direct duty, were to slip up, those on general duties would put up a

179

smokescreen to protect us. Just as an octopus retreats from an enemy behind a curtain of dense liquid. The ambassador and the consul-general would start shouting, protesting, accusing the Austrian police of slandering and provoking us. They would deny absolutely everything. They would stare the police brazenly in the face and put on a show of injured innocence. They would threaten a worsening of diplomatic relations and the end of détente. They would recall that the Red Army had selflessly liberated Austria. They would refer to the number of lives lost in the war and to the crimes of the Nazis. That was their job. They were there to cover our retreat in case we made a mistake.

But we had so far made no mistakes. All was going well. The operation we were carrying out required the combined efforts of several residencies and all the active agents in each of the residencies were drawn into the operation.

A tank engine was being transported. It had already crossed several countries in transit, going from west to east. It would arrive in Hungary, where it would change direction sharply.

The tank engine weighed a ton and a half. Our agents had got hold of it in some unknown country and had transported it across the frontier under some disguise. It had been travelling a long time, crossing many frontiers and always changing its disguise, just as a GRU undercover agent changes passports as he crosses a border.

The container with the tank engine was already in Austria, where it was described as an 'experimental power unit for irrigation systems.' There is starvation in Asia and Africa! Please allow the 'experimental unit' to pass through – help poor countries solve their food problem!

It was nerve-racking work and very hard going. A person who has never been concerned with the transport of heavy loads across state frontiers can have no idea how many bureaucrats are involved in it. And the GRU had to be sure that not one of them suspected the real purpose behind the 'experimental power unit'. If anyone among them should suddenly guess correctly he was immediately to receive rich payment for his perceptiveness and for keeping his guess to himself. Each one of them had to controlled by the GRU, if only at a distance. That was what we were doing.

One of our best officers must be due for a medal. A tank engine, and of the latest design. Not for copying, of course, but for study. Just as an American designer of racing motor-bikes would be very interested in the latest Japanese engine.

Where could I get my hands on something like that, damn it? There were plenty of interesting things about, and it was often not very difficult to get hold of them. But the Information Service of the GRU always bought up three or four identical samples in different parts of the world, and that was that. They didn't need any more. What they wanted was the very latest model, that no one could get his hands on. Sometimes you would offer them something fantastically interesting and they would turn it down. Thanks, but the GRU's undercover residency in Tunis worked faster. Thanks, we've got one already.

There was fierce competition in the GRU. Only the fastest survived.

Time passed very slowly. I was on night-duty. The light in our underground office was always the same – blue. It could be turned up or down, but it remained blue. It was 2.43 in the morning. I felt like walking around to keep sleep at bay. Normally there are no windows at all in premises occupied by a residency. In ours in Vienna there were only three in the whole vast area. You had to leave the main office and go into the corridor, up the stairs, past the photographic laboratory to corridor 'C' and from there upstairs. There were forty-eight steps. There you came to a little passage leading to the heavy door into the aerial room. In the passageway there were three windows. The place was known as the Nevsky Avenue, probably because anyone who had had to sit for hours in the depths of our fortified premises yearned to get out into the little courtyard and enjoy the sunshine. The courtyard was cut off from our working area by dozens of doors, concrete barriers and walls. It was a place where you were not allowed to discuss secret matters. Nevertheless the three windows were protected as all windows in GRU premises were protected. From the outside they looked no different from the other windows – the same grilles as everywhere. But our windows were slightly opaque, so that from the outside it was very difficult to make out what was going on inside. The window panes were very thick, and unbreakable. Moreover, thick glass vibrates less and therefore does not act as a membrane if a powerful source of electromagnetic rays is trained on it. The panes of glass seemed not to have been very carefully made – they were thicker in one place and thinner in another. But that was also deliberate. The unevenness of the glass was calculated by an electronic machine, and someone had received a prize for having invented it. Even if our windows were used as membranes the uneven glass would disperse the reflected beam in a chaotic manner and make it impossible to get satisfactory reception. None of the windows opened, of course. There was a special ventilation system which was kept under guard and which I knew nothing about. But it was clear that the windows were not used for that purpose.

In addition, every window was treble-glazed. The frames were of metal and there were liners between the metal sections, so as further to reduce vibration. From both inside and outside the glazing looked like ordinary window panes, but if you looked closely at the central frame you could see that the pane of glass was not at the same angle. Each pane was at a slightly different angle, also calculated by an electronic machine. This was to prevent the possibility of the windows being used for eavesdropping on us. The walls were even better protected, of course. Especially there, deep under the ground, where we did our work.

Outside it was as black as pitch. I knew that: I had come there only so as to be able to walk around the corridors and stairs. I was duty officer and dared not fall asleep.

The whole night shift was working practically without any participation or interference on my part. The 'TS' group worked round the clock picking up and deciphering military and government radio messages. The control group was also engaged on radio interception. But it was a quite different kind of work. The 'TS' was working in the interests of the Information Service of the GRU, picking up scraps of information out of which the command point and the central computer were continually putting together a general picture of what was going on in the world. The radio control group had different functions, though not less responsible ones. They were working only for our residency, keeping watch on what the local police were doing. The group always knew what the Viennese police were up to, how their force had been distributed round the city, and whom their plain-clothes agents were following. The radio control could always tell us if, for example, today the police had been following a suspicious-looking Arab at the railway station or that yesterday the whole force had been put on to catching a group of drug-pedlars. Very often it was not possible to work out what the police were up to, but even then the radio monitors were always ready to warn us where any particular police activity was going on.

Apart from the group intercepting radio transmissions, the radio operators and cipher clerks also worked at night. But I did not have the right to enquire into their work. So why did I have to sit there all night? Because it was so laid down. There were various different groups at work which were not subordinate to one another. So someone had to be in charge. That was why we did night duty.

I was just an ordinary operational officer of no particular distinction, but for all of them I was the incarnation of authority. It didn't matter to them whether I was a Viking or a Borzoi. I belonged to the upper class. I was much higher up the scale than any of those who had no contact with foreigners. For any of them, irrespective of their military rank, to become an operational officer was a beautiful but unrealisable dream.

'Coffee, Viktor Andreyevich?'

It was Borya, the third cipher clerk. He had nothing to do. The main receiver was silent and the receiver used for communication with agents was also quiet.

'Yes please, Borya.'

I was preparing to complete my description of the landing grounds I had selected for a *Spetsnaz* company of the 6th Guard Tank Army. On instructions from the GRU I had selected three possible places, in case of war. But since Borya had left his workplace I clearly would not be able to finish the work.

'Sugar?'

'No, Borya. I never take sugar.'

Borya worshipped at the throne of Venus. GRU and KGB cipher clerks round the world all worshipped the same lady. Borya knew that I had a lot of work to do, but he hovered around, trying to find a way of diverting my attention from the next war and of turning it to a discussion of matters concerning his religion.

'Viktor Andreyevich.'

'What is it?' I replied without looking up from my notebook.

'The dip-couriers have produced a new rhyme.'

'A dirty one, of course?'

'That's the only kind they ever have.'

'Damn you, Borya. Come on, let's hear your rhyme.'

Borya coughed and cleared his throat and then, in the pose of a great poet, recited:

> 'I walk in the dew
> My feet in the muck.
> I'm just like you,
> I just want to fuck.'

'I heard that, Borya, long before you.'

Borya was disappointed: he thought he had something new. But he wasn't upset for long.

'I'll tell you one that very few people have heard. In Leningrad there was a woman-chaser who produced marvellous verses:

> O, Leningrad,
> O my city,
> All people are whores,
> But you are holy!'

There was no getting away from him. Yet it would not be wise to get on bad terms with him. Cipher clerks were a lower class, but they were closer than anybody to the Navigator: his faithful slaves. I had no desire to hear more of his poetry, but there was no sense in cutting him off. It was better to turn the conversation in another direction.

'Did you work in the staff of the Leningrad military district?'

'No, I was in the eighth section of the staff of the 7th Army.'

'And after that?'

'Then I went straight to Vatutinki.'

'Oho!'

Vatutinki is a top-secret little town near Moscow, where the GRU's main radio-receiving centre is situated. Everything is secret there. Even the cemetery. Vatutinki is paradise. But like a real paradise, it has one inconvenience. There is no way out. Anyone who lands up in Vatutinki can rest assured that he will be buried in that same cemetery and nowhere else. A few of those who were sent to that wonderful place spent some time abroad. But their lives don't become any more varied on that account. All cipher clerks are restricted to very precisely defined areas within an embassy. Each one has his own area. For Borya it was just sixteen rooms, including the room he lived in, the main office, and the offices of the Navigator and his deputies. He was not allowed to go outside those limits. To do so was a crime—a serious one. And he could certainly not go outside the embassy. Borya would live inside that area for two years and then he would be transported back to Vatutinki, again within a restricted area. He would not travel on his own; he would be sent under guard. But Borya was lucky. Many of those who land up in Vatutinki never go anywhere. And even they are fortunate, compared with the thousands of cipher clerks working in the staffs of military districts, fleets, armies or flotillas. For every one of them Vatutinki would be a beautiful but virtually unachievable dream.

'Viktor Andreyevich, tell me something, please, about prostitutes. Because I have to go back to Vatutinki in seven months. And the lads there will laugh at me if I've been to Vienna and haven't any good stories to tell.'

'Borya, I don't know anything about prostitutes. I swear I don't.'

It was not that Borya was trying to provoke me on orders from above. He simply wanted to hear about those things. A cipher clerk who returns to Vatutinki from abroad is judged by his ability to tell stories of his sexual escapades. Everybody realises that he has been very restricted in his movements round the embassy, sometimes to only five rooms. Everybody realises that his stories are made up and that no officer would dare to tell a cipher clerk anything about what he sees going on. Nevertheless a good storyteller is appreciated in Vatutinki, as one is valued among illiterate peoples. In fact, the same thing can be observed among civilised peoples too: the Viennese shops, I had noticed, were crammed full of adventure stories about imagined planets. Anyone with any intelligence understands that they are pure invention, but they appreciate the authors of those inventions just as those who tell sexy stories are valued in Vatutinki.

'Viktor Andreyevich, come on – tell me about the prostitutes. Do they really stand out there on the street? What are they dressed in? Viktor Andreyevich, I know you don't go near them, but what do they look like from a distance?'

Before 1945 the life of a cipher clerk was different. They had complete freedom. They could go anywhere in the embassy, sometimes even outside (though with an escort, of course). But they were completely free. They even went to Vatutinki for their holidays. After they had served for a year they had a month's leave.

This meant, obviously, that a cipher clerk had plenty of opportunity to escape. In 1945 Igor Guzenko, who was a cipher clerk in the GRU diplomatic residency in Ottawa, took advantage of that freedom.

Guzenko struck the Soviet Union a frightful blow, no less serious, perhaps, than when 190 German divisions were suddenly let loose against the Red Army.

The GRU was operating as usual from the territory of one country against another. Its operation in Canada was directed against the USA. The residency in Ottawa had achieved the kind of success that no other residency in the world had achieved. The results of its work were so astounding that all the work of the GRU was handled by the First Deputy Head of the GRU, while the Head of the GRU himself took the Ottawa residency under his personal control and directed its work, reporting on it only to Malenkov. Malenkov was unequalled in the power struggle. He was the very incarnation of backstage intrigue and the concentration of power in few hands. He was an unrecognised genius. (In October 1952 Malenkov told the Party that it no longer had any need of a General Secretary. And the Party accepted Malenkov's advice, reducing Stalin from the rank of General Secretary to that of an ordinary secretary, of which there were dozens. Malenkov then told the Party that among the various secretaries one should be first. So the Party made Malenkov First Secretary and left Stalin as a simple secretary. Stalin protested, arrested Malenkov's doctor, accused him of espionage and extracted from him a confession that Malenkov was also a spy. But at that point Stalin died in mysterious circumstances, and Malenkov remained First Secretary of the Party, having liberated his doctor and labelled Stalin a madman.)

So in 1945 documents about American atomic secrets were arriving directly on Malenkov's desk. It was at precisely that moment that the cipher clerk Guzenko defected and informed the West of the GRU's achievements.

After that, the cipher clerks had a very rough time. It became impossible for them to defect in any circumstances. Even if an aircraft transporting a cipher clerk burst into flames and began to plunge to the ground, the head of the escort is obliged to shoot the man. In the same way as a diplomatic courier is obliged to break the seal on the container and press the red knob if the security of the container is threatened in any way.

'Viktor Andreyevich, is it true that they grab passers-by by the arm and invite them to have sex?' His voice told of a burning interest and anger. He was an angry cipher clerk, and every cipher clerk was as angry as a randy stallion.

Prostitution is a profession. Whoring is a hobby. Anastasia, Borya's wife, belonged to the second category. She was sitting alongside me and stroking my arm. I was driving the car and so couldn't stop her. She laughed, saying she was afraid I was going to run into a car coming the other way and was trying to help me. When there were no oncoming cars she still kept her hand on my arm and gently squeezed it, when suddenly an oncoming car appeared.

Anastasia believed in God. Her god was Venus, like her husband. But he was in a cage, while she was free to fly away. She was sitting alongside me. She had very beautiful knees.

The wives of cipher clerks had no access to any secret information and were therefore completely free. Once a month, and sometimes more often, they could go outside the embassy with a ridiculously small escort: just one operational officer. She did not, of course, have the right to be outside the embassy in the hours of darkness, and she could not be taken into big shops where she might be kidnapped. Everyone knew that she was not allowed to talk to the assistants in the shops. A knowledge of languages was forbidden, and so were attempts to communicate by gestures. But in every other way she was free.

'Vitya.' She did not call me 'Viktor Andreyevich', because she did not recognise differences of rank. She divided humanity into men and women. And men were divided in turn into those who were sexually active and those who weren't. She apparently put me into the first category. I don't know why. But she knew best. 'Vitya, we've already been in the shops and our conscience is clear. Won't you take me to see a film?'

'What kind of film?'

'A love story.'

'That's forbidden.'

'You know, Vitya, in Somalia we had a Navigator, maybe you know him, Major-general Sherstnev, and he told me that if you were sure that no third person knew about it, you could do your own thing. Otherwise life wouldn't be very interesting.'

'And you did with him things that no third person knew about?'

'I did, Vitya.'

'But we may be followed. . . .'

'Vitya, you are an operational officer and you know how to make sure. . . .'

'But that takes several hours.'

'You just try to do it by using your very best check-up route.'

She was breathing fast. She was very experienced. Once a month she would persuade the Navigator to let her go round the shops. She had been accompanied by a variety of officers. She knew that it was possible, when it was necessary, to check very quickly whether you were being followed or not.

I seemed to be sadly lacking in imagination. And without it you could only go downhill. An officer who planned his moves himself always did his best to disappear into the shadows and to let the men who were covering his tail get into the police limelight. The Austrian police were actually very well disposed towards us, but sometimes they lost their tempers. Of course, they never made a great fuss by throwing us out. It wasn't the same as Great Britain by any means, but all the same they sometimes expelled us from Austria. No fuss, no scandal. Nevertheless, if you hadn't been able to operate in Austria there wouldn't be much point in sending you to Holland where the police go about their business much more seriously or to Canada where the prospects were nothing like they had been in 1945, before Guzenko's defection.

All Vikings stayed in the shadows. But if you were a Borzoi, everybody knew you. It was natural to put the blame on the one nearest, lest the one who was further away got too near and put the blame on you. The Vikings were right to expose us, to push us to the front and to protect themselves with our lack of enterprise and ability. But I would also be a Viking. I had made up my mind to that. I wouldn't sleep at night, but I would find a way to get hold of some secrets!

The trouble was that everything they had taught us in the Academy was more than twenty years out of date and had been applied in practice many times over. I needed new tricks.

This may sound very strange, but in order to encourage us to use our imagination to carry out our illegal deeds, we were urged to read detective stories. The calculation was that it would help us develop a critical attitude to other people's deeds and decisions. The authors of detective stories are professional entertainers of the public, not professional seekers after secrets. They can cheerfully avoid the main problem, for example. How can a commander give you the job of obtaining a sample of a new weapon if nothing is known about it, nothing at all—when the world does not even suspect that such a weapon exists? Yet the GRU set out on its hunt for the atomic bomb in the United States at a time when no one else in the world suspected that it was possible to create such a weapon, and when even the President of the USA did not yet appreciate its real value.

In order to develop in us a more criminal approach to our work of intelligence-gathering, they had once taken us to a secret section of the crime museum in Moscow – on the Petrovka, No. 38. The Moscow police did not, of course, know who we were. There had been plenty of secret delegations there from the Ministry of the Interior, the KGB, the People's Control, the Komsomol and goodness knows what other organisations. There were many people who needed to develop their criminal way of thinking.

There was no gainsaying it: it was an interesting museum. What I like most of all was a machine for manufacturing money. Students at the Moscow technical college had made it and sold it to some Georgians for 10,000 roubles, saying, 'We need real money: we can always make another counterfeiting machine.' The students showed the Georgians where to put the colour, how to put the paper in and where to pour the spirit. The machine produced beautiful crisp ten-rouble notes which no expert could distinguish from genuine ones. The students warned the Georgians not to let themselves be carried away: greed ruined the priest! And not to let the machine get too hot, because that would cause the design to run. And off the Georgians went to Georgia, where the started printing money in the evenings. But then the machine broke down and a mechanic had to be brought into the gang. He opened the machine and whistled. They had been tricked. The machine was not capable of printing false money. A hundred real notes had been put into it. When you turned the handle a brand new 10-rouble note popped out. But there were only a hundred of them. Once they had all popped out there were no more. The Georgians went to the police, and the students were caught and each given three years in prison for swindling. But the Georgians got ten years apiece. For their efforts and determination to produce counterfeit money. And that was right: the students had only tricked the Georgians, while the Georgians had tried to trick the workers' and peasants' state.

People with such rich imaginations have all the luck. So what could I think up?

Chapter Twelve

The recruitment of agents is a very complicated business. Like hunting the sable, which you have to hit in the eye so as not to spoil the skin. A good hunter has no difficulty in hitting the sable in the eye. The difficulty is to track down a sable in the *taiga*.

The GRU, in its search for people who possess secret information, knows that there are plenty of such people. But a presidential adviser, a missile designer or a general staff officer are all cut off from them, by security guards, by high walls, guard dogs, secret privileges, huge pay packets. The GRU needs keepers of secrets who live on their own, without bodyguards, or who do not have any bright prospects or big salaries. It wants people with secrets who are short of money. How to find them? How to pick them out from among the millions of other people who do not have access to any secret information? You don't know? But I knew! Now I really knew – I had a brilliant idea.

The trouble was that it was impossible to get in to see the Navigator. He had been shut in his office for days, refusing to see anyone. The First Deputy was like a bear with a sore head: if you went near him, he would snap at you. He was spending practically all his time in the Navigator's office. And they were joined by Peter Yegorovich Dunayev. Officially he was a vice-consul. Unofficially he was a colonel in the GRU and the Navigator's deputy. They had now been joined by another big shot – Vice-Admiral Bondar, deputy head of the 1st directorate of the GRU. He had arrived in Vienna as a member of some delegation, not a military one – purely civil of course. But he was never to be seen among the delegates. He had more serious worries.

The whole group – the general, the admiral and the two colonels – very rarely emerged from the Navigator's office. They were like shock-workers at the pit-face, like men trying to break the output record.

Zhenya, the fifth cipher clerk, took them their breakfast, lunch and supper to the office and later went to collect the trays. Everything was cold and untouched. But he also brought out piles of coffee cups and ashtrays full of cigarette ends. What was going on, Zhenya of course had no idea. All the Navigator's coded messages were handled by Alexander Ivanovich, the first cipher clerk. But his face was always expressionless, revealing nothing.

It was quite clear from their fierce gloom that they were not discussing success but failure. And not somebody else's failure: their own. What the four of them were doing in the office was probably being called by its scientific terms: 'localisation of a failure'. In other words, it was a major disaster which had taken place. What they were up to I didn't know. I was not supposed to know. It was clear that they were cutting the threads and trying to limit the extent of the failure. How were they cutting them? One could only guess. If it was an agent who was in serious trouble, what sometimes happened was that he would be given money and a passport and told to go to Chile or Paraguay, and disappear. He would be given enough money to last the rest of his life. Whatever happened, it was vital that the GRU faded completely into the background. Someone might have to be killed. But like the anaconda snake, the GRU never killed out of a love of killing. It killed only in situations of extreme need. But it killed surely and cleanly. It was not a problem for the GRU to kill. Equally, it was not a solution this time. Things had clearly gone too far for a simple murder to solve the problem. That was why it was better at the moment not to approach the First Deputy. He would only kick me out again.

'Your kindness, Vitya, is going to be the end of you. You simply mustn't be so good to people. A person has the right to be kind to people up to a very definite limit. Beyond that point you either hit out at them or you fetch up in the mud yourself. Old Darwin even provided that rule with a scientific basis. It's the fittest and the strongest who survive. They say the theory applies only to the animal world, and they are right. But then we are all animals. How do we differ from them? In very little. Other animals don't have venereal diseases. What else? Only the smile. Man is able to smile. But the world doesn't become any nicer because of our smiles. To live means to survive. And survival is a struggle, a fight for a place in the sun. Don't weaken, Viktor, and don't be too kind, or they'll trample you underfoot.'

It was long after midnight, and there was a cool breeze coming up from the banks of the Danube. Somewhere far in the distance a plane was landing. The rain had stopped, but big warm drops were still dripping from the chestnut trees. The First Deputy was sitting opposite me, his sorrowful face resting on his hand. In fact he was no longer the First Deputy: we simply went on calling him that out of habit. And that was not all. He was now only GRU Colonel Nikolai Tarasovich Moroz, an intelligence officer operating under diplomatic cover. That wasn't very much. The majority of the officers in the GRU were colonels; there were all sorts of colonels in the GRU. It was not the rank but the actual achievements and real position that mattered. A colonel in intelligence could be just a Borzoi. Or he could be a proud and successful Viking. A colonel could be deputy to the Navigator or even First Deputy, and in some cases even the Navigator in a small residency. Colonal Nikolai Tarasovich Moroz had just been reduced from the second highest level to the very bottom. Dismissed. For such disasters in the GRU you could fetch up in the furnace, feet first. For such things you could wake up in your coffin. Anyway, the First Deputy had been dismissed. Three Borzois who had always taken care of his security had been shipped back to Moscow.

All was calm. From the outside you couldn't tell there had been any changes. Colonel Moroz's reign was over, but nobody had yet been sent to replace him. So we were being directed by the Navigator personally and through his deputies. It was not easy for him without a First Deputy but, to tell the truth, the Navigator himself wasn't making any great effort at the moment. Everything seemed to be going on its own.

Each of us endured the fall of the First Deputy in his own way and reacted accordingly. For the 'TS' officers, the radio monitors, the photo-analysts, the security men, the people who operated the security system, the radio operators, the cipher clerks and all the others who took no part in the gathering of intelligence, he remained a demi-god. He was after all still an operational intelligence officer! But among us other operational officers, there was a variety of attitudes. The captains, majors and lieutenant-colonels continued to treat him with respect. He was their equal in position and still a full colonel. Among the colonels themselves, especially the less successful ones, there were some who were inclined to jeer at him. We humans are oddly made up: those who had tried hardest to be in his good books were now the ones who did most of the jeering. They say a friend in need is a friend indeed. Nikolai Tarasovich did not take offence at the jokes being made. He didn't snap at people. Nikolai Tarasovich simply drank. He drank a lot. The Navigator paid no attention, let him drink. The fellow was very miserable. I had the impression that the Navigator himself was also drinking. Borya, the third cipher clerk, said that the Navigator was drinking in front of a mirror, locked in his office. He didn't want to drink without the mirror because he believed that solitary drinking was a serious form of drunkenness. I was not sure whether Borya was joking or telling the truth. But three months previously Borya would not have dared to make jokes like that or have revealed the Navigator's personal secrets. Our Navigator did not have such a firm hand on the situation. It was possible that the Navigator and the former First Deputy had an occasional drink together. But if so the Navigator kept it to himself, while Nikolai Tarasovich made no effort to conceal his drinking.

That evening, in the pouring rain, I ran to my car, but he, poor chap, got wet through, fumbling with the key to his Opel.

'Nikolai Tarasovich, get into my car and I'll drive you home.'

'How will I get to the embassy in the morning?'

'I'll pick you up on my way.' And off we went.

'Vitya, what about a drink?'

How could I refuse? So I drove him over to the other side of the Danube, where I had places that I thought probably few intelligence services knew. And the prices were reasonable. So we drank.

'You're too good, Viktor. You mustn't be. You help a man out in misfortune, and he will do you down in the end. They say people are beasts. I'm afraid I just can't agree with that, Vitya. People are worse than beasts. They are as cruel as pigeons.'

'Nikolai Tarasovich, everything will come right eventually. Don't upset yourself. The Navigator treats you like a brother. He will back you up. And you've got influential connections in the Aquarium and in our directorate, at the command point and in information . . . '

'That's all very true, Vitya. Only . . . it's a secret . . . I've made a big mess of things, a terrible mess . . . it went to the Central Committee of the Party, and connections in the Aquarium don't help there. You probably wonder why I'm not already back in the Soviet Union? It's because it would appear strange if there were a spy trial in one country and a lot of Soviet diplomats disappeared. Nosy journalists would make the connection at once. And that would be like admitting our guilt, and showing that we were covering up our tracks. . . . So I'm only in Vienna for the time being. When things quieten down a little and it's all forgotten they'll remove me. I shall be evacuated.'

'But what if you succeeded in recruiting an especially important agent?'

He gave me a very sad look. I felt a little awkward for what I had said. We both knew that miracles don't happen. But there was something in what I had said that pleased him and he forced a smile.

'See here, Suvorov, I've been talking too much today, and I've no right to do so . . . I'm talking because I'm drunk, but also because among all the people I know you are probably the one least inclined to do the dirty on others. Listen to me, Suvorov, and remember what I say. Our crowd at the moment are in a state of complete collapse. They are half-asleep, like after having sex. That is because the Navigator had got it in the neck and has barely survived. But I've been thrown out, and the transit of illegals through Austria has been stopped temporarily, and the documents collected are going to the Aquarium by different channels. Many of them think there's no need to do anything. They have all got lazy and careless without the firm hand of our Navigator. It won't last long. We have lost a priceless source of information, and the Central Committee will very soon remind us of the fact. The chief will be put on the rack. Everyone will be questioned. The Navigator can point the finger at anyone, and he will have to choose someone to be sacrificed on the altar. Just to teach people not to get slack. Be on your guard, Viktor. Very soon the Navigator will be brought a message from Kir, and he is terrible when he is in a rage. He'll wreck quite a few careers. And rightly so. Why on earth do you want to wait around, like a flock of sheep? Get working right away, Viktor. Tomorrow it may be too late, Just heed my advice.'

'Nikolai Tarasovich, I do have quite a good idea, but it's ages since I was able to get to see the Navigator. Perhaps I ought to try again tomorrow?'

'I don't advise it, Vitya, Not just now. He will soon be summoning everybody one at a time on to the carpet. That will be the moment to tell him about your idea. Only don't tell me anything. I am now nobody and you mustn't tell me anything. After all, I might steal your idea. I need good ideas now very badly. Aren't you scared?'

'No, I'm not scared.'

'But you ought to be, Suvorov. I'm the same sort of swine as all the rest. Maybe worse. Shall we go and find some tarts?'

'It's late, Nikolai Tarasovich.'

'Just for a short while. I could show you some super girls! Don't be stand-offish. Come on, let's go.'

Actually I was not against having a look at some girls. Although he thought of himself as a real tough, and although he had been mixed up in many dirty operations, he was still a decent chap. He was a rare exception among the thousands of two-legged beasts I came across on my way. I was more of a beast than he was. And my sexual instincts were no weaker than my instinct for self-preservation. But he was drunk, and with him I could have got into trouble. Trouble that would result in evacuation.

'It's already too late.'

He realised that I wasn't against going to see some girls, and relaxing a little in their company, but that I wouldn't do it on that occasion. And he didn't argue.

I wanted to think about anything except what was going to happen to me in a few minutes' time on the other side of the armoured door of the Navigator's office.

He was very fierce when he was angry, as Nikolai Tarasovich had said. He was especially frightening, when he had received a message from Kir in Moscow. On the Navigator's orders, Alexander Ivanovich, the first cipher clerk, had read out the message 'from higher up' to our whole crowd. It had been a very stern message.

After that the colonels were called in to be dressed down. Face to face. And after that the lieutenant-colonels. The Navigator delivered his judgments quickly. Soon it was to be my turn.

'Tell me about it.'

'Alpine tourism.'

'Alpine tourism?' The Navigator rose slowly from his chair. 'Did you say Alpine tourism?' He just couldn't stay sitting down. He went quickly from one corner of the room to another, smiling at something and looking right past me. 'Al-pine tour-ism.' He put the first finger of his right hand to his high forehead and then pointed it at me like a gun. 'I always knew you had a wonderful head.'

He sat back comfortably in his chair with his head on his hand. The orange light from the lampshade played over his eyes and I felt all the weight of his powerful brain. 'Tell me about Alpine tourism,' he said.

'Comrade general, the 6th US Fleet controls the Mediterranean. I realise that the GRU observes it from Italy, from Washington, from Greece, Turkey, Syria, the Lebanon, Egypt, Libya, Tunisia, Algeria, Morocco, Spain and France, from Malta and Cyprus, from satellites and from ships of the 5th squadron. But we could study the 6th Fleet from the inside as well as from the outside. Our observation point would be the Austrian Alps. Our experience would of course be extended to Switzerland and other countries, but we would be the first. The 6th Fleet is a goldmine. Nuclear aircraft carriers, the latest aircraft, all kinds of missiles, submarines, landing ships, with tanks, artillery and all the weapons carried by the ground forces. We could find everything in the 6th Fleet: nuclear warheads, nuclear reactors and all kinds of electronic apparatus. . . .'

He did not interrupt me.

'For an American a posting to the 6th fleet is an opportunity to look at Europe. Why fly back to America when you could spend a marvellous month's leave in Austria, Switzerland or France? After a few exhausting months under the blazing sun snow-covered mountains are exactly what a naval officer needs.'

His eyes shone: 'If you had been born in the wicked world of capitalism you would have been a successful businessman. Go on . . .'

'I propose a change of tactics. I propose catching the mouse, not when he's in his hole, but when he comes out of it. I suggest that we do not try to penetrate the especially secret places and do not try to catch some particular mouse. I suggest we make a mouse-trap. A small hotel in the mountains, which would cost us very little – 300,000 dollars, no more. To put the plan into action I need only one thing: an agent who has worked for a long time but has now lost his potential as an agent. I need one of the older men, completely devoted to our work, in whom you have confidence. I believe you must have older agents who have gone into "conservation". We will find a little mountain hotel on the verge of bankruptcy, of which there are quite a few, and we'll breathe new life into it, introducing our agent as a partner with money. In that way we will save the hotel and put the owner on his feet. When we've collected information about the hotels we'll choose one in which Americans from the 6th Fleet stay most often. The hotel would not be a place for recruitment but for studying them. A lightning recruitment could take place later, in another place.'

'To use a hotel is a rather passive approach. Somebody may stop there or not. We may have to wait a long time. . . .'

'It's like a fisherman with his line. You have to know where to cast it and what bait to use.'

'Very well. I order you to gather material about small mountain hotels which are for sale for any reason. They don't sell them if they are doing well.'

'Comrade general, I have already collected that information. Here it is. . . .'

I was no longer doing back-up work. Everybody knew that. Everybody was trying to forecast what would happen to me. Would I enjoy such privileges for long? But it was not difficult to determine my fate. You had only to watch the first cipher clerk. He knew everything. All the secrets. He was the barometer by which to judge the mood of our Navigator.

And the first cipher clerk had started addressing me by my first name and patronymic: Viktor Andreyevich. A message for you, Viktor Andreyevich. Good morning, Viktor Andreyevich. Sign here, Viktor Andreyevich.

It was an amazing change. It had never happened before with the first cipher clerk. He was not an operational officer, but he was closer than anybody to the Navigator. He had the rank of lieutenant-colonel, and he addressed only full colonels by their first names and patronymics. He didn't even bother to give the lieutenant-colonels, majors and captains any rank at all, just: here's a message for you. No more. Now suddenly he had remembered my name and had used it in public. It produced complete silence in our main office the first time he did it. Looks of amazement were shot in my direction. Seryozha— 'Twenty-seven'—allowed his jaw to drop.

The first time it happened, the first cipher clerk summoned me to the Navigator:

'The Navigator is waiting for you, Viktor Andreyevich.'

Afterwards everyone was trying to guess how I had managed to distinguish myself. I occasionally caught snatches of conversation about me: for example, that I had recruited a Chinese attaché! There were all sorts of rumours about me. But apart from myself the only ones to know what I was doing were the Navigator, the first cipher clerk and Nikolai Tarasovich Moroz, the former First Deputy. He was no longer drinking, and nobody was joking about him. Earlier, when he had been the First Deputy, he used to say: 'I order you!' Then he stopped saying anything. Now, as an ordinary operational officer, he had started saying: 'On behalf of the Navigator, I order you!' His voice had begun to ring once again. If he was again issuing orders, that meant that he had the necessary powers. Once he had begun to speak in that tone, it was clear he felt he had backing.

He had lost the title of First Deputy, which was very important. But there was something else more important – the Navigator trusted the colonel once again and depended on him. Previously the First Deputy had used his authority to hold our whole gang in his fist. Now he was doing the same again, only on behalf of the Navigator.

'Comrade general, tomorrow I shall need three men for back-up work, and on Saturday night I shall need five.'

'Take them.'

'But who?'

'Arrange it with Nikolai Tarasovich. Whoever's not busy.'

'And if there are only colonels and lieutenant-colonels?'

'Take them too.'

'But who will command them?'

'You command them. On the day the operation is carried out I authorise you to use the formula "On behalf of the Navigator".'

'Thank you, comrade general.'

Nikolai Tarasovich and I were working together. Like two real aces, with a whole squadron of people to protect us.

We were setting up a mouse-trap in the mountains. We were developing a big business. I was not at all displeased with the fact that he had been put on to my plan, and that I had been made totally responsible to him. He had experience and he had a network of agents.

With permission from the Aquarium, the Navigator had taken some sleeping agents out of 'conservation' and posted them to Austria to take part in the 'Alpine tourism' operation. We had bought not one hotel but three. The GRU didn't think them dear.

The agents taken out of conservation were divided into three categories: a group of agents with a direct channel of communication, who could pass messages directly to Vatutinki without exposing us to risk. A few others were working under the control of Nikolai Tarasovich. And one was put directly under me.

He had previously been known as 173-V-106-299. Now he was called 173-V-4I-299. He had been recruited in 1957 in Ireland. He had worked for five years on intelligence-gathering, but what he had gathered was not recorded in his case file. Between the lines you could gather that there had been great activity but small returns. Then there was a completely obscure passage in his biography. It said simply that he had been put in direct contact with the Aquarium and was not responsible to the GRU Navigator in Vienna. That period ended with his being awarded the Order of Lenin, payment of a huge bonus and his transfer to extended 'conservation' under the control of our residency.

During the years of his 'conservation' there were no meetings with him. Now he had been brought out of hibernation into active service again. He had been given some control tasks to carry out. He thought he was already in action, but in fact he was just being tested. Had he cooled off? Had he changed his ideas of his allegiance?

The Navigator is changing course. We all sense it. He has swung the wheel sharply round and is driving our ship through very stormy waters. He is taking chances. He is making the boat heel over, and that is the way to ship a lot of water. But he has a strong hand.

Something is changing. Security measures are becoming more intensive. Everybody on back-up work! A different kind of operation was afoot. Make contact with advertising agencies! Collect material about guides and hotel employees. All very secret. Make a mistake and you'll finish up in prison.

Make direct contact with advertising agents on the Mediterranean coast. What on earth have we gone into the tourist business for?

Operational officers go one after the other into the offices of the Navigator's deputies. Then they disappear for several days. To hide a transmitter in the mountains. To put money into a hiding place, more and more money. The Navigator's deputies check up on how the tasks are carried out. What on earth is going on? You can't keep going to the Navigator for advice: he is busy. Do not disturb! But where can a deputy get the right answer? Should one ask Nikolai Tarasovich Moroz? He is no longer the First Deputy, but he still knows everything. The deputies crowd into Nikolai Tarasovich's office, though he is no longer entitled to an office. He is nobody, just an officer. But until a new First Deputy arrives. . . .

Nikolai Tarasovich is a nobody. But it is better to go to him for advice and listen to his reproaches than to make a mistake. One mistake and you are for Siberia.

Again everybody is on back-up work round the clock. Night and day. Without any days off, without holidays and without let-up.

'Nikolai Tarasovich I need someone for back-up work.'

'All right, Alexander Alexandrovich, think of someone.'

Alexander Alexandrovich thought.

'Vitya Suvorov, maybe?'

'No, he can't be used for that.'

'Who, then?' Alexander Alexandrovich, a deputy to the Navigator, had only one operational officer in reserve and that is Nikolai Tarasovich Moroz. Alexander Alexandrovich looks across enquiringly at him in the hope that he might volunteer for the job. There is nobody else to send: they are all out on the job. But Nikolai Tarasovich remains silent.

'So, what? Do I have to go out on a back-up job myself? I am after all the Navigator's deputy.'

'But why don't you, Alexander Alexandrovich, just for once? If there's no one else to send?'

Alexander Alexandrovich continued to think and at last reaches a conclusion: he would send Vitali 'Aeroflot' out twice in a night.

'There you are, you see, and you said there was no one to send.'

Where on earth is the Navigator driving us? Is it wise to heel the ship over so far? Won't it capsize? No, it won't. We are well trained, from *Spetsnaz* days. Everybody into action! Alexander Alexandrovich on to back-up work. Watching over the military attaché, in a green Mercedes.

We are exhausted and getting dizzy. A mistake, and prison. For every operation a plan has to be drawn up. After every operation a report to be made. That is so that it will be easier for the inspectors from the 1st directorate of the GRU to find the culprits.

In the main office the lights are never put out. There is now no point in appointing a duty officer because the place is full of officers at every hour of the day and night.

At a desk to my left Slava from the trade mission, a young captain, is writing a report, covering up his work with his hand. He is right to do it: nobody is supposed to know other people's secrets. And how is Slava to know that I am the author of the operation he has been on? Or that a week ago the Navigator, Nikolai Tarasovich and I spent the whole night discussing every detail of it. How can Slava know that he has been covering my tail? When he came out on to that clearing in the forest I saw him and saw him quite clearly. But he didn't see me, and couldn't do so. He had no right to see me. So let him get on with his writing.

Viktor Andreyevich had a headache. His eyes ached too. He was sitting in an office and studying some hotel registers. There were a lot of them, from various hotels including those that did not belong to us. We had copies of the registers from dozens of hotels with tens of thousands of names. It was, of course, only history. But he who knows the past can make a forecast about the future. Correct or not, that's another question. But it was not possible to know what the future held without knowing the present and the past.

There were thousands of hotels in Austria and millions of tourists. If our agents obtain more registers it would be possible to feed the names into a computer to make our forecasts. But for the time being we were doing it all by hand.

A group of Japanese tourists – sixteen people. Were they of any interest? Perhaps, only I had no way of finding out. I could not know whether they were interesting or not. A pity, but I put them straight among the uninteresting ones. Besides, a Japanese tourist never returned to the same place, but was always in a hurry to see the whole planet. So I passed over the Japanese.

An English couple from London. Interesting? No way of knowing. So I passed them over too. I went to see Nikolai Tarasovich.

'Look what I've found!'

He looked, nodded his head and clicked his tongue. A single American from the little Italian port of Gaeta. What does that name mean to you? What does it mean to anybody? What would it mean to an officer of the KGB? Absolutely nothing. A little fishing village, in which there happened for some reason to be an American. Why? Who cared? No one learning that an American from Gaeta had stopped in a little mountain hotel in Austria would pay the slightest attention to it.

But we were military intelligence officers. Every one of us had started our service in an information group or department. Each of us had learnt by heart thousands of numbers and names. For every one of us such names as Pirmasens, Penmarch, Oban, Holy Loch, Woodbridge and Zweibrucken had a heavenly sound. What a joy it was to hear the word Gaeta! That little village was the base for just one naval vessel with the huge number '10' written on its hull. Now do you remember? No? It was the American cruiser *Albany*, flagship of the 6th Fleet. In it were concentrated all the secrets and all the lines of control. What a wooden head I had. Why hadn't the idea of having mountain hotels occurred to me a year ago? Quite recently an American from the little Italian village had stayed in a mountain hotel. He must have been connected with the *Albany*. We did not know who he was, but it was impossible that an American in that God-forsaken village should not know other Americans off the cruiser. Never mind if he was not the captain, or an officer, or even a sailor on the cruiser. Never mind if he was not connected with the navy. Perhaps he was a parson, or a seller of pornography. But he would have contact with sailors off the cruiser and that was the most important. If only our mouse-trap had been in place a year previously we would certainly have descended on the poor American with all our force.

A mass round-up! Dozens of spies against one victim. The victim senses that there are sharks on all sides and that there is no escape for him. Sometimes, when such a mass round-up takes place, with the participation of the entire contingent, like a wall of a Macedonian phalange, the victim cannot withstand it and commits suicide. More often he agrees to collaborate with us. If we had known about the American when he appeared in Austria, the whole irresistible might of the GRU would have been thrown at him. And if the Navigator had asked for help, then the Aquarium might have ordered the resources of several residencies to be concentrated on one recruitment. In these cases the victim shouts and struggles, coming up against our people wherever he turns. He might phone the police. Never mind, our boys can sometimes dress themselves up in police uniform. Then they can rescue him and advise him either to commit suicide or agree to the GRU's proposals. When a whole horde of us are after one man, the unfortunate victim can phone every imaginable number and always receive the same reply. Drive him into a corner. Into a dead-end. There are various kinds of corners – physical and moral, financial dead-ends and deadly precipices. Or a man can simply be driven into a corner. A naked man in the corner of a bathroom. A naked man among those who are clothed always experiences an uncontrollable feeling of shame and helplessness. We know how to drive a man into a corner, how to humiliate him, and how to praise him to the heavens too. We know how to make him throw himself over the precipice and how to extend a helping hand at the right moment.

'Lost in thought?'

'Yes, Nikolai Tarasovich.'

'Look what I've found.'

I read the entry. A British couple from the little town of Faslane, the British submarine base. If the couple lived in Faslane it was very probable that they were connected with the ships. Perhaps he was captain of a ship, or perhaps he simply worked in security at the base. Perhaps he was just a street sweeper at the naval base or near it, a milkman or the owner of a public house. Perhaps she worked in the library, or in the canteen, or in the hospital. Any of those positions would do marvellously – they would have contact with the crews, with the repair brigades and with the staff officers. If there were prostitutes at Faslane one could say with certainty that they were connected with the base too. And how! Through them it might be possible to obtain secret information that even the captains of the subs did not know.

Faslane was too small. Every one of its inhabitants was connected in some way with the base. There's a nuclear submarine base in France, but that is at Brest, a big city in which by no means everybody is connected with submarines. That is why we like to seek out very small towns in which there are military establishments of great importance, like Faslane. It would be very awkward for the GRU's diplomatic residency in London to send its lads to Faslane. The authorities in Great Britain frequently catch our people and throw them out ruthlessly. You don't even get into your stride. And the appearance of a stranger in a little town puts people on their guard. That's why we were hunting there, in Austria. Among the inhabitants of those little towns, whose names sound so sweetly in the ears of a military spy.

Night after night Nikolai Tarasovich and I spent going through the hotel registers. We could only wait and see whether one of those people would return to the same place a second time. If not we'd find others.

The hotel registers recorded the past. A pity, because you couldn't bring it back. But as we went through the books we obtained a clear idea of the scope of our future operations.

The Navigator was serious. The Navigator was severe.

'By a decree of the head of the GRU my First Deputy has been appointed.'

We all remained silent.

'Alexander Ivanovich, read out the message.'

Alexander Ivanovich surveyed us with a look which told us nothing, then looked down at a small sheet of thick, bright yellow paper:

'Top Secret. I hereby order the appointment of Colonel Nikolai Tarasovich Moroz as First Deputy Commander of the diplomatic residency of the GRU 173-V. Chief of the General Staff, Marshal of the Soviet Union Ogarkov. Head of GRU Army-General Ivashutin.'

The Navigator was smiling. The first cipher clerk was smiling. And Nikolai Tarasovich was smiling. He was again the First Deputy. I was smiling, and so were my comrades, though not all of them.

With us in the GRU, and also throughout the Soviet Army, in the KGB, and in the whole Soviet system, restoration to power after a fall from grace was a very rare occurrence. It was something like a return from the grave. Very few ever returned. When you fell, you went to the very bottom, onto the rocks.

We went up to the First Deputy and congratulated him. He no longer had to speak 'on behalf of the Navigator', he was now all-powerful in his own right.

He shook everybody by the hand. But it seemed to me that he had not forgotten those who had joked at his expense when he had started to have difficulties. And those who had joked also knew that he had not forgotten. He would remember. Not now, perhaps. But he would bide his time. Everybody knows that the expectation of revenge is worse than the revenge itself. The First Deputy was in no hurry.

'Congratulations, Nikolai Tarasovich.' It was my turn to shake his hand. As he grasped my hand he looked me straight in the eyes and said quietly, 'Thank you.'

Apart from the two of us, only the Leader and the first cipher clerk understood the true significance of that 'thank you'. A month previously agent 173-V-4I-299, who was now the joint owner of a little hotel and reporting to me, had summoned me to an emergency meeting and informed me that he had a guest from a little town in Belgium, the name of which every GRU officer dreamt of. I ought to have gone over to carry out the recruitment at once. But instead I got in touch with the Navigator and refused. I said I couldn't do it, because I was too inexperienced. For that recruitment I would have had the Order of the Red Star on my chest or another silver star on my shoulder. And in fact I had all the experience necessary. But I refused. The Navigator smiled at me and sent Nikolai Tarasovich instead. And today he was celebrating.

'Thank you, Vitya.' The Navigator was shaking my hand now. All those around us looked in astonishment, understanding nothing. Why should the Navigator suddenly shake me by the hand? What was he thanking me for? It was not my celebration. And the Navigator laid his hand on my shoulder, patted me on the back as if to say: your time will come. I was sorry to have missed out on the recruitment. At the same time I was pleased for the First Deputy, now back on top – very pleased for Nikolai Tarasovich.

The new military attaché of the Union of Soviet Socialist Republics has disappeared. Vanished into thin air. He was here, and now he isn't. He has been called back to Moscow on leave and has not returned. His green Mercedes is standing in the courtyard of the embassy. It is once again waiting for a new master.

It's only the lazy who fall sick. Is it really so difficult to get away to the woods once a month and put an end to all ills, ward off any threatening ailments? I have always managed to find time for that. Even at times of the most unrelieved footwork. Now and in the past.

I was far away in the mountains. I knew there was no one anywhere near. There were no secret hiding places and no appointments to keep. There were only ants – big brown wood ants. This was their kingdom, their city-state. In a sunny clearing between the fir trees. I took off my clothes and plunged into an ant hill, as you do into cold water. There were thousands of them, a huge crowd, a sort of Shanghai of ants. They ran all over my arms and legs. One had bitten me painfully and immediately the whole pack of them started biting me. If I stayed there long enough, the would eat me whole. But if I could stand it for just a minute it was a good treatment, like snake venom. A lot meant death, but a little was good for you. There was a good reason why the serpent was the symbol of medicine. I had never treated myself with snake venom, I don't know why. I simply never had the time. But you don't need much time for the ants. You just looked for a big ant hill and jumped into it!

The liquid given off by the glands of the ant will preserve anything from decay. The ant will bite a caterpillar and drag it into its underground storehouse. The liquid will ensure the dead body does not decay for a year or two. It will lie there as if in a refrigerator.

In the case of the living body the effect is miraculous. There will never be any wrinkles or patches on the face. The teeth do not decay. My grandfather was ninety-three when he died and he had no wrinkles and practically all his teeth. He lost only three teeth – and they were knocked out by the Reds. He ran away from them, otherwise he would have lost all his teeth along with his head.

It was not just my grandfather who exploited the secrets of the ant. The whole of Russia, and before that the whole of Byzantium, did the same. In Egypt the ant was regarded as the most important doctor. The Egyptians noticed, many thousands of years ago, how the ants preserved their food supplies and so they started pushing their hands and feet into any heaps. Later they would put dead pharaohs into swarms of ants for forty-eight hours, and a thousand years later their bodies had still not disintegrated.

Everybody knows that the brown wood ant can work wonders. But mankind is lazy! People buy an acid said to be made from ants in chemists' shops, but it is not genuine. It is made in factories. They rub it into their arms and legs. But they are silly. The ant knows where to bite you, and it is important that you are bitten in the right place. The same as with Chinese acupuncture, when they stick needles into you. They have to be in the right place.

I roared like an elk and rushed all over the place at the gallop, brushing the ants off me. Thank you very much, my friends, that is enough for one day.

The Friend of the People has disappeared. The Friend of the People is what we called the KGB navigator in Vienna. Our principal 'neighbour'. All our neighbours in the lair of Chekists look very downcast. Something is going on there. They probably don't know exactly what it is themselves. But the KGB navigators from Vienna, Geneva, Bonn and Cologne have been summoned to Moscow and for some reason have not returned. Their deputies are in charge for the time being.

The evacuation of someone is a cruel and irreversible affair. You get a message from Moscow saying that your father is not well and wants to see you before he dies. So you fly off home with an escort at your side, so that you don't run away. When you arrive in Moscow you are immediately put under investigation. And who isn't guilty of something? We've all done something wrong. So long as they've got the man, it is always possible to put together a case against him. True, they don't shoot people nowadays as they did in 1937. Or rather, they shoot people, but not on the same scale.

Where has the Friend of the People gone wrong? How are we to know? You can, of course, listen to the rumours. But rumours are put around by a special service for the purpose of obscuring the truth.

It often happens like that: you open a business and have breath-taking success. But not for long. The same thing was happening with our commercial enterprises. No sooner had we opened for business than we had a fabulous success – a recruitment, for which the First Deputy was pardoned for his earlier failure.

The First Deputy, along with a group of supporting officers, was obtaining secret information for which Colonel-general Zotov, the head of GRU Information, sent enthusiastic messages of thanks.

But just as a millionaire does not have enough money and never will have enough, or a collector is always short of just one tarnished coin, there will always be something lacking. The General Staff will never have enough secret information about the enemy, however much of it you obtain. There always remains something which is not absolutely clear about the enemy's position, about his plans and his armament. The only time when the Information Service of the GRU uses the word 'enough' is when the information you supply is inferior in quality. Then they have very soon had enough of your information, and of you too.

Our mountain hotels were not yet yielding the desired results. Results were not easy to achieve. Every month people turned up in the little hotel from places with such strange names as Minot and Offutt. Our agents in the tourist business had received lists of names of places in which practically every inhabitant must have been connected with military establishments of exceptional importance. But there were no results so far. One fish had landed in the net and that was all. And I had, voluntarily, let the First Deputy have it. I had been more important for him to register a success at the time. But nothing had come my way.

Messages from the Aquarium sounded slightly annoyed. Why don't you put number 41 on to back-up work? After all, he admitted himself that he was not ready to work independently.

Our neighbours, the Friends of the People, were having a big celebration. Some years previously an officer had defected from a Soviet naval vessel, and many KGB residencies had been hunting him down. But it was the diplomatic residency in Vienna that succeeded. It had achieved an astonishing feat and taken him back.

Well, good luck to them. They had certainly learnt how to kidnap people. But why did they not succeed in stealing any American atomic secrets, and why had they never provided Soviet industry with the plans of French anti-tank missiles, or of British torpedoes, or of German tank engines?

'Viktor Andreyevich, there's a signal for you.'

I pushed my coffee cup to one side, put my papers into my briefcase, and my briefcase into the safe. Then the key into the small safe. The combination had been changed today – one had to remember it.

'Let's go.'

The fourth cipher clerk went ahead and I followed. Down the concrete stairway to the bunker. He pressed a button, the door clicked and could then be opened. We were in a small concrete chamber. The walls were white, with a rough surface, and still bore the imprints of the boards which had been used to retain the concrete when the bunker was constructed. The doors were shut. We were being observed by closed-circuit television cameras. The cipher clerk closed the entrance door firmly: it looked like a watertight bulkhead in a submarine. The cipher clerk reached behind a curtain and dialled a number. I could not see his hand and had no right to. They said that if you dialled the wrong number a clamp seized your hand. I don't know whether this was true or just a cipher clerk's joke. Intelligence officers are not allowed to know their secrets.

The security inside the bunker was at last satisfied that we were okay, and the main door moved slowly and smoothly aside. Inside was Petya 'Spetsnaz', who waved us in. The KGB staffs its internal security force with officers of the frontier units, but the GRU uses officers from its Spetsnaz brigades. It thus kills two birds with one stone. It has a thoroughly reliable security force and at the same time it can drive the Spetsnaz men around the country from time to time to inspect the places where they may drop by parachute, the secret hiding places, the places where they can take cover, and the police stations.

The GRU's diplomatic residency in Vienna was protected by Spetsnaz officers of the 6th Guards Tank Army, trained to fight in the mountains and with special traditions. It had crossed the Great Khingan range in Manchuria on its way to the Pacific Ocean. It had travelled 800 kilometres across territory which all the experts considered to be impassable for tanks. The 6th Guards Tank Army was now in training for carrying out a lightning dash across Austria up the undefended left bank of the Rhine towards the North Sea. Compared with the Khingan, the Austrian Alps were of course just hillocks. But they had to be dealt with properly. That was why *Spetsnaz* from that Army were permanently stationed in Vienna. They had to move forward. They had to clear the way with their sharp knives.

'Good morning, Viktor Andreyevich,' Petya greeted me.

'Good morning, you scoundrel. Getting lazy in the bunker?'

'On the contrary, I'm getting wild.' Petya grinned. 'I haven't seen a bit of skirt for six months now. Even at a distance.'

'Bear up. It's worse in submarines.'

I walked down a corridor and past a number of steel doors. The corridor was hung with dozens of heavy curtains, so that you couldn't tell how long it was, whether it divided after the next curtain or turned off in another direction. We were not allowed to know. The door to the signals room was the first on the left.

It was a room with a low ceiling, also hung with curtains. The curtains may be there in case of fire, as they say, but it also means that, having been in the room, I have no idea how much signals apparatus there are.

One curtain had been pulled aside in anticipation of my arrival. Behind it was a grey box on which was carefully written: 'Transmitted by 299, received by 4I.' The cipher clerk put his key into the machine, turned it and left the room. I inserted my own key, turned it and opened a little steel door. Inside it were rows of little green lamps. One of them, with the number 83 on it, was on. I pressed a button and the lamp went out. At the same time the lamp over my signals apparatus also went out. That told the cipher clerk that a signal had been received. But he was not entitled to know what the signal was: only I was to know that. That was the number 83. Even if the clerk had known that I had received the signal 83 from agent 173-V-4I-299, how could he know what it meant?

Signal 83 meant that agent 173-V-4I-299 wanted to get in touch with me. The number 83 meant that contact – but not direct, personal contact – should take place on the first Saturday after receipt of the signal, between 4.30 and 4.45 in the morning. And the place: the Attersee near Salzburg.

Agent 299 had a great variety of signals and could summon us for personal or non-personal contact at any moment. Every form of contact had been worked out down to the smallest detail and each one had its own number. Number 83 was the code for a complete plan with various alternatives and reserve arrangements.

The best guarantee of the GRU's own security is the fact that it keeps the number of meetings with valuable agents to a minimum and if possible to nil. I had been working for ten months with agent 299, but had never set eyes on him and never would. Indirect ('non-personal') meetings with him took place two or three times a month, but I discovered from his file that in the course of twenty-one years' work with the GRU he had only had six face-to-face meetings and had met personally only two GRU officers. This was a correct procedure. The fact that there were no face-to-face meetings protected our agents from our mistakes and our officers from shocking failures and sensational pictures on the front pages of newspapers.

With a non-personal meeting, a GRU officer and his agent might be dozens of kilometres apart from one another. Neither would know where his contact was. We wouldn't use radio or telephone for transmitting or exchanging information. We'd use water or sewage pipes; sometimes two telephones might be connected to a metal fence or a barrier of barbed wire. Such 'contact sections', would be selected in advance and tested by our officers.

But for contact with valuable agents the GRU usually made use of water. The police could monitor the ether, but water was the best conductor of signals and much less open to interception. If ever the police start to monitor all reservoirs, rivers, lakes, seas and oceans, then the GRU will go over to other means of maintaining contact with agents. Its Institute of Communications will have thought up something by then.

There were drops of dew on my boots as I made my way through the tall wet grass towards the lake. The fir trees surrounded the lake like a solid fence. A solid wall. The silence was total. I had to avoid stepping on dry twigs. Why make a noise? Noise was an offence to this clean water, the crystal transparency of the sky and the pink mountain peaks above. It would always be quiet there. Even when the GRU's *Spetsnaz* arrived, there would be no tramp of soldiers' boots to break the silence, because the soft footwear of the *Spetsnaz* didn't make a noise like the nailed boots of an infantry man. Later the 6th Guards Tank Army would pass through. That would mean the rumble and roar of tanks, but only for a short time. Peace would be restored, and a cosy little concentration camp on the banks of the lake would not upset it. Perhaps I would be in charge of the camp, or perhaps just an inmate along with the local socialists and peace fighters. That's the way it has always been. Those who are the first to welcome the Red Army or want to talk peace with it are also the first to fall under its blows.

The whole earth was flooded by the dawn. It seemed delighted to welcome the sunrise. All living things rejoiced, ready to meet the surging waterfall of light which would come rushing from behind the mountain tops very soon now. Then the bird-song would rise up in a hymn to welcome the day. But for the moment all was still silent. The little diamond droplets were not yet sparkling, the pure gold was not yet running down the mountainsides, and the breeze had not yet carried down the scent of wild flowers. Nature had fallen silent in that last moment before it exploded in delight, joy and new life.

Who was there to admire it? Only I – Vitya the spy. And my agent, known as No. 299. He would be making his way to the lake from a quite different direction. I wondered whether he understood the poetry of nature? Could he listen for hours to its faint sounds? Did he realise that he and I together were making preparations for the construction of a little concentration camp on the sloping bank of the lake? Did the old man realise that he and I might become inmates of that most picturesque little camp? Did it ever occur to him that those who work very close to the mouth of the meat-grinder find themselves in it more often that ordinary mortals? Did it ever pass through his wooden head that by a trick of fate his camp number might be very similar to his number as an agent? Of course he didn't understand any of this. I had nowhere else to turn. I had been born and brought up in the system, and there was no escape. But he was helping us voluntarily, the scoundrel. If the Communists didn't trick me up against a wall and shoot me, I thought, if they didn't burn me in a crematorium or drown me in an overcrowded barge, but put me in charge of a concentration camp, I would set aside a special section for such volunteer supporters and forget to feed them. Let them eat each other first. As rats in an iron barrel eat the weakest first and then the progressively stronger ones. . . . I would let them establish each day who was the weakest. Let each of them be scared of falling asleep, lest he should be killed and eaten while he slept. Perhaps they would understand then that there is and can be no harmony on this earth. That everyone is obliged to fight for himself. My God, if they would only put me in charge of a camp.

It was time to act. I cast my line into the lake. It was very similar to an ordinary fishing line. The only difference was that you could pull out of the handle a short lead and connect it to your watch. The watch was in turn connected by wire to a little grey box. There was another lead going from the watch up my sleeve and into an inside pocket. The face of my rather original watch lit up and a minute later the light went out. That meant that the transmission had been received and was recorded on the thin wire of my recorder. The waves carrying the signals did not spread through the ether. The signals spread only within the limits of the lake and not beyond it. The message had been recorded well in advance on a tape-recorder and was transmitted at high speed. It was therefore extremely difficult to intercept an agent's message even if you knew in advance the time and place of the transmission and the frequency used. Without that, interception was impossible.

I pretended to be winding up my watch. The face lit up for a moment and then went out: the reply had been transmitted. Time to get off home.

Chapter Thirteen

'Comrade general, I have been in touch with 299 by a water contact. He informs us that there are not likely to be any guests at his hotel in the next few months from places that interest us.'

'That's bad.'

'But 299 is not wasting his time. He has established friendly relations with the owners of neighbouring hotels and sometimes, on some pretext or other, he has an opportunity of looking at their reservation list.'

'You don't think that's dangerous?' The Commander knew that it was not dangerous, but he was obliged to put the question.

'No, comrade general, it's not dangerous. 299 is very smart and experienced. And he tells us that in a nearby hotel' – I took a piece of paper and wrote down the name of the hotel, because I did not have the right to say aloud any dates, addresses, names of places or people. Even in 'safe' rooms we had to write such things down on paper, sometimes saying aloud some dates or names having nothing to do with the case—'in a nearby hotel a room has already been reserved for a man.' Again I wrote the name down. 'Two years ago he stayed in an hotel which now belongs to us. We've got a certain amount of information about him and even a photograph, though not a very clear one. His hobby is mountain climbing, for which he travels to Austria and possibly also to Switzerland. He works in Spain, in a town called. . . .''

I laid a piece of paper in front of me and with a gesture of triumph inscribed the name in big letters? 'Rota'.

He looked at me, scarcely daring to believe his eyes. Then I wrote down once again that short but fascinating name, which every intelligence office dreamt of and which sounded so crystal clear to every one of us? 'Rota'!

The general laughed. I laughed too. In the world there are hundreds of places in which we are interested. Any one of them would be a real find for us and would mean that fate was smiling on us. But I had had a real bit of luck – 'Rota'!

'Shall I check your knowledge?' he asked with a laugh. He was joking, of course, because you couldn't be a GRU officer without knowing the main features of that base. At hearing the word Rota the brain of any officer of the GRU reacts like a computer and begins to produce short phrases and precise figures: water area – twenty-five square kilometres; harbour protected by breakwater of 1500 metres; three piers, each 350 metres long; depth of water at piers – twelve metres; ammunition store – 8000 tons; storage for petroleum products – 300,000 tons; aerodrome – one runway of 4000 metres. As for the fact that it was a base for American nuclear submarines—everybody knew that.

The Navigator strode round the office, rubbing his hands.

'Write a request.'

'Very well.'

A man from the little Spanish village of Rota. I knew nothing at all about him. It wasn't even clear if he was an American or a Spaniard. But I made my 'request'. The next day that request would be fed into the GRU's big computer, which would tell us everything it knew about him.

The GRU's big computer was the produce of the creative genius of American engineers and had been sold to the Soviet Union by short-sighted American politicians. America received millions for the big computer, but lost billions. The big computer knew everybody and was very clever. It would swallow down a colossal quantity of data about the whole population of the earth. It had a voracious appetite. It could devour whole telephone books, lists of university graduates and of employees of an astronomical number of firms. It was insatiable. It would take in millions of newspaper cuttings about births and deaths. But that was not its only nourishment. It had access to vast quantities of secret documents. It was the business of every one of us in the GRU to see that that voracious American offspring was never hungry.

Perhaps the information about the man from Rota would be disjointed, inadequate. Perhaps the big computer would give us no more than his date of birth, perhaps the date when his name first appeared in a secret telephone directory, and perhaps the name of the bank in which he kept his money. But even these disconnected pieces of information would be quite sufficient for the GRU command point to despatch some messages to places where it might be possible to obtain some more facts about him. Some of our Borzois might run down his parents, his school friends, or his birthplace. So that when I met up with him in a little hotel on the shores of a lake I would know more about him than he thought. I hoped I would soon meet him. For the sake of convenience he had already been given the number 713 or, in full, 173-V-4I-713. That would let everybody who was entitled to know that the man in charge of him was intelligence officer Forty-one of the Vienna diplomatic residency of the GRU.

Time was flying past like an express train, deafening you and hurling you back from the rails. Once again, day and night ran together into a sort of black and white whirlpool. There was a transit case from the Lebanon; establishment of contact with some people recruited in South Africa; an impersonal contact with some invisible 'friend' recruited by goodness knows whom; back-up for undercover operators; and another transit for Ireland. Both the Navigator and the First Deputy refused to let me be diverted on to unimportant jobs. But far too often there were especially important jobs, like backing up illegals or a large-scale operation, when everybody had to take part, including the Navigator's deputies. Then nobody was given special treatment. Everybody had to be involved, even twice in a single night. Receiving a transit case from France. Another from Honduras. Don't you realise how important it is?

Suddenly the wheel stopped turning. Leafing through my diary, covered with entries, suddenly I came across an almost empty page, with only one entry on it: 'Work with 713.' And that referred to that very day when I was sitting in my chair, my head still buzzing round with thoughts of meetings and dead-letter boxes and non-personal meetings.

I looked at that brief entry for a long time, then picked up the telephone and, without dialling any number, asked:

'Comrade general, could you possibly spare me a few minutes?'

'Won't it wait till tomorrow?'

'I have already been trying to see you for several days.' I was lying, because I knew he had no time to check up on me. 'But today is the last day.'

'What do you mean – the last day?'

'Not even the last, comrade general, but the first.'

'Listen, damn you, I can't at the moment. But come and see me in half an hour. If there's somebody waiting to see me, tell them to go to hell in my name. Got it?'

'I've got it.'

Later, I gave the Navigator the route I proposed to take and the tricks I intended to resort to to throw the police off my tail. And I reported everything I now knew about 713.

'All right, then. That's not bad. I wish you luck.'

He stood up, smiled at me and shook me by the hand. The third time in four years.

The roads were jammed with holiday-makers, and I was in a hurry. I was counting on getting to the hotel by late afternoon so as to leave the evening free for putting my plan into action. I had been driving down the main road for five hours. From time to time I had been held up by enormous traffic jams, but as soon as the road was clear I pressed on as fast as the car would go, overtaking everybody on the way. As the sun began to set I left the highway and took to a narrow mountain road, without reducing my speed. A white Mercedes appeared around a corner and there was a screech of brakes and a cloud of dust as it left the hard road for the edge. The driver dazzled me with his lights, deafened me with his horn. A woman in the back of the Mercedes pointed a finger to her temple to tell me I was out of my mind. I didn't need her to tell me that. A touch on the brakes on the corner; they screamed in protest; the car swung across to the wrong side of the road; I took my foot off the brake and pressed the accelerator down to the floor. I was darned sure they didn't get my number: they didn't have time to see it. I was already round the corner, hands firmly on the wheel. Even if I had gone over the edge I wouldn't have let go. Meanwhile the car was making noises to indicate that it didn't approve of the treatment I was giving it. At the first crossroads I took to a really narrow road through a dark forest. A long scramble uphill, followed by a long descent, deep into a mountain valley. Then the road began to get wider. I needed no map: I had a good idea of that part of the country and could guide myself by the setting sun, now crimson. Its jagged edge was already touhing the line of trees on the horizon.

It was already quite dark when I arrived at the hotel. It was situated on the shore of a forest lake at the foot of a long mountain slope. In winter, no doubt, the place was full of brightly coloured ski-suits. But now, in the summer, there was just peace and quiet. Cold air was coming down from the mountainside and someone had covered the lakeside meadow with a soft coverlet of white mist. But I had no time to admire the beauties of nature. I went straight to my room on the second floor. At first I couldn't get my key into the keyhole. But then I took myself in hand, opened the door, threw my suitcase into a corner and gave myself a shower. I was really dirty after a day's driving. Once I had freshened up and restored my circulation with a rough towel, I put on a suit, freshly cleaned and pressed, and tied a brightly coloured scarf round my neck. A glance in the mirror told me that I had far too tense a look on my face – there was a leaden look in my eyes and my lips were tightly pursed – when I ought to be wearing an expression of carefree happiness. I did my best. And so downstairs, though not too quickly. People would never believe that this was one of the most exhausting days in my very demanding life, in which I knew neither high days nor holidays. And let no one think my working day was over: there was much more to come.

In the hall downstairs a band was playing, loud and fast. Bright lights played on the walls, on the ceiling and on the faces of the happy people who were expending their energies for the sake of amusement. Suddenly the sound of a trumpet rose above the whirlpool of noise, deafening everyone with its wail, while the rhythm of the band held the whole crowd in its power. The beat of the music was echoed in the crystal glasses standing on the tables.

On my hand I felt the cold of a glass which I raised, flashing and sparkling, in front of me and smelt its sharp aroma, and at that moment the whole raging storm of noise and light was caught in it. Smiling at the dancing bubbles, I hid my face behind the glass and cast my eyes slowly round the hall, trying not to reveal the tension I felt. I finally caught sight of him out of the corner of my eye – the man who featured in the green file as No. 713. I had seen him only once before, and then only in a small snapshot. But I recognised him all right. I lowered the glass slowly to my lips, suppressed my smile, caught a whiff of the intoxicating smell, and just as slowly turned my face in his direction. At the same time he turned towards me and our eyes met. I put on an expression of pleasant surprise and greeted him with a gesture of recognition. Taken aback, he looked around, but found no one behind him. Then he looked at me again with the unspoken question: who are you signalling to? To you! – I reply dumbly – who else? Then, pushing the dancers aside and carrying my glass high above my head like a torch of freedom, I made my way across to him.

'Hello! I never expected to meet you here. Do you remember that marvellous evening we had in Vancouver?'

'I've never been to Canada.'

'Oh, I'm sorry,' I said, embarrassed and looking closely into his face. 'There's such bad lighting here and you are so like someone I used to know. . . . Please forgive me.'

I made my way back to the bar, and for the next twenty minutes I watched the dancers. I tried to follow the simpler movements: there has never been time in my life for dancing. But as soon as I felt a pleasant warmth spreading through my body I joined the dancing throng.

The longer I danced the better my body performed the required twists and turns, or so it seemed to me. Anyway, no one paid any attention to me. The happy crowd welcomed everyone and forgave everything.

I've no idea when he left. It was very late when I went upstairs, among the last to leave.

The alarm clock woke me early next morning, but I lay in bed for a long time, my face buried in the pillow. I was suffering for a chronic lack of sleep. Five hours of sleep cannot make up for months of insomnia.

Then I made myself hop out of bed, put in fifteen minutes of painful gymnastics, and then submit to the torture of a shower alternately boiling hot and freezing cold. Anyone who does that regularly looks fifteen years younger than his age. But that wasn't what I was after. I had to look cheerful and full of life, as befitted an idle layabout.

I went downstairs before anyone else and set about reading the morning papers, assuming as careless an air as I could.

First to arrive for breakfast were an elderly American couple. Then there was a woman of uncertain age and uncertain nationality with a stupid and unusually aggressive little dog. Next appeared a group of grinning Japanese festooned with cameras. And then *he* appeared. I smiled and nodded to him. He recognised me and nodded back.

After breakfast I went back to my room. The clearner had not yet been in. I hung the 'Do not disturb' notice on the door, let down the blinds and stretched myself out on the bed with a feeling of great relief. I had long dreamt of enjoying such a day with nothing to do in a hurry. I tried to recall all the details of the previous day, but I got no further than having a blissful smile on my face. I was probably still smiling when I fell asleep.

That evening I again danced my feet off with all the others. He sat in the same place as before, alone. When I caught sight of him I smiled and winked, inviting him to join the madding crowd. He smiled and shook his head.

In the morning I was the first down to the breakfast room. He was the second.

'Good morning,' I said, offering him the morning papers.

'Good morning,' he replied with a smile.

The front pages of the papers were full of news about Idi Amin, the president of Uganda. We exchanged a few brief comments, smiled at each other and went in to breakfast. It was most important now not to frighten him. I could of course have already taken the bull by the horns, but I had several days to play with, so I chose to make the 'smooth contact'. There was a great deal that we did not know about the man, and even watching him at a distance for a few days would provide a lot of useful information. He was alone, he did not chase after women, he did not throw his money about but did not count the dollars, and he was a cheerful fellow. This last fact was very important, because gloomy types were the worst to recruit. He didn't get drunk but drank regularly. He read a lot of books. He watched and listened to the latest news. He understood and appreciated a joke. He dressed smartly but did not overdress. He wore no articles of jewellery. His hair was not always neatly combed – and that was enough to tell you something about his inner self. His jaws were often tightly closed – a sure sign of self-control, discipline and strength of will. Such a person was difficult to recruit but easy to work with later. Quietly, for a long time, I studied his facial expression. I particularly needed to know all about his eyes: they were spaced wide apart and large; his eyelids did not droop and he had little bags under his eyes. His pupils moved slowly from one position to another and remained fixed in one place for a long time. He lowered his eyelids slowly and would raise them just as slowly. He would look long at something but not always attentively. More often than not it was an absent look rather than a penetrating one. In the study of a man's character special attention is given to the muscles of his mouth in various situations: in a smile, in anger, in annoyance or when relaxed. But even a smile can be condescending, scornful, contemptuous, happy, ironical or sarcastic; there's the smile of a winner and the smile of a loser, the smile of someone who has landed in an awkward situation and a threatening smile, nearer to a grin. But in all these situations the muscles play a part. The way those muscles work is a mirror put to the person's soul. And all those details are much more important than a knowledge of his financial and official difficulties, even if these are useful too.

213

When it was dark I threw a rucksack into my car along with thigh boots and fishing rods and set off for a distant lake to fish. At dawn the First Deputy emerged from the reeds, sat alongside me and cast a line into the water. There was nobody about, the water was warm just before the dawn and a slight mist was rising from it, pink from the rays of the rising sun, though the sun was still not visible.

The First Deputy loathed fishing. He was particularly upset by the fact that there were people in the world who were willing to handle worms. He simply couldn't touch them. It was another matter if he was ordered to. But he was the senior of us, and in any case there was no need for him to take them in his hands. He cast the line in with an empty hook. He was terribly tired. His eyes were bloodshot and his face grey. For the sake of having a brief meeting with me he had obviously spent the whole night at the wheel. Yet he had plenty of his own important business to do. He just couldn't stop yawning as he listened to me. At the end of my story he stopped yawning and even gave me a little smile.

'It's all going well, Viktor.'

'Do you think I'll be able to recruit him?'

For the third time in my life I was favoured with the sort of look that a tired teacher bestows on an unusually stupid pupil. My teacher rubbed his bloodshot eyes and said: 'Listen, Suvorov, there's something you don't seem to understand. In this sort of business you must never ask permission. If you ask me for it I shall refuse. One day you will become a First Deputy of even a Navigator, but just remember that even then you must never ask anyone for permission to do something. If you send a request to the Aquarium the reply will always come too late, if only for technical reasons. I may know a great deal about your man, but I cannot *feel* what he's like. You speak to him directly, and your intuition alone is what will help you. In this situation neither I nor the Navigator nor the Aquarium wish to assume the responsibility themselves. If you don't succeed in recruiting the man, it's your mistake for which you will not quickly be forgiven. If you slip up and get arrested during the recruitment, that will also not be forgiven. Everything depends on you alone. If you decide to go ahead and you recruit the man, then it will be your medal, you will receive the praise, it will be your success and your career. And we shall then back you up. Remember that the Aquarium will always be in the right. And remember that the Aquarium is always on the side of those who are successful.

'If you break the rules and get into difficulties you will end up before a GRU tribunal. If you keep carefully to the rules but have a failure, again it is you who will be to blame, on the grounds that you applied the rule book too dogmatically. But if you are successful, everybody will back you up and forgive you everything, including breaches of our most important rules, on the grounds that you applied the rules in a creative and flexible manner, ignoring out-of-date and obsolete rules.'

'If you're sure of success, go ahead and recruit the chap. If you are not sure, then drop it for the moment. Every officer dreams of such a chance. But it's up to you.'

'I'm going to recruit him.'

'That's different talk. So just remember: neither I nor the Navigator, nor the Aquarium approve your intentions. We simply know nothing about them. If you get into difficulties we shall say that you are a stupid young man who exceeded his authority and that you deserve to be posted to the space centre at Plesetsk.'

'I understand.'

'Then I wish you well.'

So as to look like a real angler he took a few of the fish I had caught and disappeared into the reeds.

It was evening and I was having a drink with No. 713. He had no idea that he had long ago been allotted a number, that the big computer had devoted special attention to him, that quite a number of GRU officers were gathered around the mountain hotel, and that the Aquarium had sent one of the GRU's leading psychologists, who had analysed a short film that I had taken. But 713 was not to know that the movements of his face muscles had been studied by some of the most successful psychiatrists in the secret world of intelligence.

We were drinking and laughing and talking about all sorts of things. I began to talk about the weather, about money, about women, about success and power, about the preservation of peace and the prevention of a major nuclear catastrophe. There had to be some subject on which he had strong views and would begin to talk about. It was most important that he should talk more than I did. I needed a key to loosen his tongue, a subject that interested him. We went on drinking and laughing. Then the key was found. He was interested in sharks. Had I seen the film *Jaws*? Not yet, I said. Ah, what a film! The shark's jaws appear on the screen when the audience least expects them. Terrific effect. We laughed again. He began describing the habits of the shark for me.... an amazing creature.... more laughter. He then tried to guess my nationality. Greek? Yugoslav? A mixture of Czech and Italian? Or of Turk and German? 'No', I said, 'I am a Russian.' More laughter. 'Then what on earth are you, a Russian, doing here?' 'Oh, I'm a spy!' 'You've come to get me into your network?' 'Yes,' I said, and we both laughed till our sides ached.

Then he suddenly stopped laughing.

'Are you really Russian?'

'Yes, I am.'

'And are you really a spy?'

'Yes, I am.'

'And you are out to recruit me?'

'Yes, it's you I'm after.'

'Do you know all about me?'

'Not everything. But something.'

He remained silent for a long time.

'Has our meeting been recorded on film, and are you planning to blackmail me?'

'Our meeting *has* been filmed, but I do not intend to blackmail you. Perhaps that doesn't fit in with what is written in spy stories, but blackmail has never yielded positive results and so it is not used. At any rate in my service.'

'Your service is the KGB?'

'No. The GRU.'

'I never heard of it.'

'So much the better.'

'Listen, Russian, I swore an oath not to give any secret information to foreign states.'

'You don't have to give any secrets to anybody.'

'Then what do you want from me?' He had obviously never met a real spy, and quite simply he found it interesting to talk to me.

'You could write a book.'

'What about?'

'About submarines at the Rota base.'

'You know I'm from that base?'

'That's why I'm recruiting you and not the people at the next table.'

Again we laughed.

'It seems to me a bit like in a film.'

'It's always like that. I also never thought I should fetch up in intelligence. Anyway, good night. Waitress, the bill please.'

'Wait a minute, Russian – I write a book and what then?'

'I publish the book in the Soviet Union.'

'In a million copies?'

'No. Just forty-three.'

'That's not many.'

'We pay you 17,000 dollars for each copy. We do not sign any contract with you. We pay ten per cent immediately. The rest immediately on receipt of the manuscript, if, of course, it throws some light on matters which interest our readers. Later on the book might be published in English. If there are things which might not be of interest to the Western reader, that could be left out of the American edition. So there would be no handing-over of secrets. Just freedom of the press and nothing more. People write not only about submarines but even about the CIA. And nobody brings them to court for that.'

'And they are all paid by you as well?'

'Only some of them.'

I paid the bill and went up to my room to get some sleep.

Chapter Fourteen

It is a very pleasant, even a unique feeling that you experience when you return to your own strongly protected base after having been out on your own recruiting an agent.

My absence for a week had been noticed by our whole crowd of officers. If an intelligence officer was away for three days, it was obvious that he had been backing up someone else. But if he was away for more than a week? Where had he been? Everybody knew that he must have been recruiting someone.

As I walked down the corridor our whole company of spies made way for me, falling silent as I approached. I had to bite my lips to stop myself from smiling. I was not supposed to smile before receiving the Navigator's congratulations. It was not good behaviour.

My colleagues also observed the traditions. Mobody asked me awkward questions, nobody smiled at me and nobody congratulated me. You were not supposed to congratulate anybody before the Navigator did so. Of course, nobody knew what to congratulate me for, though everybody realised that there was some good reason. Everybody sensed that I was now riding high, everyone could see a crown sparkling with diamonds on my head.

It was very pleasant to know that nobody was envious of me. There was understanding and respect and rejoicing. And there was pride in me and in all of us. There goes Vitya over the red carpet right into the general's office, and we are glad for him, for we have also walked over that carpet, or if not then we shall cross it in just as proud and dignified a manner.

The band of spies watched me and made way for me. Everybody seemed quite happy and relieved that I had returned and had not landed in trouble, had not been caught or tied up, not buried like a bear in hibernation or hounded by dogs like a wolf.

The door of the Navigator's office opened at my approach. The Navigator himself greeted me on the threshold. All very simple. He stepped aside and invited me in: come in, Viktor Andreyevich. On the surface nothing had changed, yet such treatment was very unusual. And then, when in the total silence someone gave a deep sigh, the Navigator turned and laughed. And with him everybody laughed at that honest sigh.

The rules of the GRU categorically forbid anything about the work of one officer to be revealed to other officers, about either successes or failures. Navigators keep strictly to the rules. They know that no one should know more than he needs to know to carry out his duties. But in that case, how was it possible to maintain an atmosphere of fierce competition inside the secret organisation? That was why residents devised all sorts of tricks to evade the rules and to demonstrate to the whole company their approval of some people and their dissatisfaction with others. They always found ways of doing it.

In my case, immediately behind me there appeared in the corridor the sixth cipher clerk in white gloves carrying a silver ice-bucket with a bottle of champagne in it.

The whole company greeted the appearance of the ice-bucket and the starched napkins with a murmur of approval. The boss had found a good way of getting round the rules. And see what heights Vitya Suvorov, the scoundrel, had soared to. He was really on his way up. The young Borzois' eyes shone as they spoke of my take-off. But the older – and wiser – officers shook their heads. They knew that the moment of success was the most difficult in the life of an operational officer. Success was preceded by a savage straining of one's resources and a superhuman concentration of attention at every word, every step and every breath. In the course of recruiting someone an officer summoned up all his willpower, his character and his knowledge to strike the blow at his victim, and at that moment of greatest tension and concentration of will against the person being recruited he had to be aware of everything going on around him.

Success meant relaxation, and a sudden relaxation of tension could end in catastrophe, breakdown, hysteria, deep depression, crime and even suicide. The older officers are wise enough to know that.

The Navigator knew too. That was why he was both happy and severe. He pointed to some non-existent mistakes of mine and warned me not to overdo the rejoicing. But how could I not rejoice? No. 713 had agreed. He had taken the money. And he had gone away with a list of questions which had to be dealt with in the book. (In the American edition many of those details might be omitted.) He had taken the ten per cent and was in our hands. He would soon spend the 73,000 dollars and would then want to get hold of the rest. Experience had taught the GRU that there were a lot of people who were keen to get the ten per cent and do no more. But every one of them, once having had a taste of money for which they worked and risked little, did the job conscientiously and received the remainder. There were no exceptions to that rule.

I was not sure why it was, but success did not give me any great pleasure. Those folk are probably right who say that you experience happiness only as you are scrambling up to success. As soon as you achieved it you no longer felt happy. There were very few happy people among those who had achieved success. There were many more of them among the ragged and dirty, the hungry vagrants, than among film stars or leading politicians. And there were more suicides among world-famous writers and poets than among street cleaners.

I felt bad, and I didn't know why. I was now ready for anything. I wondered why nobody ever tried to recruit us? If only an American diplomat would come up to me now and say: 'Hey, you, let me recruit you!' I would say yes. I would honestly say yes. He would be terribly surprised, knowing the habits of the GRU. Listen, you fool, my American friend would say, do you realise what's waiting for you if this falls though? I know, I would reply cheerfully. 'Come on, recruit me, you damned capitalist. I'll work for you without pay. Everything the American intelligence service gives me, I'll stick into your pocket! I simply want to risk my neck.' Isn't it exhilarating to walk along the edge of a precipice, to dice with death? After all there are idiots who try to ride bucking broncos and who dance about in front of bulls. Not for money, for the pleasure.

Come on, recruit me, my enemies! I'll go along with you.

Why don't you say something?

Screening, screening, and yet more screening. We were sick and tired of the continual screening.

It was easy to check up on the background of the friends we had recruited. They were continually being monitored by the Information Service, without, of course, its knowing their names, histories or the jobs they had. The same question could be dealt with by someone who was thousands of kilometres away from the matter in which the GRU was interested: information about the plans of the German General Staff could come from Geneva, but also from Tokyo or from Nicosia. And no source had the slightest idea about the existence of the others or of their capabilities. If the information provided by one source were markedly different from that provided by others, it meant that there was something wrong with that source. It couldn't be the other way round: that there was something wrong with all the other sources – that they were swallowing some disinformation and only one was producing the truth. In any case, if the same piece of apparatus was delivered from different corners of the globe and if, when it was copied, it gave the desired results and satisfied the needs of the Army, there was no need to worry. Even if our friend had been recruited by the other side, even if he was a double agent. Never mind. He would have provided what we needed, and if the intelligence service on the other side thought it worthwhile to pay so dearly simply to trick us, let them. We gladly accepted such gifts. But the moment the gifts turned out to be of poor quality, with faults in them, Information would quickly tip us off about it.

The Aquarium did not screen only our friends, but us as well. They checked up on us frequently, tediously and hypercritically. Another method had been devised to deal with us, that of straightforward provocation. In the course of my training and work the Aquarium had played many of those tricks on me. They were always concerned to find out how I would react, and I always reacted correctly: I would report immediately and precisely to my Navigator everything that had happened to me and to my friends. If I caught sight of a friend of mine in a wood, I would report it to my chief. If nothing happened to my friend, that meant that he had been on an operation in the wood, or perhaps he had been there simply so that the commanding officer could check on whether, if I saw him, I would report it at once. They were always trying to catch me out, to see which I held dearest – the Aquarium or my friend. It was the Aquarium, of course. Just try not reporting – if it turned out to be only a means of checking on you, that would be the end of everything and you would be on the conveyor and on the way out.

In fact they had recently been checking on me even more, so that I was permanently taking part in such screening. Now, for example, I had abandoned my car and was picking my way through a lot of puddles in the dark. My feet were cold and wet. I promised myself that when I returned home I would get into a bath and lie there for an hour and have a good soak.

In my pocket was a quite small packet, inside which was a Bible. It was a tiny little book printed on very thin paper. Such editions were produced by various religious societies so that they would be easier to import into the Soviet Union. I was to drop the Bible into a letter-box which was belonging to Vovka Fomichev. Fomichev was a captain and an assistant military attaché and one of us – that is to say a man from the Aquarium, recently arrived. Whether he realised it or not, the Aquarium was now playing a whole series of dirty tricks on him to test him. I was on my way to his house.

He would take the Bible out of his mail box in the morning. All sorts of religious communities and organisations were always pushing them on us. He would hardly be likely to know that this time it was we who had dropped the packet into his box. Perhaps the little book would attract him, or perhaps he might try to hold on to it to do a little business, because in Russia people are mad to get hold of such little books and will pay huge sums for them. The next day was a holiday and Fomichev would not have to go to work. So we would see what would happen – would he report the matter straight away in the morning or would he wait till Monday, or would he perhaps not report it at all – either hanging on to it or quietly throwing it away lest he should get into unnecessary trouble? Any course of action except the first – an immediate report – would be the end of him. It would mean the conveyor.

It was cold and wet and the wind was blowing the leaves along the pavement. But once a leaf fell into a puddle it stuck there, to be swept away next day by a street cleaner. There was no one about – only I, a lonely spy belonging to a huge network. I was checking up on one of my colleagues, although it was difficult to say who was checking whom. Vovka Fomichev was a friend of mine. We had twice been out on joint operations together. He worked skilfully and confidently. But, who could tell – he was a recent arrival and perhaps had been given some special task? Maybe I was now being checked with his assistance? He had certainly made friends with me. He wanted to acquire experience. But maybe I was again being tested. I could drop the packet in the letter-box and then try to

220

drop him a friendly hint that he should report the matter at once. But that would be the end of me and I would be put on the conveyor: so, they would say, a friend means more to you than our glorious Soviet military intelligence service?

The house in which Vovka Fomichev lived was large and very smart. It housed a large number of diplomats from various countries. It was of course under police surveillance, the main entrance at least. It was possible that it wasn't watched, but it was better to assume that it was and to base one's plans on that assumption. So I did not go in by the front entrance, but through some dark rear courtyards past some tidy rubbish bins and into an underground garage. We had keys to a great many garages and entrances to buildings in which diplomats usually lived. I could also get into any hotel in Vienna without difficulty. We had a huge cupboard full of keys. Wherever our colleagues from the Aquarium go they always take a copy of the keys. Most important was to keep a careful record of them so as to be able to find the key you needed at the right moment. On that occasion I had three keys in my pocket. If necessary I could have got into Fomichev's flat. He was not to know that three years previously, a rather unsuccessful predecessor of his had lived there and had made copies of the keys for the GRU. Unfortunately he had not had the resources to do anything more heroic, and he had been evacuated in disgrace and thrown out of the General Staff.

Cats fled in various directions away from the rubbish bins with painful squeals. That was a good sign, because it meant that there were no other people nearby. But perhaps there was a hidden television camera? There was no light – they were saving electricity. Why have a light in a rear courtyard? But a TV camera could operate with infra-red rays. That was why I had my coat unbuttoned so that my tie-pin was visible. It looked like an ordinary tie-pin: an expert would have had difficulty proving that it wasn't. But it was covered with a special paint so that if in the darkness infra-red rays were directed on me the tie-pin would light up, reacting to the infra-red light. By turning round I could even establish the position of the hidden camera. If I had found that I was being observed I would simply have relieved myself among the rubbish bins and strolled away. But the tie-pin did not light up. I was not being observed, so I took a key and carefully put it into the keyhole. The door slid quietly aside and I was in a vast garage with hundreds of cars.

I moved very carefully, but not stealthily, like a thief. If anyone saw me they should think that I had just driven in, parked my car and was going home. I opened the steel door with another key. Then I went up in the lift from the underground garage to the top floor and waited there for a few minutes, listening carefully. The whole house was asleep; not a door banged, no lift moving in the lift shaft. I looked at my watch. If I was being followed my visit to the building had to remain a puzzle. Perhaps I had come for a meeting with an American diplomat, or perhaps some woman was waiting for me. If I was being followed, then even my real purpose – to drop the Bible in the letter-box – might appear to them as camouflage and they would have to ponder it for a long time, because I had spent so much time at the top.

The lifts were silent in their shafts and no one was walking up or down the stairs: I was quite sure of that.

So then I went cautiously down the stairway. I did not walk on my toes nor even on the whole sole of my shoes. I touched the floor only with the outside welts of the shoes, like a clown making his legs into a ring. I had soft soles which did not squeak, but it was better to walk as I had been taught. Like that your footsteps were never audible. I reached the bottom floor where in the marble vestibules there were dozens of letter-boxes. I knew which one I needed, but I looked around at the names on a lot of them, then stood close up to them and dropped my packet in the right opening, covering several of them with my body. Anybody watching behind me could hardly have known which box I was interested in or what I had put in it.

With a look of boredom, as though I had found nothing of interest, I went down the stairs into the undeground garage.

Anyone who uses the same path for entering and leaving a place is displaying a lack of taste in conspiratorial work. I have acquired that taste. It is not like a taste for wine, nor a taste for sex, nor a taste for a fight. A taste for a life of conspiracy is not like any other, and I like it. I understand and appreciate it. I have it. It was not a lack of taste which sent me again into the dark garage. It was simply that I had no better way out.

I was suffering again from lack of sleep. When would I ever get enough sleep? My eyes were bloodshot. But I turned up in the office at six o'clock in the morning. It was Sunday, and I was waiting for Vovka Fomichev. If he turned up even earlier than me, that would be magnificent. But there was only Sasha 'Aeroflot' yawning in a corner. His eyes were also bloodshot. He had probably also been laying a trap for someone, perhaps even for me. He was probably waiting for someone who was due to drop in, out of breath. He started making excuses to me, saying that he had had to finish making out some expenses in a hurry. I realised, of course, that what he said was possibly true, but not the whole truth. It was some other demand that had brought him into the embassy at six on a Sunday morning. I told him that I had three operational reports still to be typed for the next post. It was actually true. But he would understand that it was not the only reason which had dragged me to the office. He pretended to be working, but was keeping an eye on the clock. I put on a show and watched the clock too, but furtively. I laid out some documents on my desk and stared at the wall. It was a pity we were not allowed to have windows in the places where we worked.

At ten a.m. the First Deputy summoned Sasha 'Aeroflot' to his office, leaving me alone in the main office. At 11.32 the Navigator appeared.

'Well, what happened?'

'Comrade general, I deposited the gift without incident. But he has not reacted yet.'

I could tell by the expression on the Navigator's face that they had not been testing me but Vovka Fomichev. An elementary provocation, and he had taken the bait. For some reason or other, having found a Bible in his letter-box, he had not reported it to his chief. So what would he do if something serious happened to him? Would he report it? He was clearly a danger to our organisation and to the whole Soviet system.

'Viktor Andreyevich, go off home and have a rest. Come back at six this evening.'

'Very good.'

People all over the world have days off – days when nobody goes to work. Soviet diplomats have two such days every week. Saturday and Sunday.

But the GRU does not have days off. Nor does the KGB. So there you have the picture. On every free day some of the diplomats do not turn up at the embassy. But the others – the greater number – do. So it becomes clear to everyone who is a pure diplomat and who is not so pure.

To prevent this happening, all kinds of tricks have been devised to get the pure diplomat into the embassy on a free day, to use his broad friendly smile as a screen and to conceal the work of the residency. On a free day the embassy becomes a veritable ant-heap. It's a clever arrangement. It is on the free days, and only on the free days, that the mail from the Soviet Union is distributed. Letters and newspapers. Everyone needs to read *Izvestia*, because it publishes the currency exchange rates. Everyone is busy calculating, trying to work out whether to change his currency now or to wait. The exchange rates jump up and down, and what the position of the Soviet State Bank will be in a week's time is known to God alone and no one else, not even the chairman of the bank.

Another feature of the Soviet embassies throughout the world at weekends is the special shops which are open and sell goods at remarkably low prices. The whole Soviet colony flocks to the shop to buy. And again, on Sundays there are lectures. Again they crowd into them, not because they like the lectures but because you get a good mark if you attend. Nobody forces you to attend the lectures: it's your own business. But if it should appear to someone that Ivan Nikonorovich, for example, appears rather apathetic and isn't particularly interested in politics, he is likely to be sent home – evacuated. Suddenly one night there's a ring on his doorbell and a message: your father is very ill and wants to say goodbye to you. An escort steps up to Ivan Nikonorovich and, whether he wants to be at his father's deathbed, or not, he is on his way to the plane.

They also show films in Soviet embassies on Sundays. Recent ones and others not so recent. Again people turn up in great numbers. Attendance is a sign of high political awareness and unbreakable ties with your socialist motherland.

So there are always plenty of people in the embassy at weekends. Nowhere to park your car. But I parked mine. I had a special place reserved for me.

The Navigator and I were strolling round the grounds, which were vast. As we chatted we kept glancing towards the gates from a distance. Pyotr Yegorovich Dunayev, the vice-consul, and Nikolai Tarasovich Moroz, first secretary at the embassy, were also strolling around but appearing not to notice us. They had good reason to be there, because an evacuation was about to take place. The assistant Soviet military attaché in Vienna, GRU Captain Vladimir Dimitrievich Fomichev, was unreliable. A plane had already been summoned to Vienna. A very limited number of people were to take part in the evacuation: the Navigator – that was his decision – I – because I had taken part in the test and knew about Fomichev's unreliability – and Colonels Dunayev and Moroz, deputy and First Deputy to the Navigator.

Fomichev's grey Ford swept smoothly through the gate: the assistant military attaché had arrived for the cinema, with his wife. Why on earth, Volodya, did you not rush down here with your tongue hanging out? Why didn't you bring the Bible with you? Why did you conceal it? What use was it to you? There is no God, and it's time you knew it. All those inventions about God are just vile anti-Soviet rubbish. There's no going to Heaven after you die. Heaven has to be built here on earth. If you think there will be Heaven after death you automatically dissociate yourself from the active construction of Heaven on earth. We can forgive illiterate old women for believing that, but not you. You're for the conveyor. They will get the truth out of you. Why did you hide the Bible? What did you want it for? Perhaps you didn't hide it. Perhaps you were afraid of getting into trouble. So you took it and threw it into a rubbish bin, thinking no one would find out. But we know everything! You must report everything that happened to you. The GRU will never forgive you for being silent.

The Navigator's deputy strolled slowly across to the gate. There was only one way of getting into the embassy and it was the only way out. It was already cut off for the assistant military attaché. There was a guard on the gate, but the guard knew nothing and would know nothing so long as the assistant military attaché did not try to escape. If he did, then the mousetrap would spring shut in his face. The Navigator and the First Deputy were ambling towards the library, not hurrying. Near the library was an extra entrance to the bunker.

I would stay a little longer where I was.

Then Borya, the third cipher clerk, hurried across to the parking lot. Borya did not know what was behind it all. His job was to go up to Fomichev, salute and say: 'Vladimir Dimitrievich, there's a message for you.'

I watched from a distance.

Now Borya was near his car and Fomichev got out. The expression on his face was not visible. He was saying something to his wife; then he gave her a quick kiss. She went off alone to the cinema. He certainly didn't know that he had kissed his wife for the last time. He was now regarded as a criminal. He had not reported to his commanding officer that the bourgeois world had tried to seduce him and divert him from the right path. He would not, of course, be shot for that. But he'd be sent to prison. He wouldn't get a long sentence – five years for an attempt to deceive the resident. They would add something when he was in prison. They always add something for people like that. And, if he ever got out of prison (we have a special prison of our own), it was unlikely that his wife would want to see him. She would throw him over. I studied her face once at a diplomatic reception at very close quarters. She would throw him over.

Time for me to move.

Through the steel door, along the corridor and down the stairs. Another door, the one with the grinning skull. Down again, into the bunker and the main office. Another corridor, into the small office, another corridor with doors to right and left. He was now in the First Deputy's office. I rang the bell. The First Deputy's face appeared round the door, which he used as a shield. You couldn't see what was going on inside the office.

'What do you want?'

'Do you need any help?'

'No. Go and watch the film, Viktor Andreyevich. We can cope.'

'*Au revoir*, Nikolai Tarasovich.'

'*Au revoir.*'

Down the corridor, up the stairs and into the little office. . . .

'Vitya!' The First Deputy was running after me.

'Yes,' comrade colonel.'

'Vitya – I completely forgot. Wait till the end of the film and meet up with his wife Valentina. Tell her that her husband is off on an urgent job that will take a couple of days. Don't upset her. Say it's a secret operation. Fix it so that she doesn't suspect anything. And take her home. In the meantime move his car from the parking lot and hide it in the underground garage. Here are the keys. That's it. See you tomorrow.'

'Tomorrow, Nikolai Tarasovich.'

Valya Fomicheva was a very special woman – the sort that people turned to look at and follow with their eyes. She was quite short, with hair cut like a boy's. Huge, captivating eyes. A rather capricious smile. There was something mischievous hovering around the corners of her mouth. There was undoubtedly something of the devil in her, but you couldn't say what. Perhaps all her charm was devilish. Why on earth had Volodya chosen such a wife? A beautiful wife – somebody else's wife. Who in the embassy didn't look at her? They all had their eyes on her. In the city too. Especially men from the south, Frenchmen and Italians. Especially tall, thick-set men with a touch of grey in their hair. Her compact figure gave them no peace. I even found it rather awkward to travel in a car with her. If we stopped at a crossroads reproachful glances would be directed at me, as if to say: why do you need such a beautiful woman?

But she was certainly not mine. I was driving her home because her husband was already on the conveyor. He was already giving evidence. They would extract the necessary confessions from him here in Vienna. Then he would land in the Aquarium, in the huge glass building on the Khoroshevskoye highway.

For the moment Valya, his wife, hadn't the slightest idea about all that. He had gone off into the night, on a job. It didn't worry her: she was used to that. She was more interested in telling me about the wonderful new raincoats that the whole of Vienna was wearing. They had streaks of gold in them, and were really very attractive. Such a coat would suit her well. She would look like the Snow Queen and disturb our peace with her cold, contemptuous look. She compressed a lot of authority into her tightly closed fists. There was no doubt that she would dominate anyone who came her way, despite the fact that she was very fragile, and if you squeezed her she would shatter like a crystal vase. With a woman like Valya Fomicheva you should never spend more than one night, before you throw her over and get away. Otherwise she would make you her slave, bend you and bring you to your knees. I know women like that: there was one just like it in my life. Also small and fragile. People also turned to look at her. I left her myself, without waiting for her to drive me out, to deceive me and get me on my knees.

It was silly of Captain Fomichev to have fallen for such a woman. I knew for sure that she despised him, while he, out of jealousy, spied on her. Yielding to a passing mood, she had agreed to become his wife, and even now, on the conveyor, he was thinking only of her. One question would not leave him alone. Who was now driving her home? He had no need to worry: it was I, Vitya Suvorov. I had no need of her. I avoided such women. In any case, Vienna was not the place to go in for such things. We judged each other too strictly and followed each other too closely.

'Suvorov, why do you never smile at me?'

'Am I the only one who doesn't?'

'Yes. Everyone smiles at me. Are you afraid of me?'

'No.'

'Suvorov, you *are* afraid of me. But I'll make you smile.'

'Is that a threat?'

'No, a promise.'

We were both silent for the rest of the trip. I knew that it was not a GRU provocation. Women like her talked that way naturally. Moreover, the GRU couldn't be keeping an eye on me just then. GRU operations were carefully prepared and carried out. They differed from operations carried out by other intelligence services by their simplicity. The GRU never went after two hares at the same time. That was why the GRU was so successful.

'I hope, Suvorov, you are not going simply to drop me near my house. I am a beautiful woman – I know that. I might be raped on the stairway. You would be held responsible.'

'That doesn't happen in Vienna.'

'All the same, I'm afraid to be alone.'

She was afraid of nothing in this life. I knew such women. Wild animals in skirts. At the age of sixteen she had surely carried a heavy knife in her strong little hand. If anything had gone wrong she would have been ready to use it, the little devil. Maybe she had used it, who could tell?

We were alone in the lift. She said with a laugh:

'Are you sure that my Volodya is not coming home tonight?'

'He's out on an operation.'

'And you're not afraid to leave me alone at night? Someone might steal me.'

The lift came to a gentle halt. I opened the door for her and she took her key.

'What are you doing this evening?'

'Sleeping.'

'Who do you sleep with, Suvorov?'

'I sleep on my own.'

'And I am alone too,' she sighed.

She stepped across the threshold and suddenly turned to me. Her eyes were flaming. Her face that of a pure little schoolgirl. That is the most treacherous mind of woman. I hate them.

All evacuations are carried out by plane. It's very quick and there is only one police control to go through.

They are also always carried out in the daytime. At night the police are more suspicious, and in the morning a new shift comes on with renewed strength. In the evening planes do not usually leave on long flights. So the afternoon is best.

The former GRU captain and assistant military attaché was sitting on a stool, his head hanging down. He was not tied down; he was just sitting. But he no longer had any desire to shout or make a fuss. He had already gone through the first stage of the conveyor: he had confessed. Yes, there had been a Bible in his letter-box. No, he was not interested in religion. Yes, he had been afraid of reporting it, because too many such reports were bad for his record. Yes, he had thrown the book into a rubbish bin – the third one from the left. The Bible was already lying on the table. Everything had been found. The Bible was in a cellophane cover.

227

While I had been driving his wife home they had already extracted from him the first layer of evidence. Yes, he admitted, he had concealed things from the Navigator before. He had visited prostitutes – on four occasions. But no – he had had no contact with Western intelligence. Nor had anyone tried to recruit him. No – he had not given away any secret information.

Evacuation was the answer.

'Hand me the spirit.'

Instead of surgical spirit we usually used ordinary Gordon's gin out of the Navigator's bar.

'Syringe.'

It was a one-shot injection. It looked like the one *Spetsnaz*. But this was not 'Blissful death', simply 'Bliss'.

'Spirit.'

The place where he had had the injection had to be carefully swabbed to avoid infection.

We were in the departure lounge of the airport. The roar of aircraft engines; the polished floor; and the souvenirs, lots of souvenirs. Dolls in national dress, Ronson lighters. Then came the ticket barrier. Any baggage? No baggage – just a short stay. Passports, please!

Our passports are green. 'In the name of the Union of Soviet Socialist Republics, the Minister of Foreign Affairs of the USSR. . . .'

Carry on.

There were three of us: the former captain, myself and the vice-consul. On the surface we were just seeing him off, but in fact we were directly in charge of him. And over by a kiosk with a lot of bottles was the Consul-general of the USSR, covering us at a distance, in case we needed protection or someone to frighten off the authorities.

Then our flight was announced. A long line of passengers, and a toothy stewardess. Wait a moment, please! Let the diplomatic mail go through: it's yours in any case. Carry on to the plane.

We walked across to the aircraft, a TU-134. There were two sets of steps up to it. The rear ones for most of the passengers; the ones at the front for VIPs and the diplomatic mail. For us, that meant. Another stewardess at the plane's door, also with prominent teeth. What had she to smile at? But how could she know that the former captain was no longer a VIP? How could she know that he was not smiling because he fancied the stewardess's backside, but simply because he had been given a shot of 'Bliss'.

There were two big diplomatic couriers standing at the steps. They knew what sort of a load they had to deal with. They were armed and made no secret of it. That was international diplomatic practice, laid down at the Vienna Congress of 1815.

They helped the former captain up the steps. For some reason his feet didn't seem to find the steps very easily. He was dragging his feet. But never mind: they would help him. At the doorway the two big fellows turned the former captain sideways: they couldn't get in the door three abreast. I again caught sight of their faces. The former Soviet diplomat was smiling with a gentle good-natured smile. Who was he smiling at? At me, perhaps?

So I smiled back.

Chapter Fifteen

'Put it on,' the Commander ordered, and I put the transparent helmet over my head. He did the same, and we now looked like astronauts. Our two helmets were joined by flexible transparent tubes.

It was impossible to overhear what was being said in the commander's office, even theoretically. But if, in addition to all the other security arrangements, he ordered you to use the special device for talking, it meant that the conversation would deal with something exceptionally interesting.

'You are doing very well, and not only at intelligence-gathering. You recently went through a series of tests organised by the Aquarium and myself. You had no idea that you were being tested, but you passed through them brilliantly. You are now in the highest category as far as trustworthiness is concerned.'

If that was true it meant that the GRU was somewhat over-estimating me. I knew I had sinned in the past: I was no saint. But perhaps the Navigator was not telling me the whole truth. He was, after all, known as 'the cunning one'.

'The GRU is entrusting you with the carrying out of an extremely important operation. In the near future an agent known as the Green Friend is due to arrive in Vienna. He is a very important man for us – just how important you can judge from the fact that Colonel-general Meshcheryakov is controlling him personally in Moscow. Who the Green Friend is I do not know and have no right to know. You, of course, have even less right to know. You'll remember that we never meet these people face to face. The Green Friend, like the others, operates through a system of dead-letter drops and signals. The GRU is, however, ready to have a meeting with him at any moment, and we have to be sure that contact can be made in any circumstances and at any time. So once every few years we arrange check-up meetings. He receives an urgent summons and keeps an appointment, but we do not actually make contact with him. We simply observe him from a distance. The fact that he reacts to the invitation provides the GRU with confirmation that our communications system is working properly. Moreover we are able to check what security there is around him. We are about to conduct such an operation now.

'The head of the GRU has given orders that you are to be in charge of the operation. We shall take a room for you in an hotel. You will spend two days with a large group covering your tail to make sure you are not followed. Travel the whole country. Drop your car in Innsbruck and disappear – vanish into thin air. Return to Vienna like a ghost and carry out a final check on your tail.

Enter the hotel through the restaurant and slip upstairs to the room, where everything will have been prepared for you.

'There will be a Minox camera with a telescopic lens and a "Mikrat 93" film loaded in it. The film has two layers of emulsion on it, one of which has already been exposed with pictures of Austrian military aerodromes on it. You will be using the other layer. If you are arrested try to rip the film out of the camera and expose it. But if you don't succeed in doing that and they develop it they will get only pictures of aerodromes and the developer will destroy what you have taken. Let them think you are just a small-time spy. All clear?'

'Yes.'

'Right, then listen to this. The Friend will show up at a certain time at the window of a shoe shop. You will be a hundred metres from him and eighteen metres higher up. You will take a picture of him when he appears. I don't know who he will be. He might even be a woman dressed as a man, or a man dressed as a woman. Don't be surprised if it's someone in filthy clothes or with uncombed hair. That's all the better for the job. For half an hour before he is due to appear you are to snap any activity that strikes you as suspicious.

'You will recognise him because he will appear at precisely the time and place agreed. He will have a folded newspaper in his right hand, and that will serve as both a recognition signal and also as a sign that all is well. If the newspaper is in his left hand, that's a danger signal. He is keeping the appointment, but he doesn't know whether we will meet him or not. If he is being followed he may abort the meeting, and in that way protect our officer and save his own skin at the same time. If he is being watched by the police it is in his own interest to reduce the number of contacts with us. If in five minutes nobody makes contact with him he will go away and will keep another appointment when we request it. Perhaps in ten years and on the other side of the world. And perhaps once again we shall only be checking up on him without actually meeting him. Anything not clear?'

'All is clear.'

'Finally: I shall let you know without warning, just before it begins, the time and place of the operation. In the time that remains until the operation you are not allowed to have any contact with foreigners. If you are forced to have any contact, report it to me personally. Nobody, not even the first cipher clerk, knows anything about the case. The telegram from Moscow was in my personal code. You must have no other camera with you in the hotel room apart from the one I shall give you before the operation. Another camera might cost you your head. Be careful with the Minox. It has been loaded in the Aquarium and sealed. The seal is practically invisible: be careful not to damage it. What the Friend looks like you are not allowed to tell anyone, even me. The sealed Minox will go to the Aquarium in the diplomatic mail and will be opened there and the film developed by a special process. Have you understood everything?'

231

'Everything.'

'Then repeat it all to me from the beginning.'

The hotel room had been chosen by someone who knew his job. I had a corner room, so that I could watch three quiet side-streets at the same time. There was the shoe shop. There was practically no traffic in the adjoining streets. Three hours and ten minutes remained until the Friend was due to appear.

Some thoughtful person had prepared everything I might need: the telescopic lens for the Minox, about as big as an electric torch battery; a big pair of Zeiss binoculars; an Omega chronometer; a selection of light filters, a map of the city and a thermos flask with hot coffee. The Minox itself I had brought with me in my pocket.

There it was, in the palm of my hand: a little chromium-plated rectangle with little knobs and windows. All the world's intelligence services had been working with the Minox for half a century. It was a Minox that Philby used when he was spying for the Soviets against the British. It was a Minox that Colonel Penkovsky used when he was spying for the British against the Soviets. And there it was in the palm of my hand – the tiny, finely made Minox. I fitted the telescopic lens and tried it out. I only wanted to measure the distance. For such a small camera a hundred metres was a big distance. If my hand shook everything would be blurred. The Minox had not been invented for this kind of work.

The time passed very slowly. The lid of the thermos, which served me as a cup, had steam rising from it. A fat woman left a house and went down the street. Nothing of interest. A postman passed by on his bicycle. Then the streets were quite empty. A black Mercedes went down the street with a man in the back seat dressed in white robes: the representative of some poor country on his way to a meeting to demand money from richer countries. Diplomats from rich countries were also on their way to meetings. But the richer ones had more modest cars – they drove Fords and Volkswagens. The experts say that in the future the gap between the rich and the poor countries will get bigger. They should know. A bigger gap will mean that the diplomats from the poorer countries will travel in Rolls-Royce limousines, while the diplomats from the richer countries will probably switch to bicycles to save money.

The fine hand on the very precise little chronometer went slowly round and round. The fat woman went past again. Again the sound of the tyres of a huge black limousine with tinted glass windows: some poor diplomat going to beg for aid. I again swept the street with the Zeiss binoculars, so as not to miss anything, to memorise the numbers and the faces. There were not many of them. To memorise every little sign of life, every change. I had the Minox

232

ready cocked, like an anti-aircraft gun on a tank, constantly prepared for action. Anything suspicious would be on film. The frames on a Minox film are tiny, so that you can get a great many on a short film.

But what on earth was that? I hadn't quite taken in what was going on. I was suddenly overwhelmed by an awareness of something terrible and irreparable. A very elegant Citroën had stopped on the street. I would have recognised it among a thousand other cars – it was the First Deputy's Citroën. A woman got out of it, bent down quickly towards the First Deputy and kissed him. And that was the moment that my little Minox snapped. The woman got into a Fiat sports car and drove off. The First Deputy had long disappeared from the street.

I sat in an armchair and bit my lips. The woman was certainly not the First Deputy's wife. I knew his wife. Nor was the woman a secret agent. The Navigator knew the time and place of every operation, and he would certainly have banned all operations in my vicinity at that time. So it meant that the GRU was again trying me out. They had stuck me in that stupid room and put on a little comedy for me. Now they were waiting to see whether I would report the offence committed by the man I admired so greatly or whether I would try to cover up for him. That was why they had given me a camera, to be able to tell whether I had hesitated for even a moment or had used the camera immediately. They would also be able to tell from the photo whether my hands had been shaking or not.

But I had other reasons for biting my lips. Another possibility remained. That quiet side-street was very suitable for secret encounters of all kinds. Very few people were aware that I was sitting there in the hotel behind heavy shutters. Even the First Deputy might not know, if he had not been involved in the operation. And his mistress? An American woman? Or English? She was obviously foreign. Soviet women are not allowed to have cars when they are abroad. Certainly not sports cars. What would they need sports cars for? All cars belong to the Soviet state and are to be used only by those who are working to protect and increase the might of the state. If all this was not some kind of show put on to test me, then it was the end for the First Deputy. He faced a dismal end. It was the conveyor for him, the whole works. But it could be just a test for me. There had been plenty of them. I had acted exactly as I should have done – quickly and decisively. My unseeing eyes looked out on an empty street. Nobody was disturbing its peace. Only an unpleasant-looking, rather bent figure with a newspaper in his hand was hanging around the window of the shoe shop. Goodness knows what the fellow could find to interest him there.

I leant back in my chair and stared at the ceiling. Then suddenly I leapt up, overturning the thermos. I grabbed the Minox and feverishly pressed the release. That was *him*! Damn it all, that was the Green Friend. Once, twice, and then again the shutter clicked. To hell with all the Friends, along with Colonel-general Meshcheryakov, the First Deputy and his whore. Time was up. The Friend threw his newspaper into a rubbish bin and disappeared round the corner.

233

The quality of the photos might turn out to be unsatisfactory and that would reveal my mental state. That would draw attention to the fact that I did not want to report on the First Deputy and that I had hesitated.

I stood up. I removed the telescopic lens from the camera. I packed the thermos, the lens, and the binoculars into a parcel and dropped them into a bowl. Somebody else would clear up after me. The Minox I held firmly in my left hand. Like that it would be easier to rip the film out if I were arrested. Ah, if only they would arrest me. Perhaps I could simulate being seized by the police? No, that wouldn't work. The Consul-general would phone the police and be told that no one had attacked me. Then I should be put on the conveyor.

I went out on to the street where the bright sunlight blinded me. No, in this joyful world things just couldn't be that bad. It had been a routine check-up. A typical GRU provocation. And I had not taken the bait. At the Academy they had organised much worse check-ups for us. The lives of our closest friends were at stake. Then later it was explained that it had been just a little bit of play-acting thought up by our chiefs. Many of us didn't pass those tests, and I did. And we were forgiven for a few minutes' hesitation. We were, after all, only human.

'Where did the Friend appear from?'

I thought for a moment – should I tell a lie or not?

'I didn't notice, comrade general.'

'You had a chronometer. Did he not turn up exactly on time?'

I remained silent.

'Did something confuse you? Was there something suspicious? Something you couldn't understand or explain? What put you off?'

'Your First Deputy. . . .''

A look of bafflement, then of pain appeared in his eyes.

'. . . your First Deputy was at the meeting place twenty-two minutes before the Friend appeared . . . with a woman.'

The bones on his fists stood out unnaturally white. His face was white too. Silently he studied the wall behind me. Then he asked, quietly and calmly:

'You did not, of course, manage to take a shot of him?'

It was difficult to tell whether he was asking a question or making a statement. Perhaps he was threatening.

'In fact, I did.'

I was afraid to look him in the eyes, so I looked down at my feet. The time dragged dully, unwillingly on. The clock on the wall ticked on – tick, tick, tick.

'What are we going to do?'

'I don't know,' I said, hunching my shoulders.

'What are we going to do?' He brought his fist down on the desk and at the same time I was sprayed with the spit from his mouth as he shouted : 'WHAT SHALL WE DO?'

'Get ready to evacuate him,' I said suddenly and crossly into his face.

My shout calmed him down and he went quiet. He became just an unfortunate old man upon whom a great sorrow had descended. He was a strong character, but the system was stronger than any of us. It was stronger than all of us. The system was all-powerful. Any one of us could come under its inexorable axe. He was looking into emptiness.

'You know, Vitya, in 1964 Colonel Moroz saved me from a death sentence. Since then I have taken him with me round the world. He recruited women. But such women! Such is life. He was very fond of them, and they fell for him too. I knew that he had a little something on the side. I knew he had a mistress in every city. I forgave him. But I knew that he would come unstuck one day. I knew. How can you hide such things in Austria? Can we do the evacuation between us?'

'Yes, we can.'

'Get the syringe from the cupboard.'

'I've got it.'

He pressed the button on his intercom: 'The first cipher clerk.'

'Here, comrade general,' came the reply.

'The First Deputy to me.'

'Very well.'

'Sit down,' said the Navigator in a tired voice. He was already sitting at his desk, his left hand on the desk-top, his right hand in a drawer. That's where it stayed. I was standing behind the chair in which the First Deputy was now sitting. The fact that the Navigator's hand was in the drawer told the First Deputy everything. And my presence told him that it was I who had observed him and had reported something back. He stretched out his whole body until his bones cracked and then quietly put his arms round behind the back of the chair. He knew the rules of the game. I slipped the handcuffs on him, then carefully turned up the sleeve of his jacket, undid the gold cuff-link and exposed his arm. I dipped a white napkin in gin from a green bottle and swabbed the place where the needle was to enter. I then filled the syringe with the slightly opaque liquid and inserted the needle carefully beneath the skin. Then I removed the needle and again wiped the arm.

With a nod of the head the Navigator indicated that I was to leave. I left his office and as I closed the door I heard him say, in a voice empty of emotion:

'Tell me all about it. . . .'

I felt ill, really ill.

Nothing like it had ever happened to me before. Only weak people feel ill. It is they who think up thousands of illnesses and give in to them and so waste

235

their lives. It is weak people who invented headaches, sudden attacks of weakness, fainting fits and pangs of conscience. There are no such things in reality. All those troubles exist only in the imaginations of the weak. I don't include myself among the strong. I am just normal. And a normal person doesn't have headaches or heart attacks or nervous breakdowns. I have never been ill, never moaned and never asked anyone for help.

But on that occasion I felt very bad. I had an unbearable depression, a deadly depression. I could have killed someone!

I was sitting in a little inn – in a corner, like a cornered wolf. The table-cloth on which I had placed my elbows was checked. Red and white. A clean table-cloth. A big mug of beer. The beer was like brandy in colour. It was probably very different in taste, but I couldn't taste anything. There were two lions standing on their haunches carved on the sides of the beer-mug. They were holding a shield in their paws. A beautiful shield and beautiful lions. Their pink tongues were sticking out. I was very fond of all sorts of cats: I loved leopards and panthers and black cats and grey cats. I also liked the lions depicted on the sides of the beer mugs. The cat is a beautiful animal, even domesticated. Clean and strong. A cat differs from a dog by its independent spirit. And how flexible they were! Why did people not worship cats?

The people in the inn were all very cheerful. They probably all knew each other and were smiling at each other. Opposite me there were four healthy-looking peasants, with feathers in their hats and leather shorts down to their knees, held up by braces. They looked a very tough bunch with their ginger beards. There was already no room on their table for the empty beer mugs. They were laughing. What were they laughing about? I would have liked to hurl my beer mug into those laughing faces. Who cared if there were four of them or that they had fists like my regimental commander, as big as beer mugs themselves.

Should I have a go at them? Let them kill me here on the spot. Let them crack my skull with an oaken stool or an Austrian beer mug. But they wouldn't kill like that. They would throw me out of the bar and call the police. So should I have a go at the police? Or what about Brezhnev, who was due to arrive in Vienna soon to meet poor misguided Carter? Perhaps I might go for Brezhnev with an axe? Then they would certainly kill me.

Only was it really worthwhile, dying at the hands of a policeman or of one of Brezhnev's secret bodyguards? It was another matter to be killed by good strong people like those over there.

They were still laughing.

I have never really envied anybody. But now black envy slithered into my mind like a snake in the grass. How I wanted some shorts like theirs and a hat with a feather. I already had the mug of beer. What else could a man want to complete his happiness?

They were rocking with laughter. One of them started to cough, and that stopped his laughing. Another one stood up, with a full mug in his hand, the froth coming over the top. He was also laughing. I looked him straight in the eyes. I don't know what there was in my eyes, but when he met my stare the powerful Austrian, leader of the whole company, fell immediately silent, his face fell and his smile faded. He also looked me straight in the eyes with a fixed intent gaze. His eyes were clear and directed right at me. He compressed his lips and put his head to one side.

Whether it was because my look had a cold, deathly air about it, or whether he had the impression that I was about to ruin myself, I do not know. I don't know what he was thinking, but when his eyes met mine, that tough-looking peasant seemed to lose some of his fire. Everyone around him was laughing; the drink was having its effect. But he stood there with a long face, staring at the ground. I even began to feel sorry for him. Why had I with one glance spoilt the man's whole evening?

How long they stayed there I was not sure, but they finally stood up and left, the biggest one being the last to leave. He stopped in the doorway and looked at me, frowning. Then suddenly he heaved his whole mighty frame across to my table. He was an intimidating as a tank in battle. My jaw froze in anticipation of a crashing blow. But I wasn't in the least afraid. Go ahead, Austrian, hit me! I had really wrecked his evening, and for that in our country you inevitably get punched in the face. That's a tradition. He came up to me, his huge belly blocking the light. Hit me! I shan't resist. Hit me, don't spare me! He gripped my left shoulder with his huge fist and gently squeezed it. It was a powerful hand, but warm and friendly, not at all leaden. And it was as though human sympathy flooded through that hand. With my right hand I gripped his arm and squeezed it gratefully. I didn't look him in the eyes, I don't know why. I looked down at the table, while he made his way to the exit, clumsily and without turning round. A strange character, a being from another planet. But a human being, nevertheless. A good man. A better man that I was. A hundred times better.

What on earth was happening to me? What changes had taken place? What were these sudden leaps? I was feeling better – because of the beer, no doubt. Or perhaps it was because of the huge horny hand that had grabbed me by the shoulder and held me back from the brink. But what exactly was the matter with me? Why had the bright world become so dark for me? Perhaps it was what the weak called pangs of conscience? But it couldn't be: I had no conscience. It wasn't troubling me: why should it, after all? Because I had betrayed the First Deputy? True, he was a decent chap. But if I hadn't put him on the conveyor, he would have done the same for me. That was the sort of job we had. By reporting on the First Deputy I had protected the GRU from all sorts of accidents. For such acts Kir in the Central Committee would say thank you. They would remove the First Deputy and send another one. Was it worthwhile getting upset about? If everyone just gave in to his own feelings the whole system would collapse. As it is, it stands firm and gets stronger. And its strength lies in the fact that it immediately gets rid of anyone who weakens, anyone who lets his feelings have their way.

Had I weakened? Undoubtedly. Had I made an enemy in the Navigator? It was certain. And had anyone seen me? Possibly. Could any outsider have seen what I was going through? Of course he could. If I was looking depressed, if my arms were hanging loose, if I pulled a long face – that was all visible. If the Austrian had understood that I was in a bad way, an experienced intelligence officer who might have been following me would have understood long ago. After the evacuation of the First Deputy the Navigator was quite capable of having a tail put on me, just to make sure: how was Number Forty-one behaving? Was he showing signs of weakness?

Something had happened to me, and for several hours I had lost control of myself. If the Navigator got to know about it, I could expect to be evacuated the same night. The next regular plane was in three days' time. I would spend those days locked in the photographic laboratory, it was likely that I would finish up in the darkness that very night. Even an ordinary aircraft on which the navigation instruments momentarily fail is grounded. The same applied to an intelligence officer, only more so. A spy who had lost control of himself was dangerous and had to be removed at once.

I walked slowly from the inn to my car. If you want to find out for certain whether you are being followed, behave as calmly as you can. Keep looking down. Reassure those who are following you. Then you will see them because, once put off their guard, they will give themselves away. For many years now I have behaved like a fighter pilot, constantly scanning the rear-view mirror. I look behind more than ahead. It's part of my job. But not now. Now I wanted to give anyone who might be following me an opportunity to relax and be less vigilant. I simply drove my car straight ahead, without any tricks or turns, or any attempt to slip into side-streets.

I drove along the Danube embankment, over a bridge and then along the river again. I didn't hurry or indulge in sudden bursts of speed, and I didn't make for the railway line. (It's easy to check whether you are being followed along the railway.) I drove around the centre of the city, using wide roads in the general stream of the traffic, so making it easy for someone to follow me, although very difficult for me. From the Schwedenplatz I made for the Aspernplatz. There I turned sharply into the first side-street on the left in the direction of the main post office, then another turn to the right. There I had to stop at traffic lights. I knew they were there. But did the fellow who was following me?

I stood at the lights, alone, in the narrow winding side-street. . . . In a second the lights would turn green. Round the corner hurtled a battered green Ford with a screech of brakes. There was a young man at the wheel who had not known about the lights round the corner and hadn't thought I would be waiting for him there. I now moved off slowly with the lights at green. I just managed to catch sight of his bespectacled face in my driving mirror. Yes, I knew that face. He did not have a diplomatic number on his car, but he was a

Soviet diplomat. I had seen him in a delegation at the conference on arms reduction in Europe. I had not thought he was one of our number. I had thought he was a straight diplomat. But what was a Soviet diplomat doing, dashing round the city in his working hours? Why had he come shooting round the corner at such breakneck speed? He could easily get fined.

I was not hurrying any more. I wore an expression of complete indifference on my face; I noticed nothing and reacted to nothing. The Ford had not turned up again, or maybe it had, but I wasn't going looking for it any more. Once was enough for me. It was perfectly clear to me that I had been followed. There was not the slightest doubt about that.

The driver of the Ford was probably wondering now whether I had seen him or not. Had I recognised him? He would be comforting himself with the thought that my mind was probably elsewhere, that I hadn't looked behind me and so I couldn't have seen him.

I wondered how many cars the Navigator had sent to follow me. Certainly more than one. If there had been only one car after me, there would have been at least two men in it. Since there had been only a single person in the car, it meant that there were several cars. That was obvious. And being followed could end up only with being sent back to Moscow.

One had to understand the reasoning of the men in charge of the GRU. If a man lost control over himself after some trifling incident, it meant that he might so the same again some day. At a critical moment, perhaps. And maybe he had already lost control over his actions in the past? Perhaps enemy organisations had already taken advantage of this?

They would come to get me later in the night. If I were in the Navigator's place I would do exactly the same: first, have me followed immediately after the incident, and, second, once I was convinced that something had gone wrong, give instructions for 'evacuation'.

I was not going to the embassy. To go there would mean handcuffs and an injection, immediately. I was going home. I needed to prepare myself for the inevitable, and to meet my fate with dignity.

I locked the door of my flat from the inside and left the window slightly open. If I lacked the courage to meet them face to face I would jump out of the window. I was seven floors up and that was quite sufficient. But that was the easy way out and I was having second thoughts about it. It was the way out for the faint of heart, for those who feared the conveyor. If at the last moment I got cold feet, then I would use that escape. A proud GRU officer had recently dodged the conveyor by that very same means: he had thrown himself out of a window onto the pavement in the very centre of Paris. Another GRU officer based in

London had been working with the very important group in Switzerland. He had made some mistake, but didn't want to go on the conveyor. So he opened his veins.

It was all very well talking now. All the same, I wouldn't go out through the window. That was no way for me. So I stood up and closed it firmly. I would neither go on the conveyor nor jump out of the window. When they knocked I would open the door and get my teeth into the throat of one of them.

What was left for me to do? Theoretically I might be able to go underground and make myself a hiding-place somewhere in the mountains. They had trained me well in *Spetsnaz*. . . .

I glanced at my watch and a shudder went up my spine. It was twelve minutes past midnight. I knew the ways of the Aquarium. An evacuation usually started at four o'clock in the morning. The Aquarium always struck at dawn, just as Hitler did. That was when the deepest sleep came. They might, of course, start earlier, but then they would have to have started placing their people already. It might be too late for me now. It was quite possible that a couple of men were biding their time on the landing one floor up. There would be another couple at the exit and of course someone in the garage. The main group would be waiting somewhere nearby. I didn't have much of a chance. All I could do was to go carefully out of the flat without calling the lift; walk down two or three flights; and only then get the lift down. I could take the lift right into the underground garage and then drive out, not by the exit, but by the entrance, if I could get the door open from the inside.

I unlocked the door silently, then very carefully began to turn the handle. It was all-important that the door shouldn't squeak. I took a deep breath and pulled the door towards me. A shaft of light from the corridor shone wider and wider on the floor of my room. Holding my breath I drew the door towards me further. It squeaked, quietly, sadly and long.

I had managed it. My car was now parked some way away, from my home, standing in a dark corner among a mass of other cars on a huge parking lot. But I could see my own house very clearly. So far there was nothing suspicious taking place around it. Everything and everybody was asleep. Then, after I had been watching for a long time and seeing nothing, at four o'clock exactly a light came on in my flat. It was what I had expected.

I was in a forest. A cold, grey dawn. Patches of fog. A ground frost. I was not yet running anywhere. I was there simply to have time to think.

There was something bothering me: the choice I was faced with. It was a very difficult choice – to resist or not to resist. The Soviet system had destroyed many people, including some very powerful leaders. It is still not clear to historians why people like Tukhachevsky, Yezhov, Berzin and Yagoda* went to their deaths like lambs to the slaughter. But not everybody behaved like that. General Vlasov created the Russian Liberation Army with a million volunteers. Raskolnikov simply escaped abroad. All those who tried to put up resistance to the system have been placed by history into the category of foul traitors. So I was faced with a choice: to surrender without a fight, like a lamb, or to become a foul traitor. As far as the system is concerned I am guilty of nothing, but I am down for evacuation and that would inevitably be followed by the conveyor. If I were to shout that I was innocent, it would change nothing. Millions had done the same before me.

So if I didn't want to be a lamb, I should have to become a traitor. That would be terrible, if I were not a traitor already. Because, after all, I had been a traitor for a long time and it was inevitable. That was how it would be seen. Exactly the same as with my leaders. All those who had not fled abroad, but had continued faithfully to serve Lenin, had later turned out to be traitors. All the people around Lenin – Trotsky, Zinoviev, Kamenev, Rykov, Bukharin and Tomsky – had turned out to be a gang of hired murderers, traitors and spies. What had Lenin been? Lenin had been the leader of that foul gang. All those who had served Stalin so faithfully had also turned out to be traitors, spies and killers – Yagoda, Yezhov, Beria, Tukhachevsky and Blyukher. Then Stalin himself, as it later appeared, was the greatest criminal of all time and all peoples. Those who faithfully served Khrushchev turned out to be enemies, profligates and criminals, too – Molotov, Kaganovich, Serov, Korotchenko, Shelest, Shelepin, Bulganin. Khrushchev himself turned out to be a fool and chatterbox. What did it all mean? Sooner or later any one of my leaders could be toppled from Olympus and declared to be a spy, a traitor, a profligate, a killer, a fool or a chatterbox. And anybody who had served those traitors and spies would also be labelled a criminal. So I had nothing to lose. I had already been serving those people – I was already a traitor and a criminal. To escape from them was a crime, but it was a lesser crime than to stay with them.

The forest was all around me. What was I thinking about? Nothing. Ideology? To hell with ideology. I was not guilty. I had done nothing wrong. My teeth ground together, my fists were tightly balled. I had to get out. I would get out, but where? I could stay in the mountains, live in a cave. I was trained for it. Or maybe I could go to another country, to Britain. It was a country that Penkovsky had served well, and it would make a nice surprise for the chief of the GRU. Britain still kicked out the Soviet diplomats it didn't like. A hundred at once, the last time. My leaders respected that strength. I respected that strength.

But did Britain need me? I had no way of knowing unless I asked. Should I phone the ambassador first? I'd never get through. I knew how embassies worked. What I had to do was contact a deputy. I knew where the British

* See V. Suvorov, *Soviet Military Intelligence*, London 1984.

diplomats' villas were. There was a group of them all together in one particular district. I'd go to the first one I saw.

The British diplomat's house was large and white, with a colonnaded porch. The driveway was covered with gravel, the garden luxurious. I was not shaved and I was wearing a black leather jacket. I had no car, and I was not in the least like a diplomat. In fact I was already no longer a diplomat. I no longer represented my country. On the contrary, my country was now searching for me all over the place.

The British diplomat's house was not at all like other houses. There was no door-bell. Instead there was a polished brass fox's head as a door-knocker. It was very important for me that the master of the house should answer the door and not one of his servants. I was lucky. It was Saturday; he was not at work and there were no servants.

'Good morning.'

'Good morning.'

I held out my diplomatic passport. He leafed through it, handed it back to me and invited me in.

'I have a message for Her Majesty's government.'

'Please go to the embassy.'

'I cannot go to the embassy. It's too public there and I have to speak to someone who can make a decision. That's why I want to pass this letter by your hand.'

'I refuse to accept it.' He rose and opened the door for me. 'I am no spy and please do not involve me in these spy games.'

'This is not espionage ... any more. This is a letter for Her Majesty's government. Whether you accept it or not, I am now going to telephone the British embassy and say that a letter for the British Government is here in your house ... I shall leave it here and you can do what you like with it.'

He gave me a look that promised no good to me.

'Give me your letter.'

'Give me an envelope, please.'

'You don't even have an envelope?' he said in astonishment.

'Unfortunately not.'

He placed before me a quantity of paper, envelopes and a pen. I pushed the paper aside and took out of my pocket a bunch of cards with the names and addresses of cafés and restaurants. Every spy always carries a supply of a dozen such cards. Rather than explaining to a new contact where you were to meet, it was much easier to hand him a card, making it clear that you were inviting him to the address written on it.

I looked quickly through them and chose one. For a few seconds I pondered what to write. Then I took the pen and wrote down three letters: GRU. I put the card into an envelope, stuck the envelope down and wrote the address in

Russian letters: 'To the Government of Her Majesty'. On the envelope I stamped my personal seal – '173-V-4I'.

'Is that all?'

'That's all. Goodbye.'

Once again I was in a forest. I kept driving the car further and further. Now an encounter with the local police might also be dangerous. The Soviet embassy might have informed the police that a Soviet diplomat had gone mad and was careering round the country. They might inform Interpol that I had stolen a million and was running away. They might deliver a protest to the government, saying that the Austrian authorities had seized me by force and that I must be returned immediately, or else. . . . They knew how to make loud protests. I now needed to talk to the British embassy by telephone and to explain the situation, before some village policeman stopped me and summoned the Soviet consul. Then it would be too late to explain anything to anybody. After the first meeting with the consul I would begin to foam at the mouth and laugh or cry, and they would send a special aircraft for me. So long as I was not foaming I was going to keep trying. I knew where there were some out-of-the-way telephones.

'Hello, British embassy, I have sent a message. . . . I know that you will not connect me with the ambassador, but I need to speak to a responsible person . . . I don't need to know his name – you decide. I have sent a message. . . .'

At last they found someone.

'Hello . . . who is that speaking?'

'I have sent a message. The person with whom I sent it knows my name . . . '

'Is that so?'

'Yes. Ask him.'

The phone went silent for some time, then came to life again.

'Do you represent your country?'

'No, I represent only myself.'

Again the phone fell silent.

'What do you want?'

'I want you to open the envelope at once and pass the message to the British government.'

The phone fell silent, apart from some heavy breathing.

'I can't open the envelope because it's not addressed to me but to the government. . . .'

'Please open it. It is I who signed it. I signed it like that so that its contents should not be known by certain people. But I give you the right to open it. . . .'

Deep in the depths of the telephone there was some whispering.

'It's a very strange message. Some kind of restaurant. . . .'

'No, not that. . . . Look on the other side.'

'There's also a rather strange message – just some letters.'

243

'That's what you have to transmit.'

'You are off your head. A message of three letters cannot be of any importance.'

'It will be up to Her Majesty's government to decide whether it's important or not.'

Silence again. Then some crackling and hissing at the other end. And then: 'I have found a compromise. I won't send a radio message, but I will send your message by diplomatic mail!' His voice sounded like that of a schoolboy who had just solved a difficult problem.

'To hell with you and your British compromises. My message may be important or not, it's not for me to decide, but it is certainly urgent. An hour from now, and possibly even sooner, it will be too late. However, you should know that I am a very persistent person and once I've started something I don't give up. I shall call you again, in fifteen minutes. Please show the ambassador my message.'

'The ambassador's not here today.'

'Then show it to anyone you like. Your secretary, for example. Perhaps she reads the papers. Perhaps she could suggest what you should do. . . .'

I then hung up on him.

I kept on the move, avoiding buildings and people until I could phone again. I kept humming to myself the awful tunes of 'The Wolf Hunt'. Only recently I had felt like a trapped animal, but my strength had now returned. I clutched the steering wheel with all my strength, as a pilot diving to his death grips his controls. I knew that I would not surrender. I had a strongly built car with which I would smash anyone who tried to block my path. If the worst came to the worst I had a heavy spanner and a huge screwdriver. I was ready to sell my life dearly. I would die, but in battle!

I called the British Embassy again. My second and last attempt. I had seldom asked anybody for anything twice, and never three times, and I never would.

I had very little time left. I had promised to phone in fifteen minutes, but I had left it for forty-three minutes because there had been a car standing near the telephone I had intended to use and I had to go elsewhere.

'Is that the British Embassy?'

'Yes.' But now everything had changed. The 'yes' was snapped out sharply, like a military command. Then came a man's voice that I recognised: 'Is everything all right with you? I have been worried because you took so long to call. . . .'

'About my message. . . .'

'Your message has been transmitted,' he interrupted me. 'It was a very important message. It's hardly credible, but we've already received a reply from London. They are waiting for you. . . . We need you. Are you ready?'

'Yes.'

'Is the address on the card you sent the place to meet you?'

'Yes.'

'There is no time on the card – does that mean we should meet you as soon as possible?'

'Yes.'

'That's what we assumed. Our official representatives are already waiting for you there.'

I said 'thank you' in Russian for some reason. I don't know whether he understood me.

Index